Little Nothings
MY SHADOW
IN THE DISTANCE

D1596312

Little Nothings

MY SHADOW
IN THE DISTANCE

LEWIS TRONDHEIM

ISBN 978-1-56163-609-9
Library of Congress Control Number: 2010291580
© 2009 Trondheim
Rights arranged through Sylvain Coissard Agency, France.
© 2011 NBM for the English translation
Translation by Joe Johnson
Lettering by Ortho
Printed in China

1st printing July 2011

Comicslit is an imprint
and trademark of

NANTIER • BEALL • MINOUSTCHINE
Publishing inc.
new york

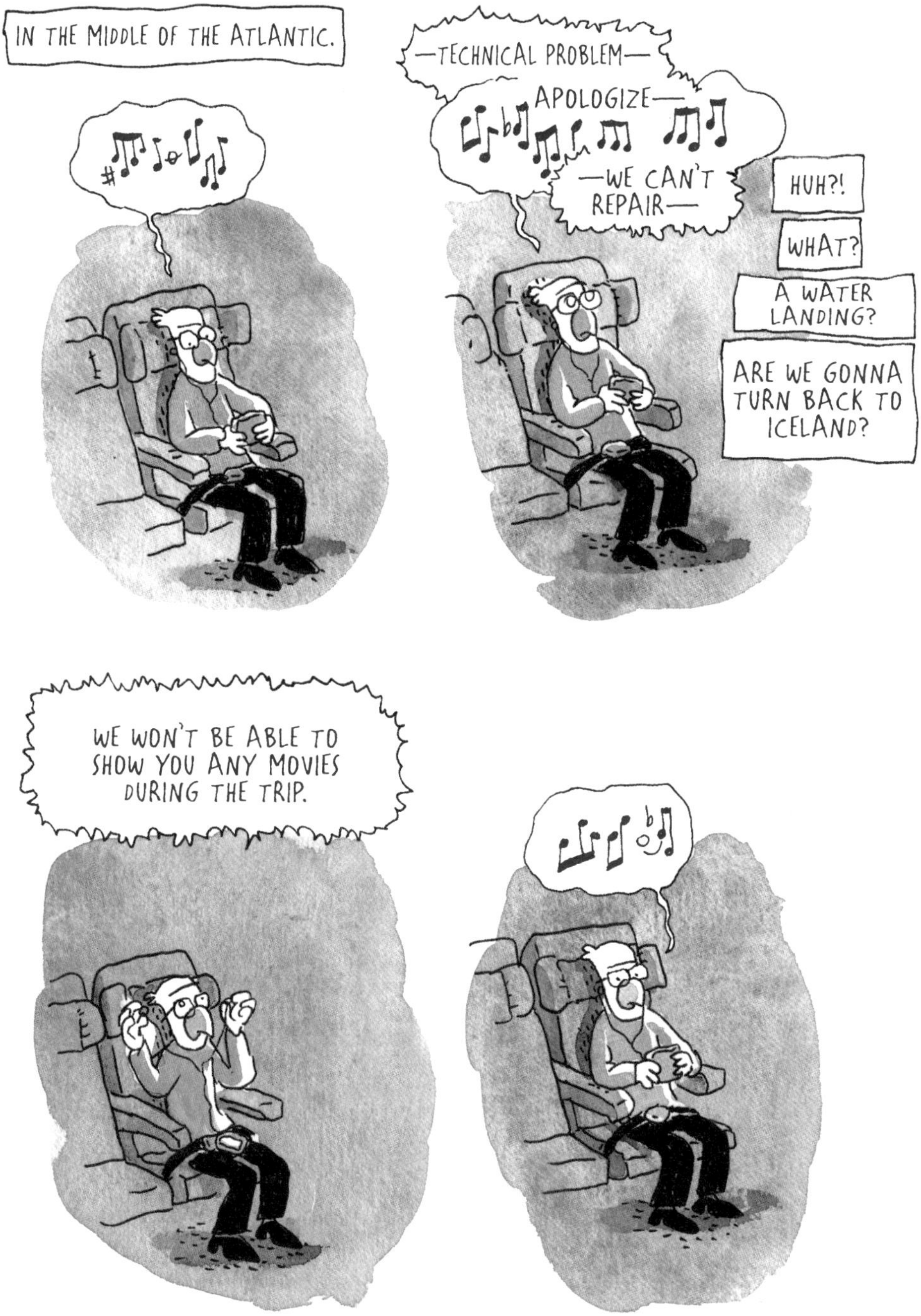
IN THE MIDDLE OF THE ATLANTIC.
—TECHNICAL PROBLEM—
APOLOGIZE—
—WE CAN'T REPAIR—
HUH?!
WHAT?
A WATER LANDING?
ARE WE GONNA TURN BACK TO ICELAND?
WE WON'T BE ABLE TO SHOW YOU ANY MOVIES DURING THE TRIP.

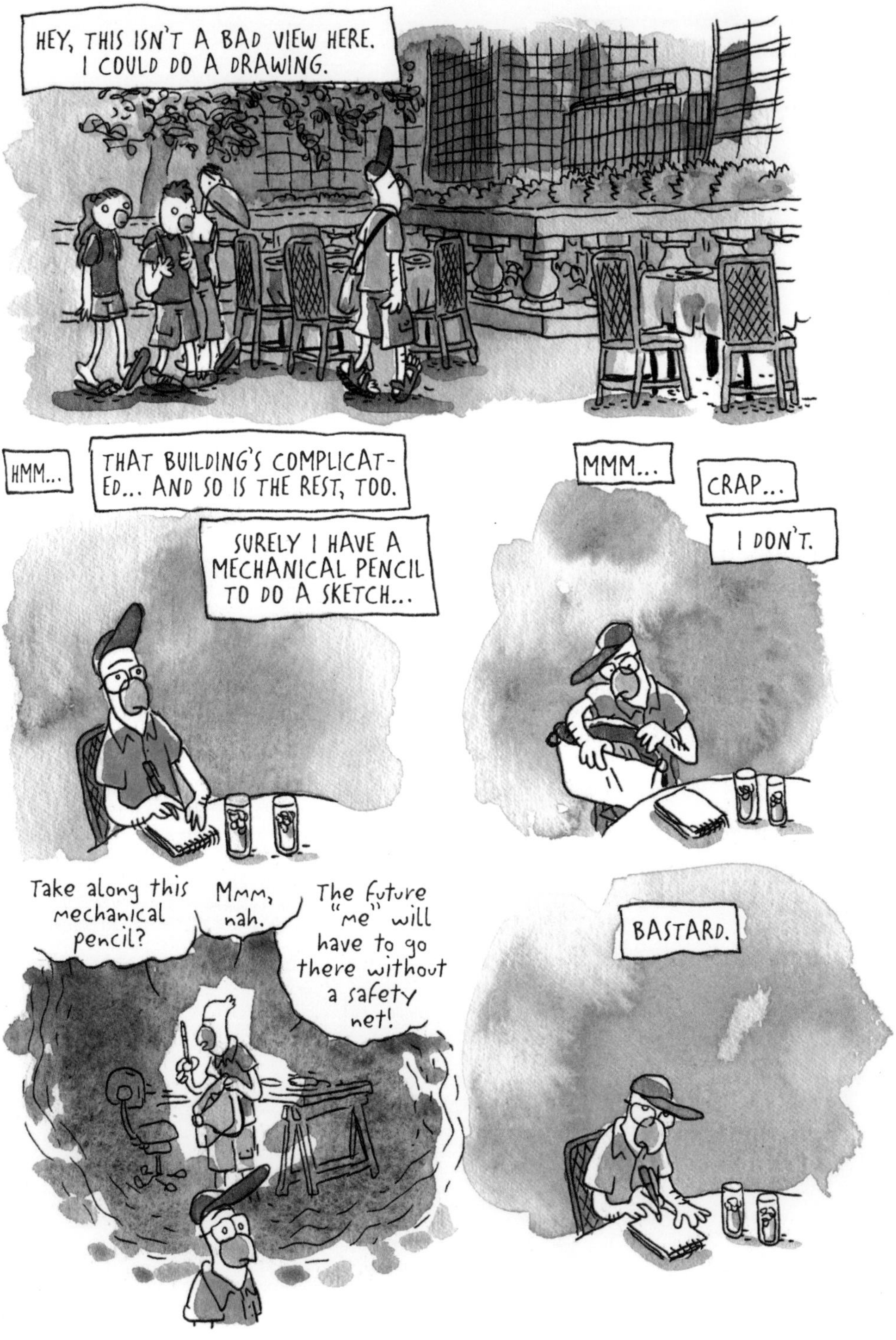
HEY, THIS ISN'T A BAD VIEW HERE. I COULD DO A DRAWING.
HMM...
THAT BUILDING'S COMPLICATED... AND SO IS THE REST, TOO.
SURELY I HAVE A MECHANICAL PENCIL TO DO A SKETCH...
MMM...
CRAP...
I DON'T.
Take along this mechanical pencil?
Mmm, nah.
The future "me" will have to go there without a safety net!
BASTARD.

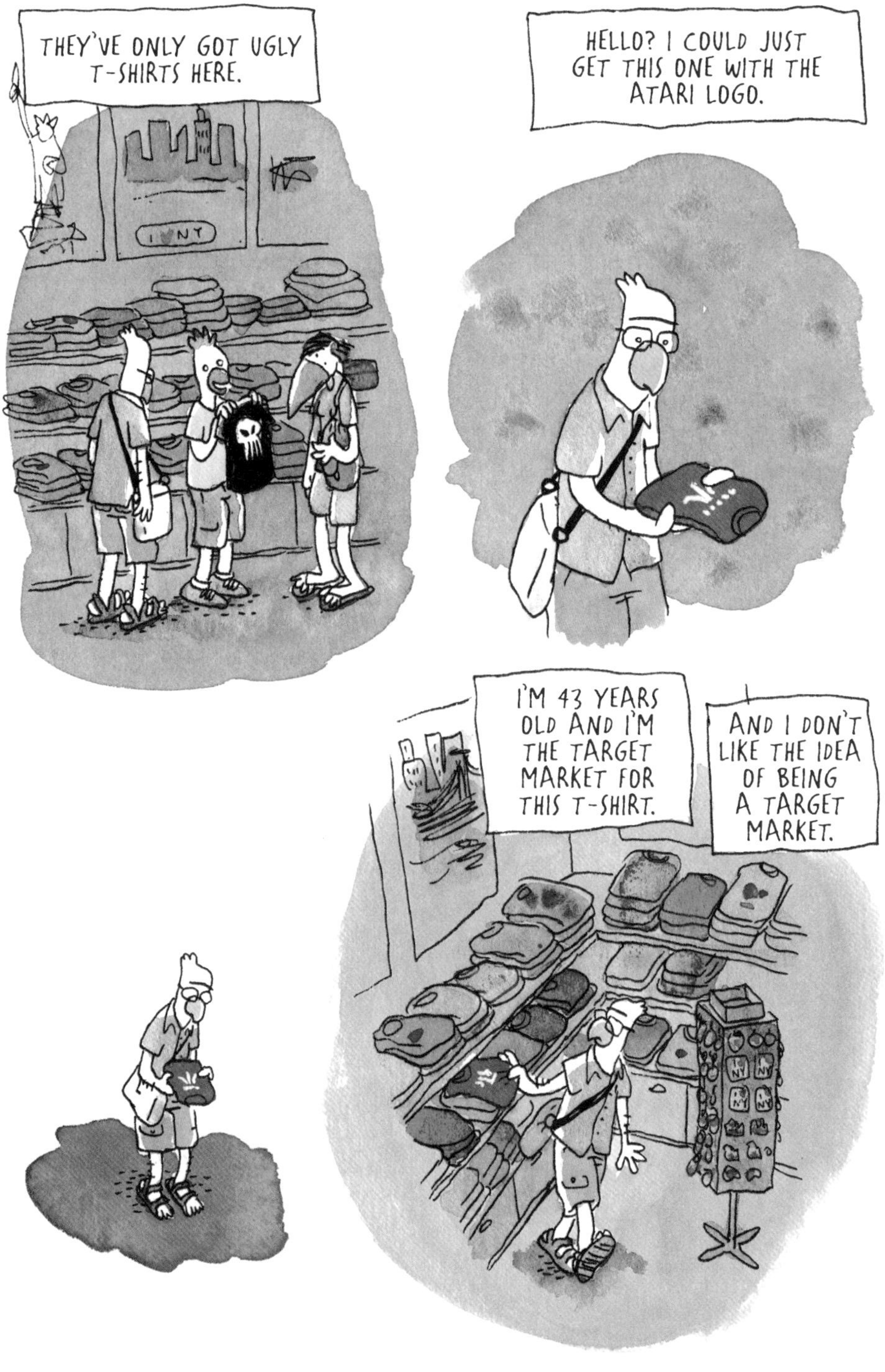
THEY'VE ONLY GOT UGLY T-SHIRTS HERE.
HELLO? I COULD JUST GET THIS ONE WITH THE ATARI LOGO.
I'M 43 YEARS OLD AND I'M THE TARGET MARKET FOR THIS T-SHIRT.
AND I DON'T LIKE THE IDEA OF BEING A TARGET MARKET.

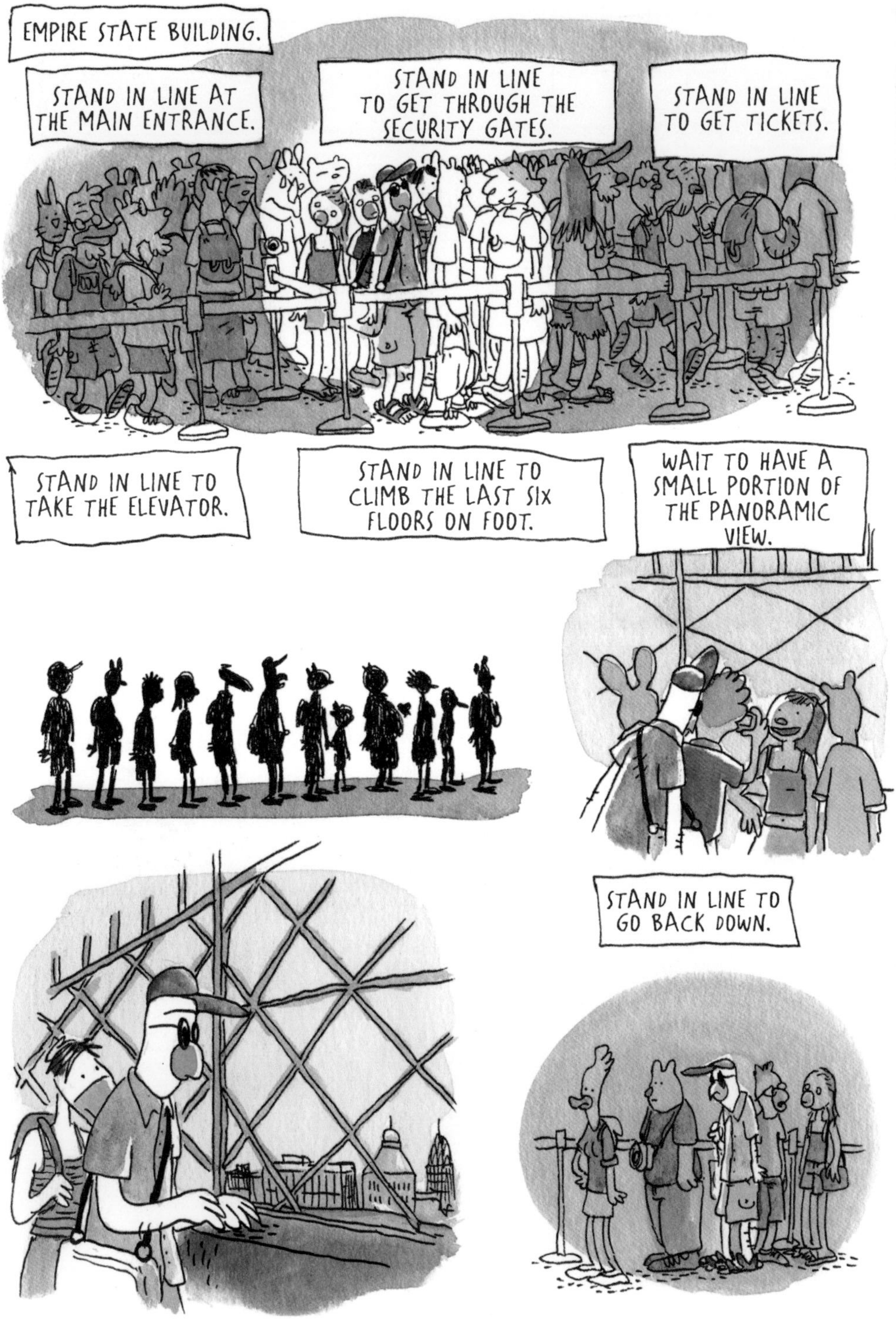
EMPIRE STATE BUILDING.
STAND IN LINE AT THE MAIN ENTRANCE.
STAND IN LINE TO GET THROUGH THE SECURITY GATES.
STAND IN LINE TO GET TICKETS.
STAND IN LINE TO TAKE THE ELEVATOR.
STAND IN LINE TO CLIMB THE LAST SIX FLOORS ON FOOT.
WAIT TO HAVE A SMALL PORTION OF THE PANORAMIC VIEW.
STAND IN LINE TO GO BACK DOWN.

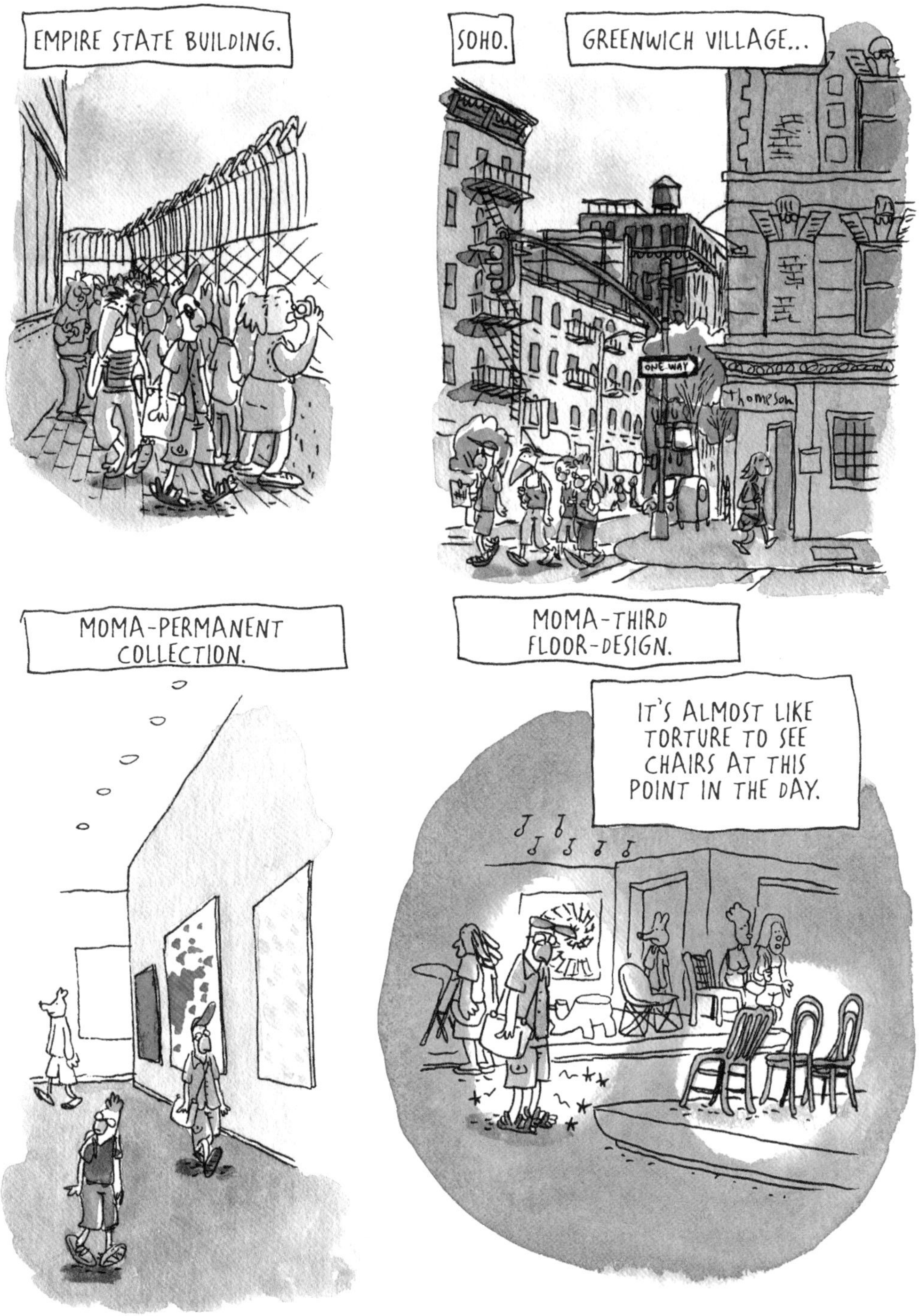
EMPIRE STATE BUILDING.
SOHO.
GREENWICH VILLAGE...
ONE WAY
Thomeson
MOMA-PERMANENT COLLECTION.
MOMA-THIRD FLOOR-DESIGN.
IT'S ALMOST LIKE TORTURE TO SEE CHAIRS AT THIS POINT IN THE DAY.

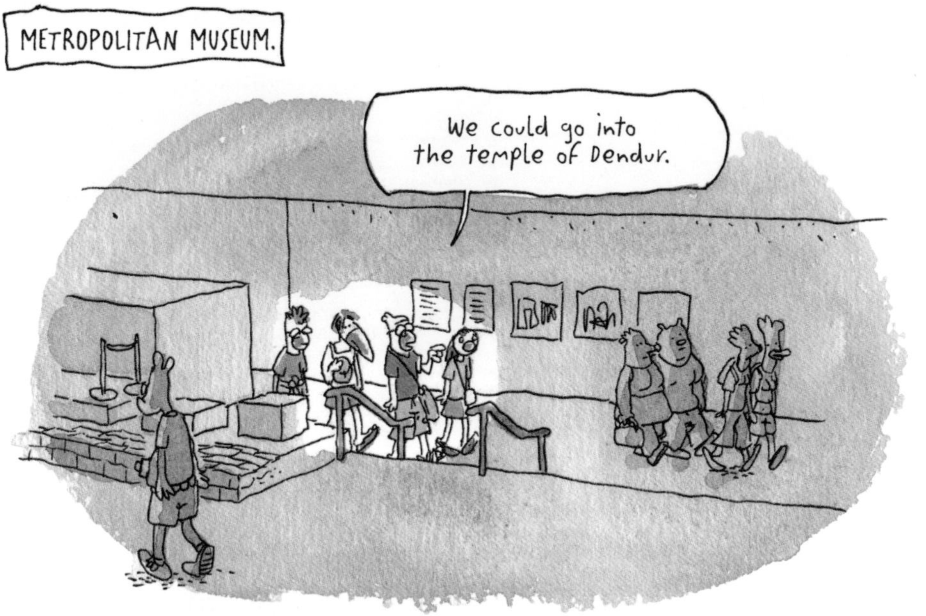
METROPOLITAN MUSEUM.
We could go into the temple of Dendur.

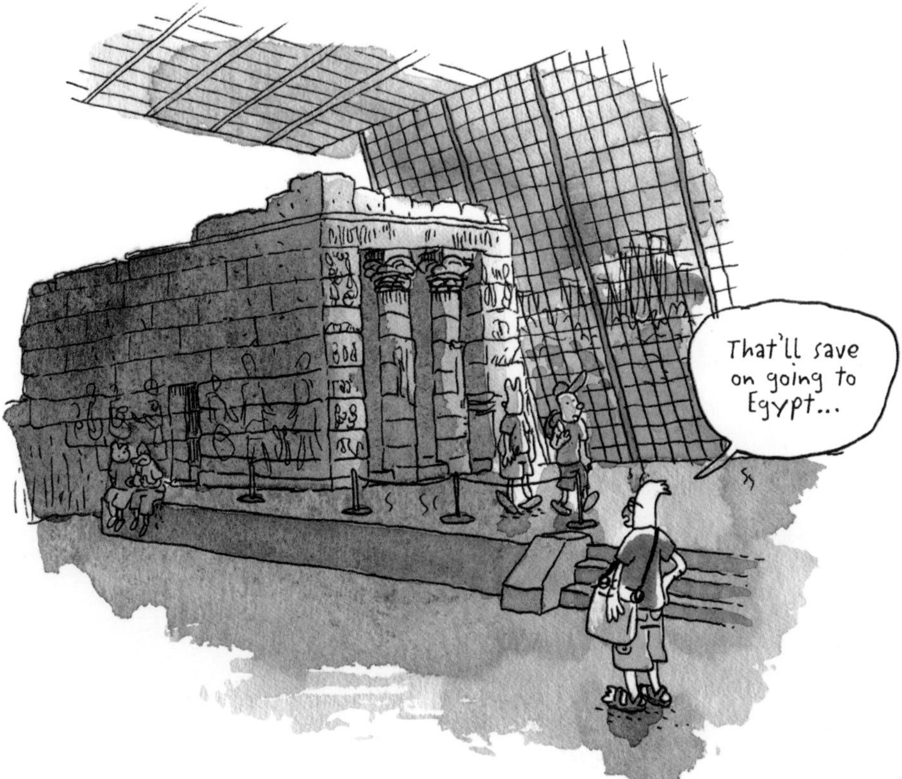
That'll save on going to Egypt...

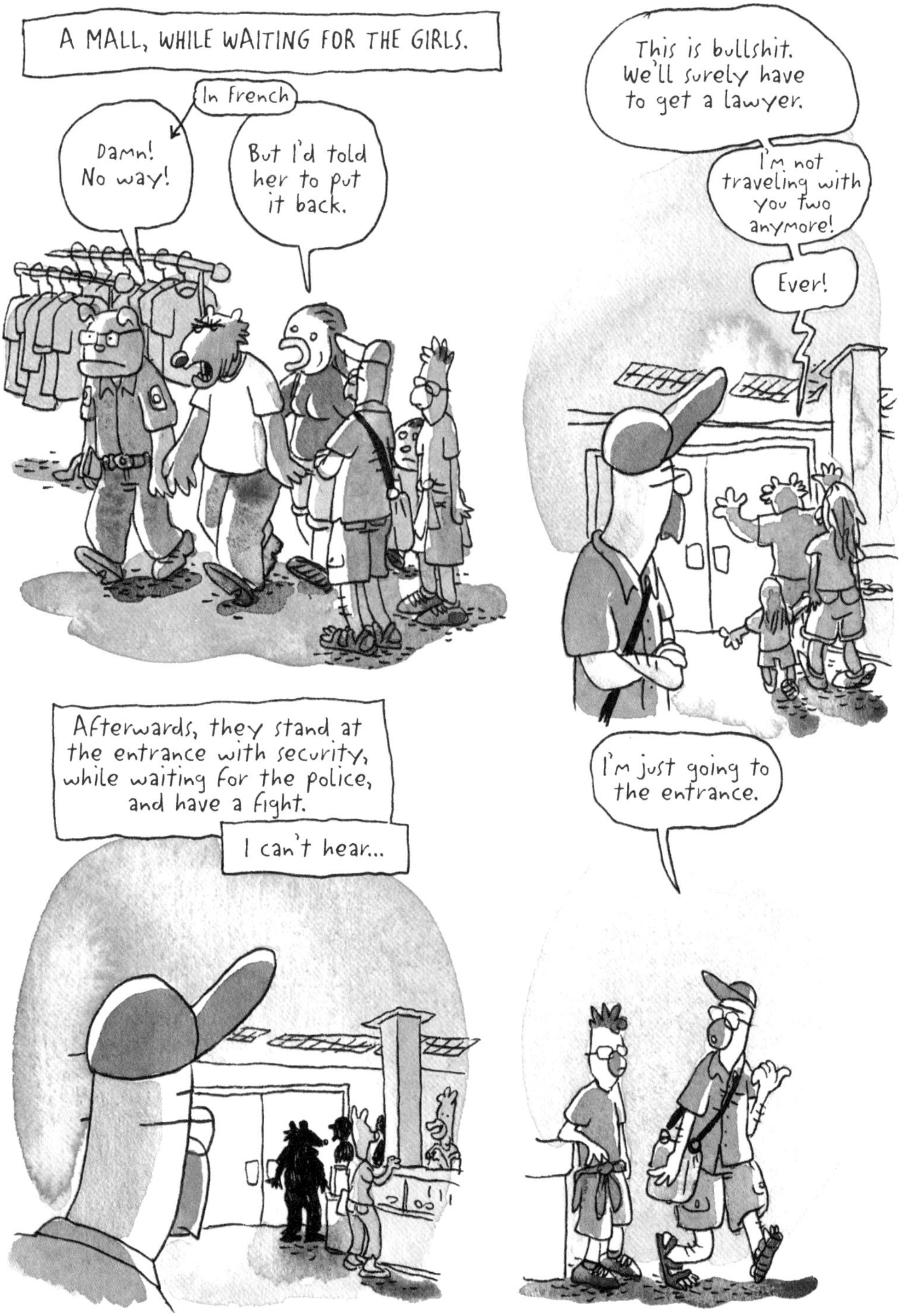
A MALL, WHILE WAITING FOR THE GIRLS.
In French
Damn! No way!
But I'd told her to put it back.
This is bullshit. We'll surely have to get a lawyer.
I'm not traveling with you two anymore!
Ever!
Afterwards, they stand at the entrance with security, while waiting for the police, and have a fight.
I can't hear...
I'm just going to the entrance.

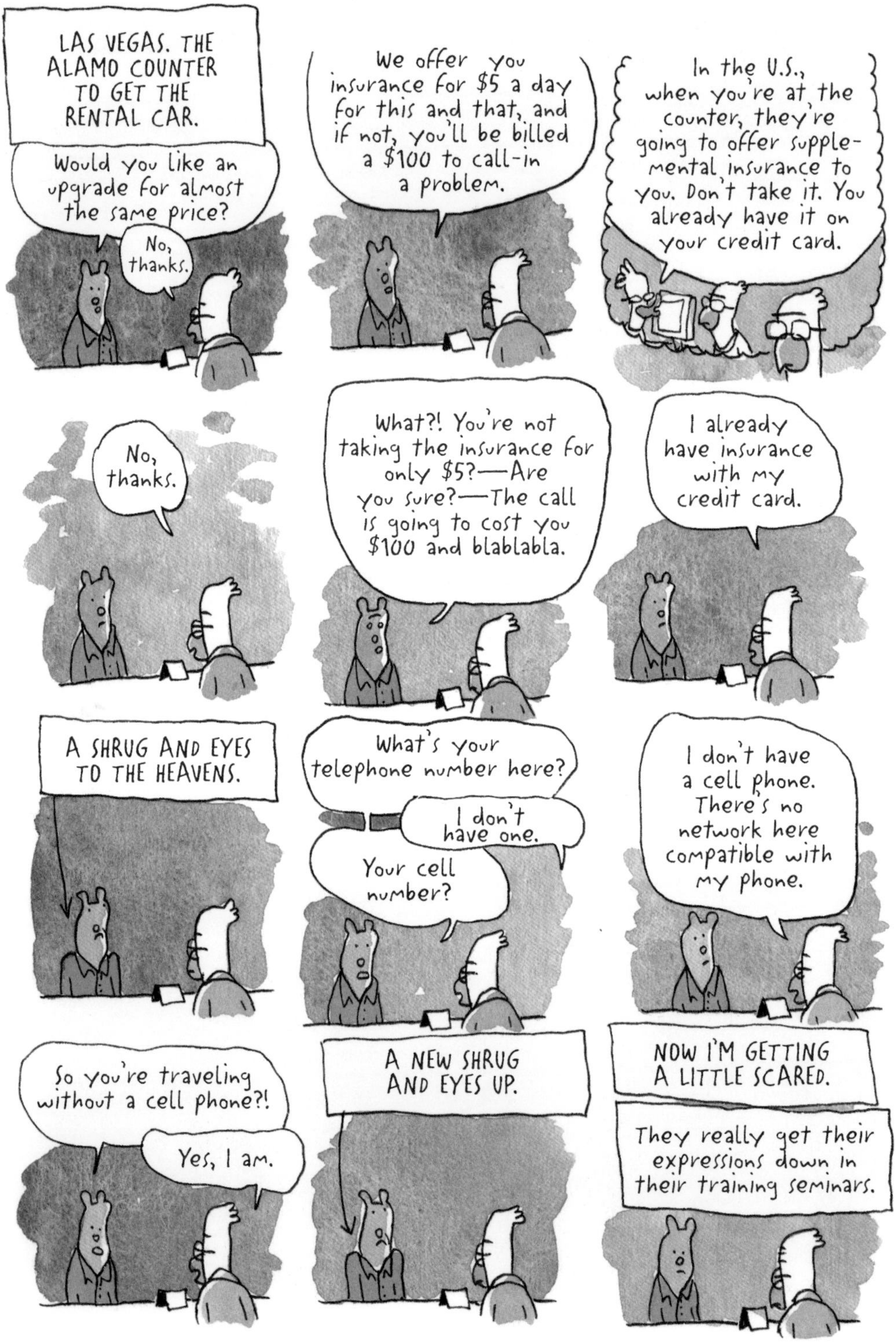
LAS VEGAS. THE ALAMO COUNTER TO GET THE RENTAL CAR.
Would you like an upgrade for almost the same price?
No, thanks.
We offer you insurance for $5 a day for this and that, and if not, you'll be billed a $100 to call-in a problem.
In the U.S., when you're at the counter, they're going to offer supplemental insurance to you. Don't take it. You already have it on your credit card.
No, thanks.
What?! You're not taking the insurance for only $5?—Are you sure?—The call is going to cost you $100 and blablabla.
I already have insurance with my credit card.
A SHRUG AND EYES TO THE HEAVENS.
What's your telephone number here?
I don't have one.
Your cell number?
I don't have a cell phone. There's no network here compatible with my phone.
So you're traveling without a cell phone?!
Yes, I am.
A NEW SHRUG AND EYES UP.
NOW I'M GETTING A LITTLE SCARED.
They really get their expressions down in their training seminars.

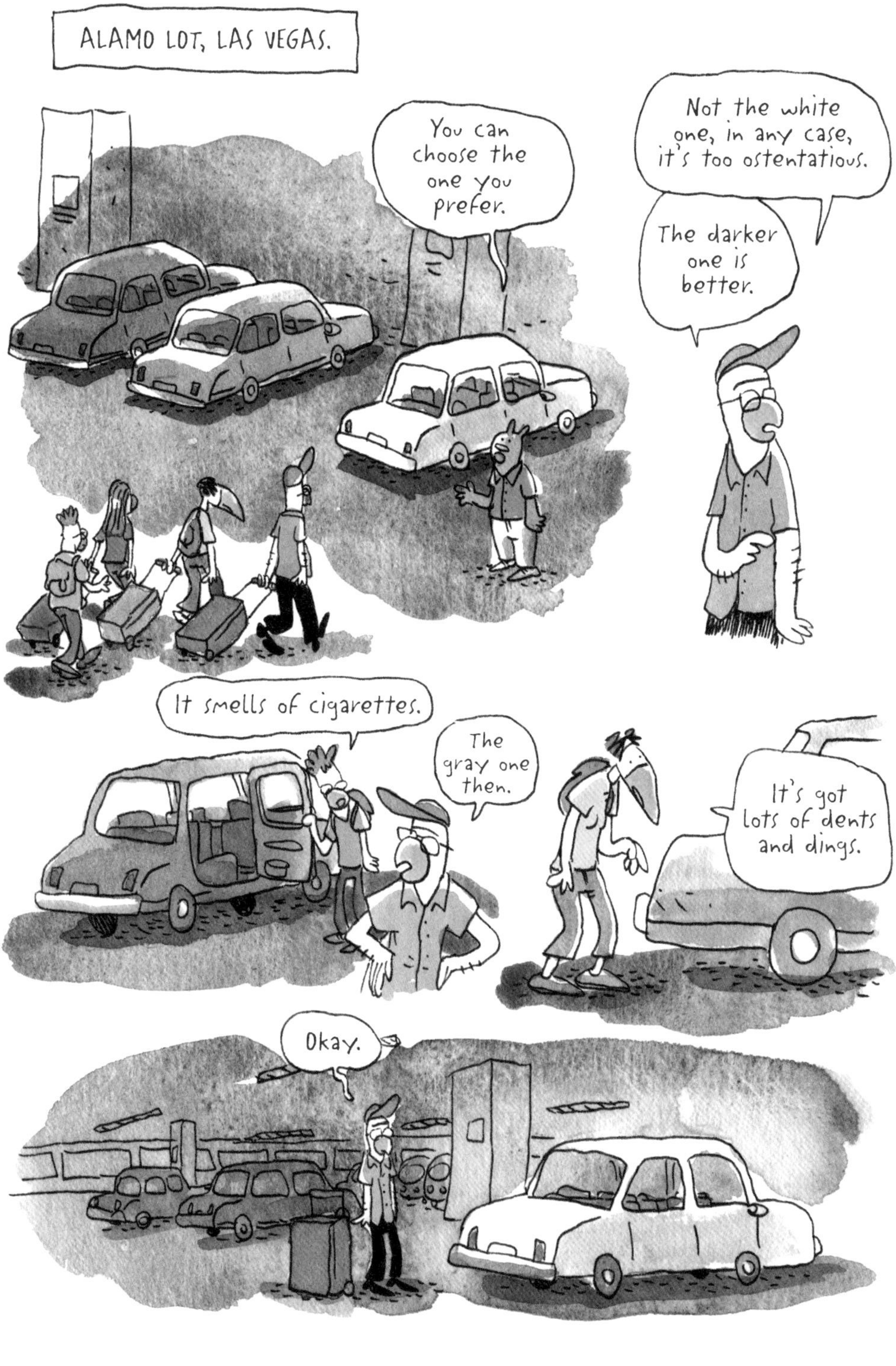
ALAMO LOT, LAS VEGAS.
You can choose the one you prefer.
Not the white one, in any case, it's too ostentatious.
The darker one is better.
It smells of cigarettes.
The gray one then.
It's got lots of dents and dings.
Okay.

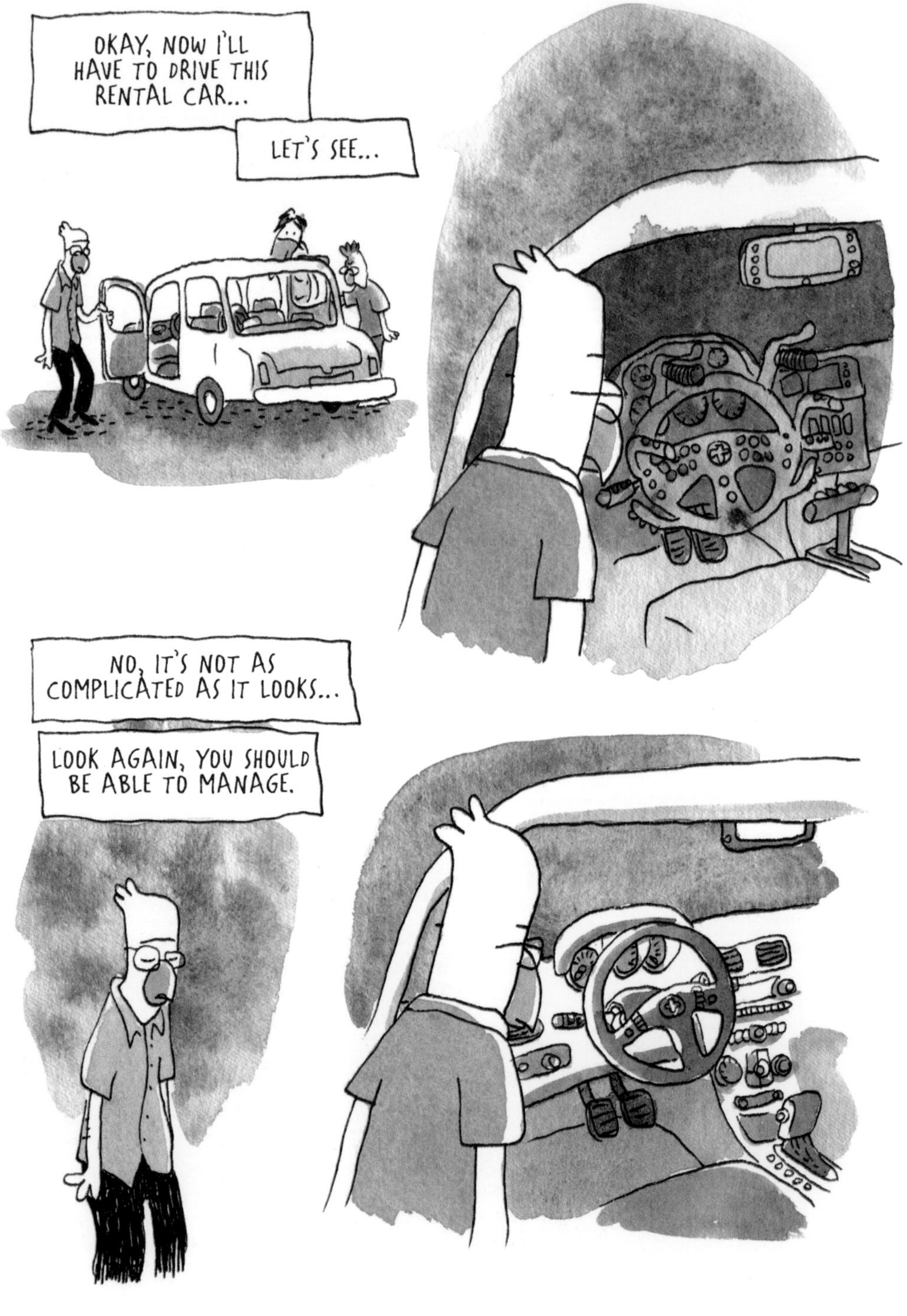
OKAY, NOW I'LL HAVE TO DRIVE THIS RENTAL CAR...
LET'S SEE...
NO, IT'S NOT AS COMPLICATED AS IT LOOKS...
LOOK AGAIN, YOU SHOULD BE ABLE TO MANAGE.

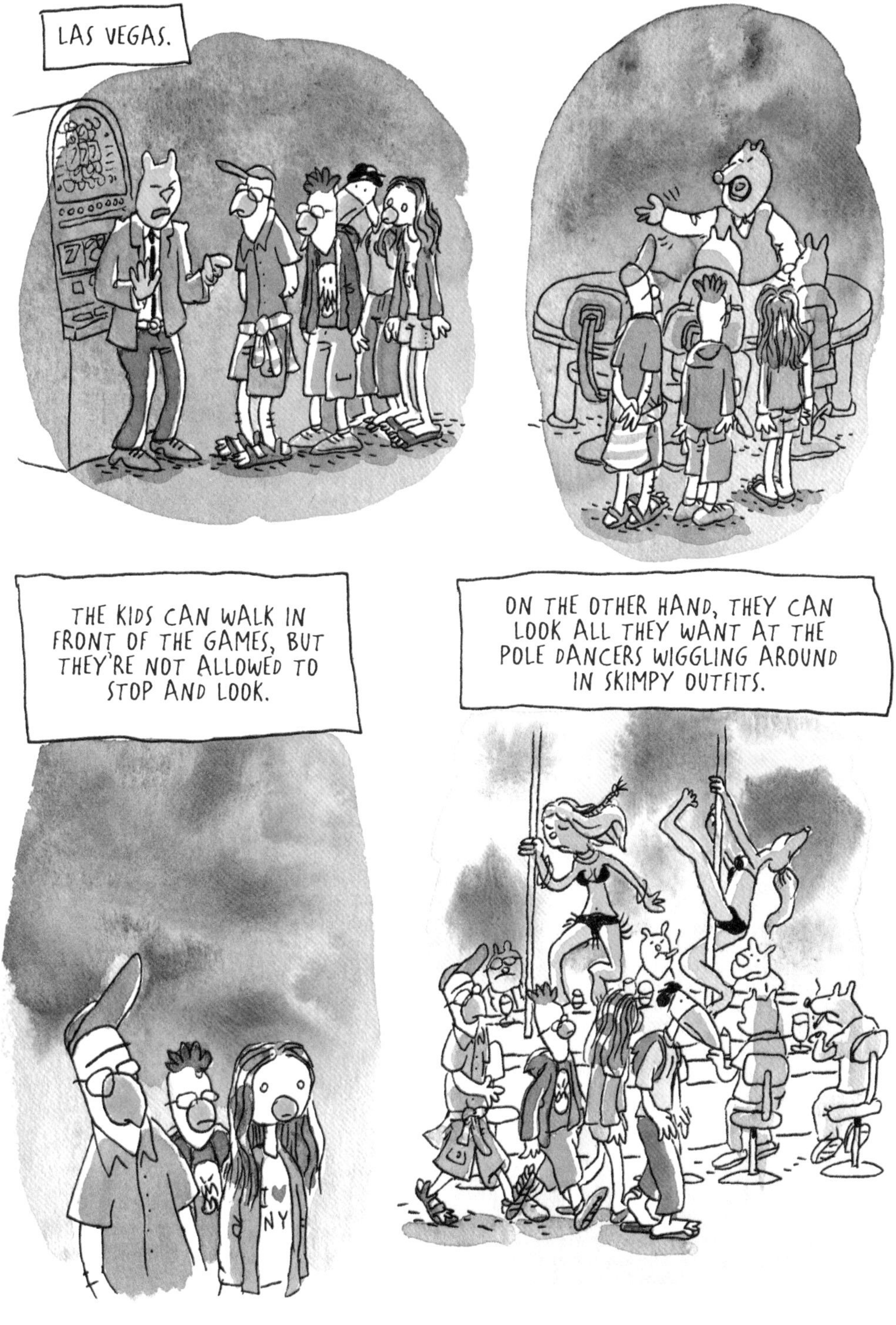
LAS VEGAS.
THE KIDS CAN WALK IN FRONT OF THE GAMES, BUT THEY'RE NOT ALLOWED TO STOP AND LOOK.
ON THE OTHER HAND, THEY CAN LOOK ALL THEY WANT AT THE POLE DANCERS WIGGLING AROUND IN SKIMPY OUTFITS.
I ♥ NY

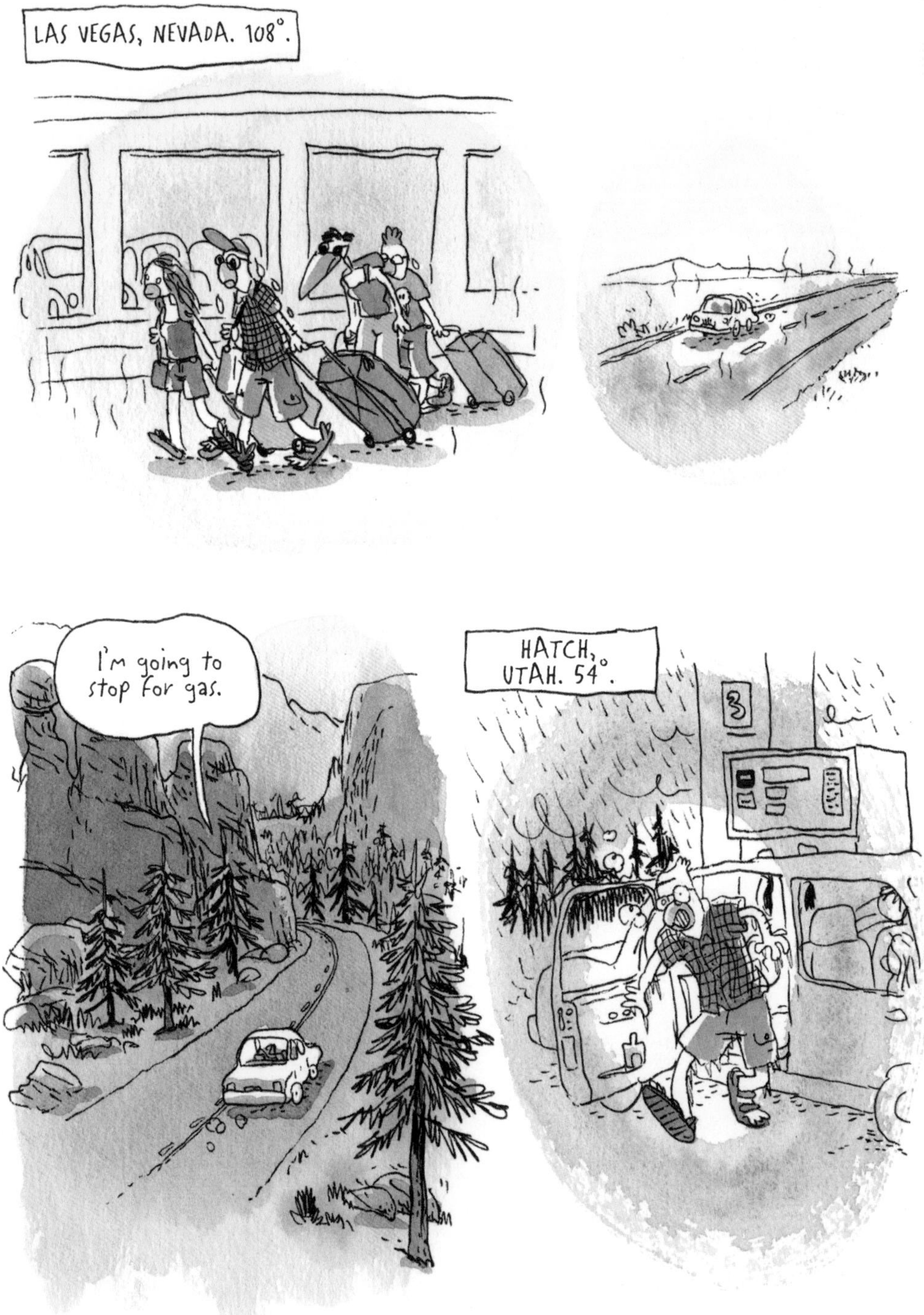
LAS VEGAS, NEVADA. 108°.
I'm going to stop for gas.
HATCH, UTAH. 54°.

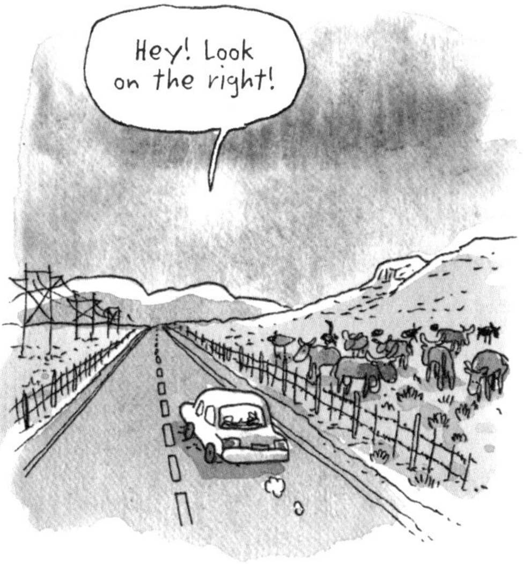
Hey! Look on the right!

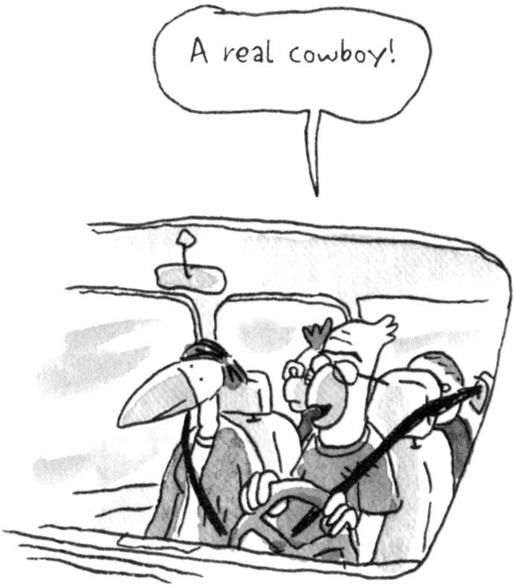
A real cowboy!

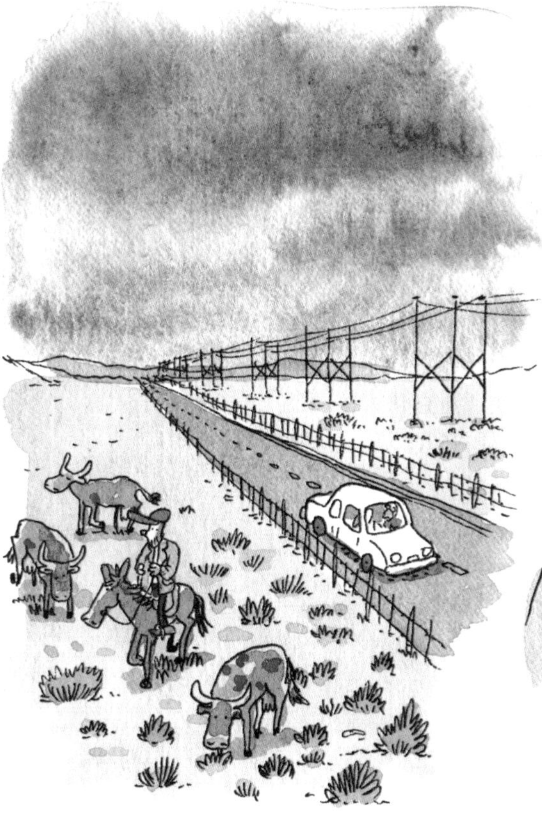

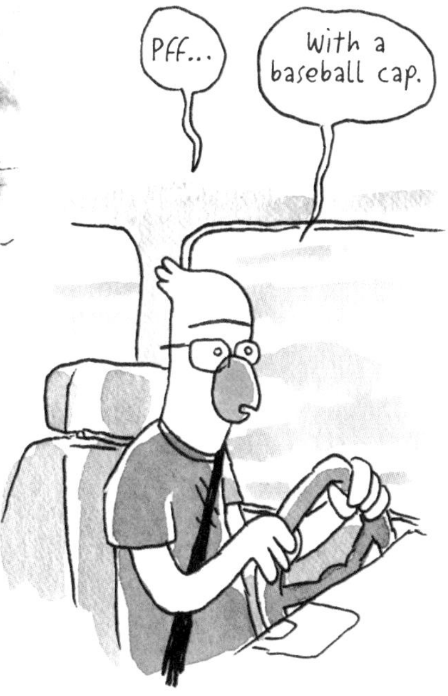
Pff...
With a baseball cap.

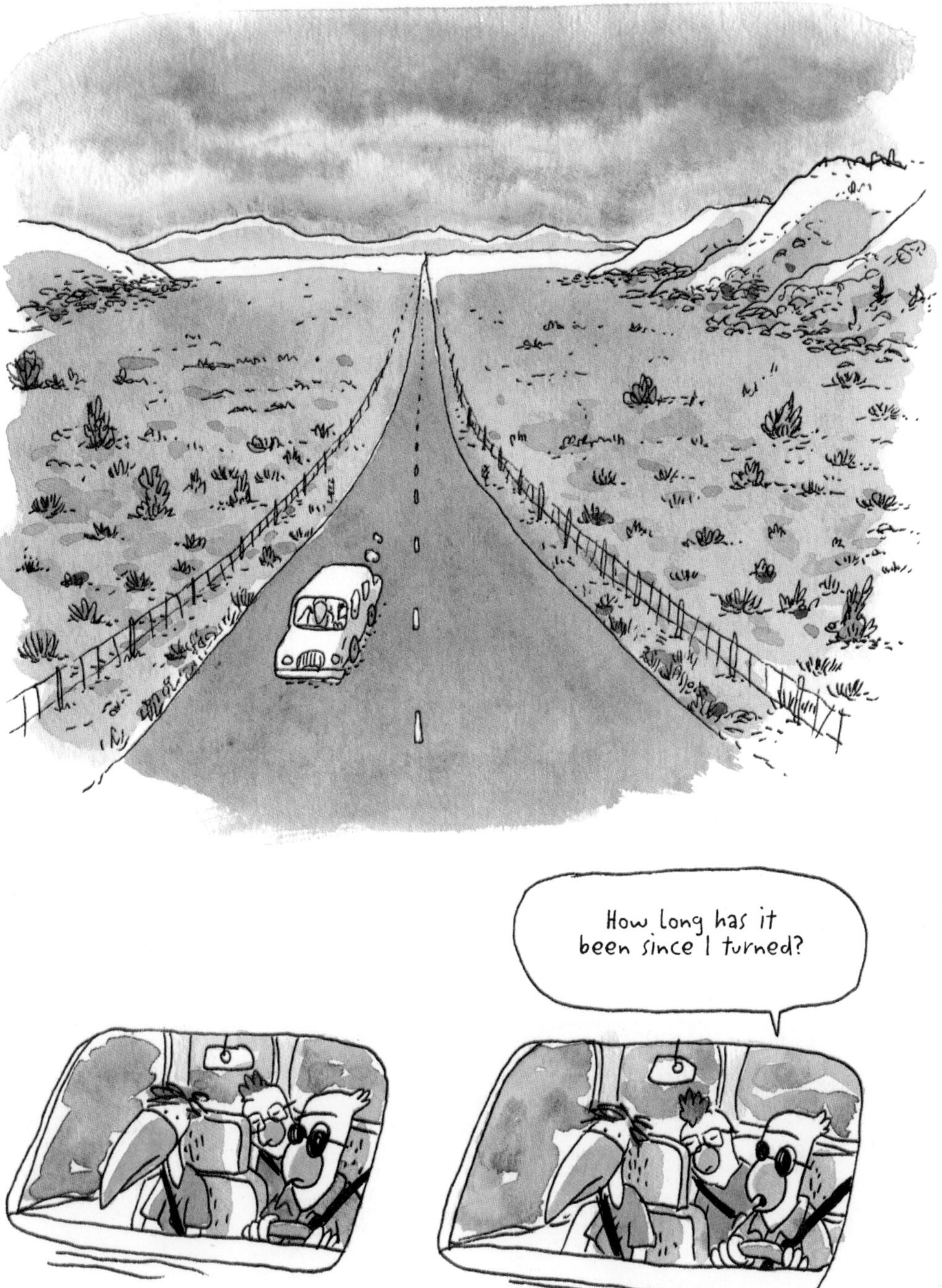
How long has it been since I turned?

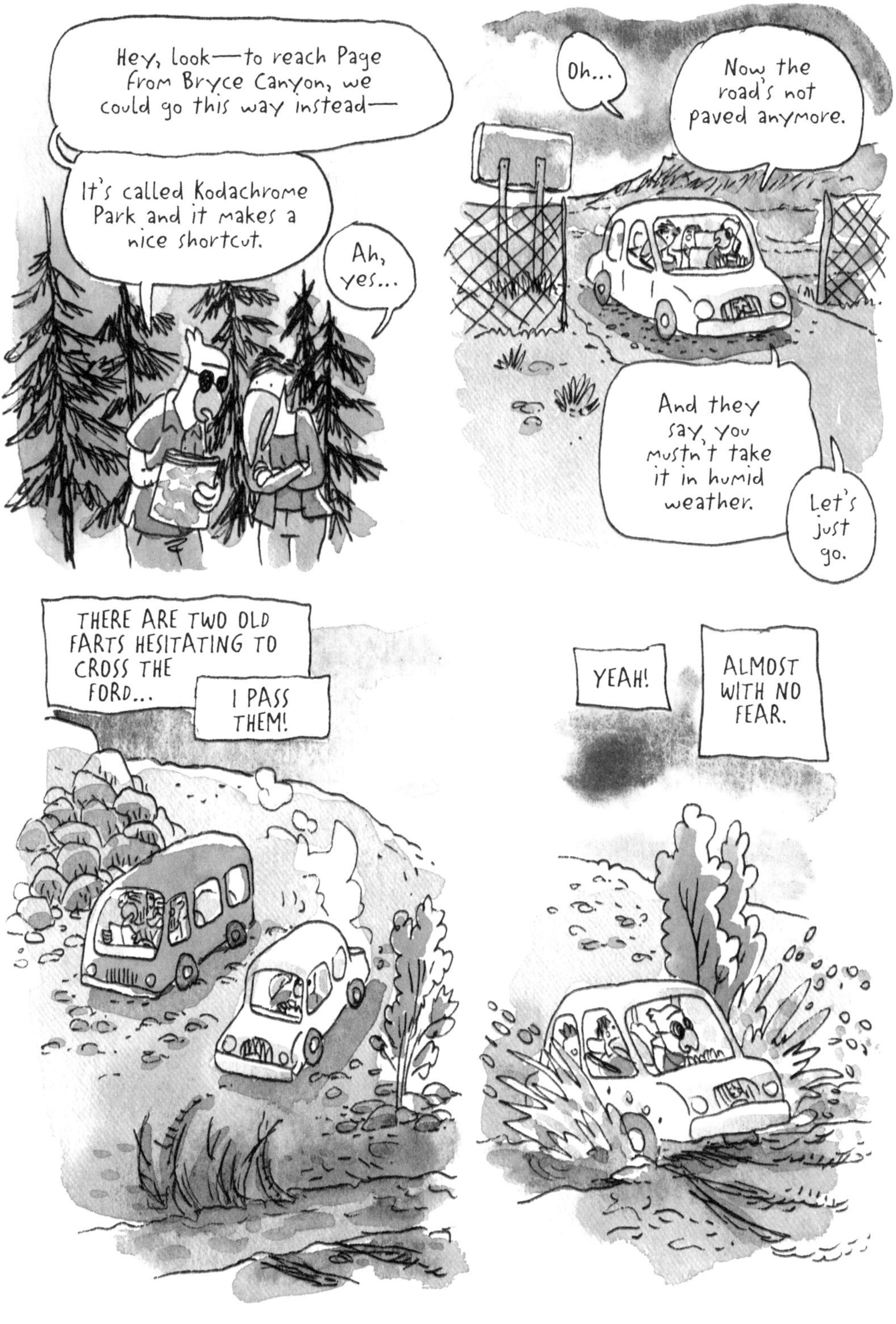
Hey, look—to reach Page from Bryce Canyon, we could go this way instead—
It's called Kodachrome Park and it makes a nice shortcut.
Ah, yes...
Oh...
Now the road's not paved anymore.
And they say, you mustn't take it in humid weather.
Let's just go.
THERE ARE TWO OLD FARTS HESITATING TO CROSS THE FORD...
I PASS THEM!
YEAH!
ALMOST WITH NO FEAR.

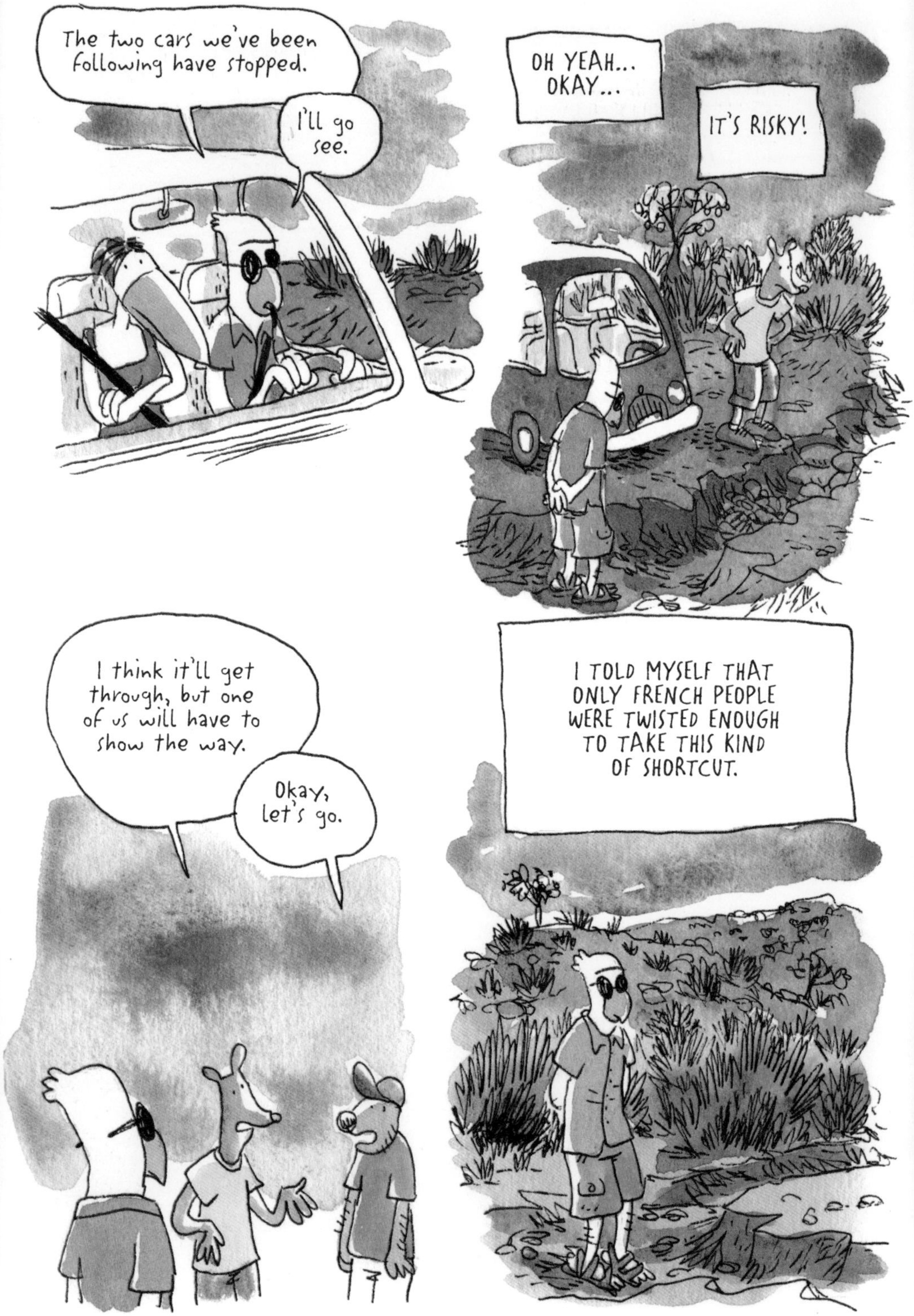
The two cars we've been following have stopped.
I'll go see.
OH YEAH... OKAY...
IT'S RISKY!
I think it'll get through, but one of us will have to show the way.
Okay, let's go.
I TOLD MYSELF THAT ONLY FRENCH PEOPLE WERE TWISTED ENOUGH TO TAKE THIS KIND OF SHORTCUT.

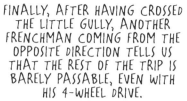

FINALLY, AFTER HAVING CROSSED THE LITTLE GULLY, ANOTHER FRENCHMAN COMING FROM THE OPPOSITE DIRECTION TELLS US THAT THE REST OF THE TRIP IS BARELY PASSABLE, EVEN WITH HIS 4-WHEEL DRIVE.

WE DECIDE TO TURN AROUND EVEN THOUGH WE WERE ALMOST THERE.

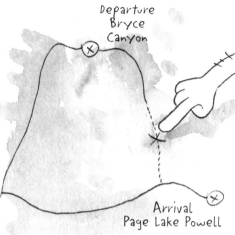

Departure
Bryce
Canyon

Arrival
Page Lake Powell

GREAT VICTORIES SOMETIMES INCLUDE TACTICAL RETREATS...

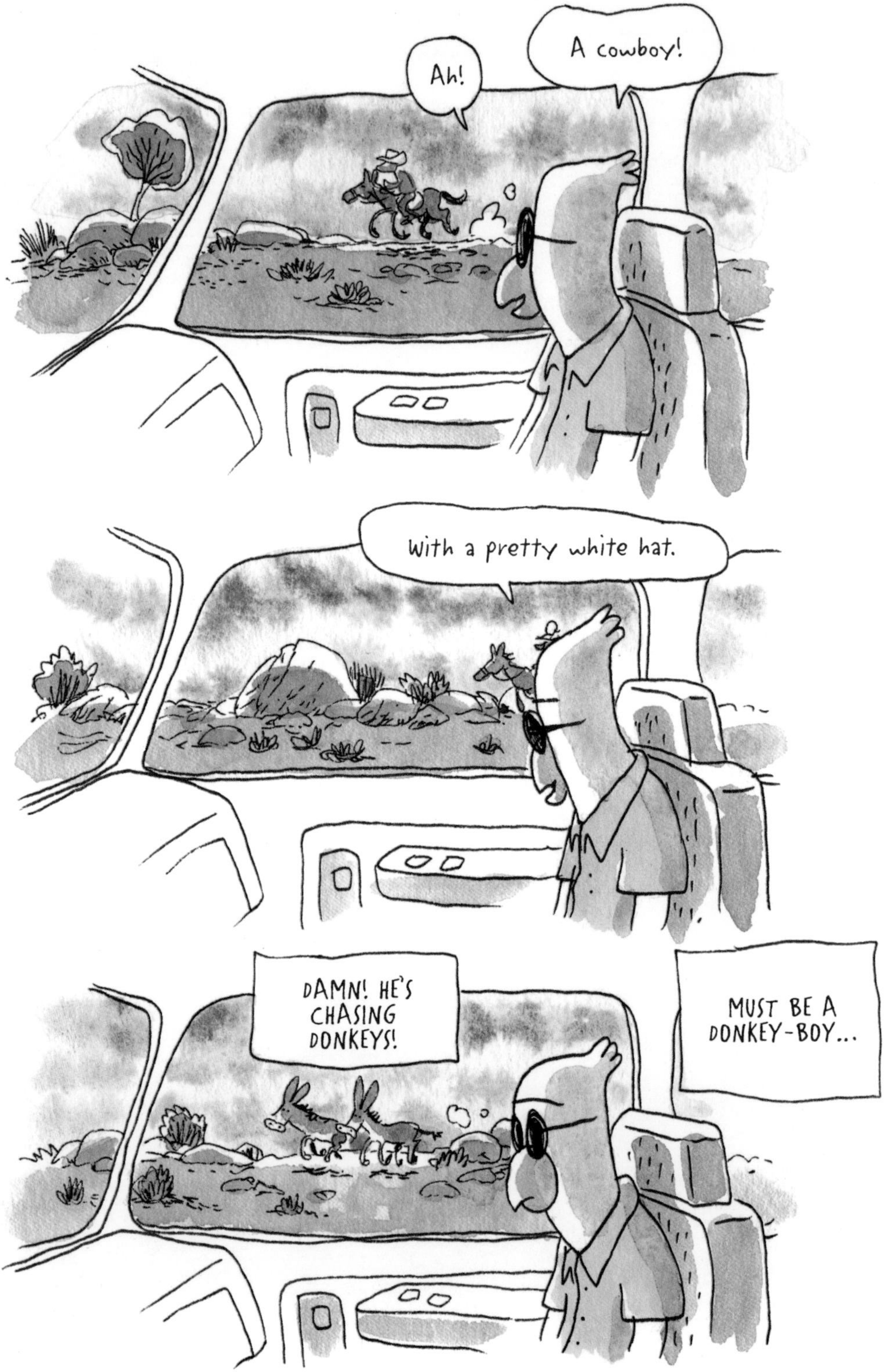
Ah!
A cowboy!
With a pretty white hat.
DAMN! HE'S CHASING DONKEYS!
MUST BE A DONKEY-BOY...

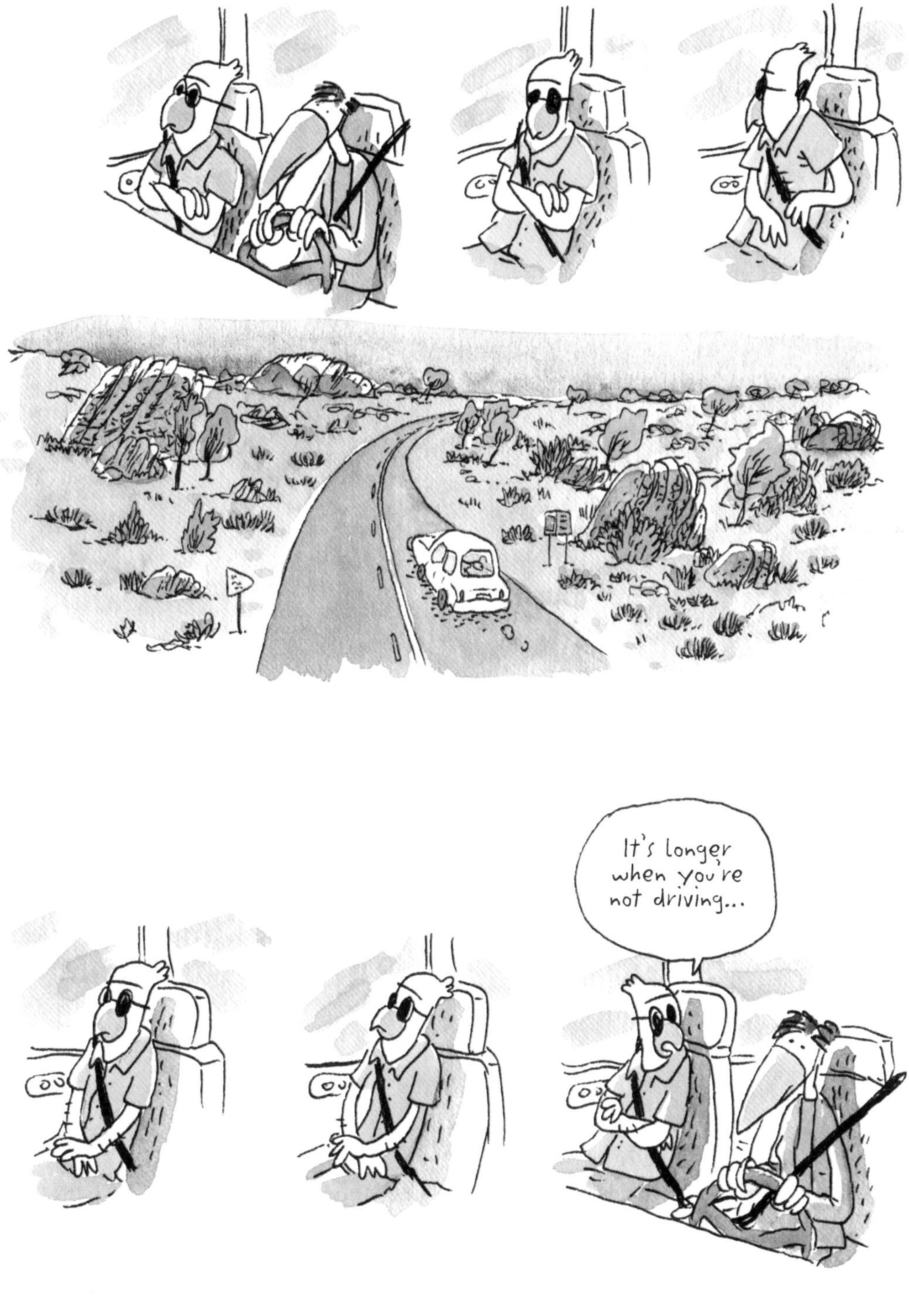
It's longer when you're not driving...

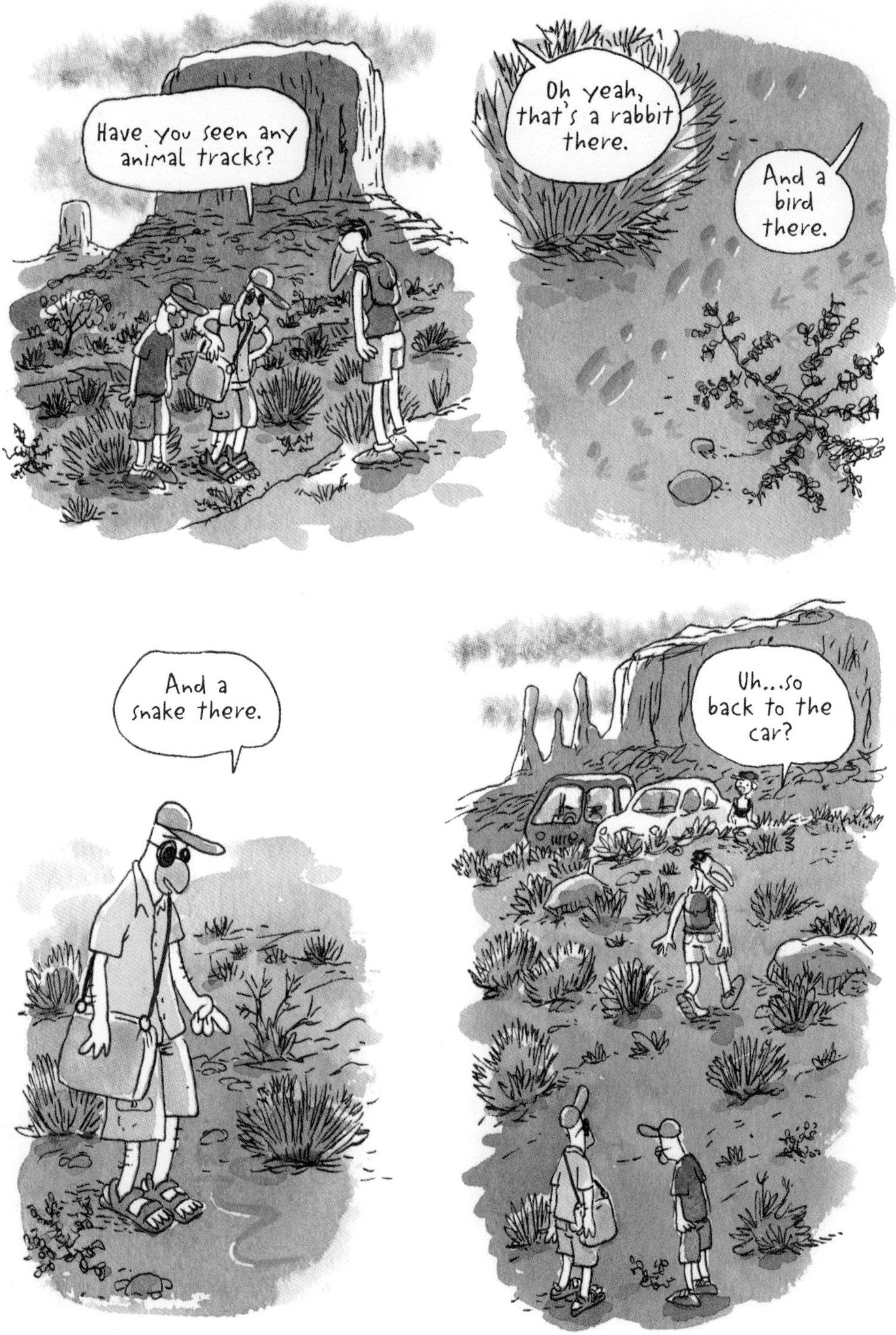
Have you seen any animal tracks?
Oh yeah, that's a rabbit there.
And a bird there.
And a snake there.
Uh...so back to the car?

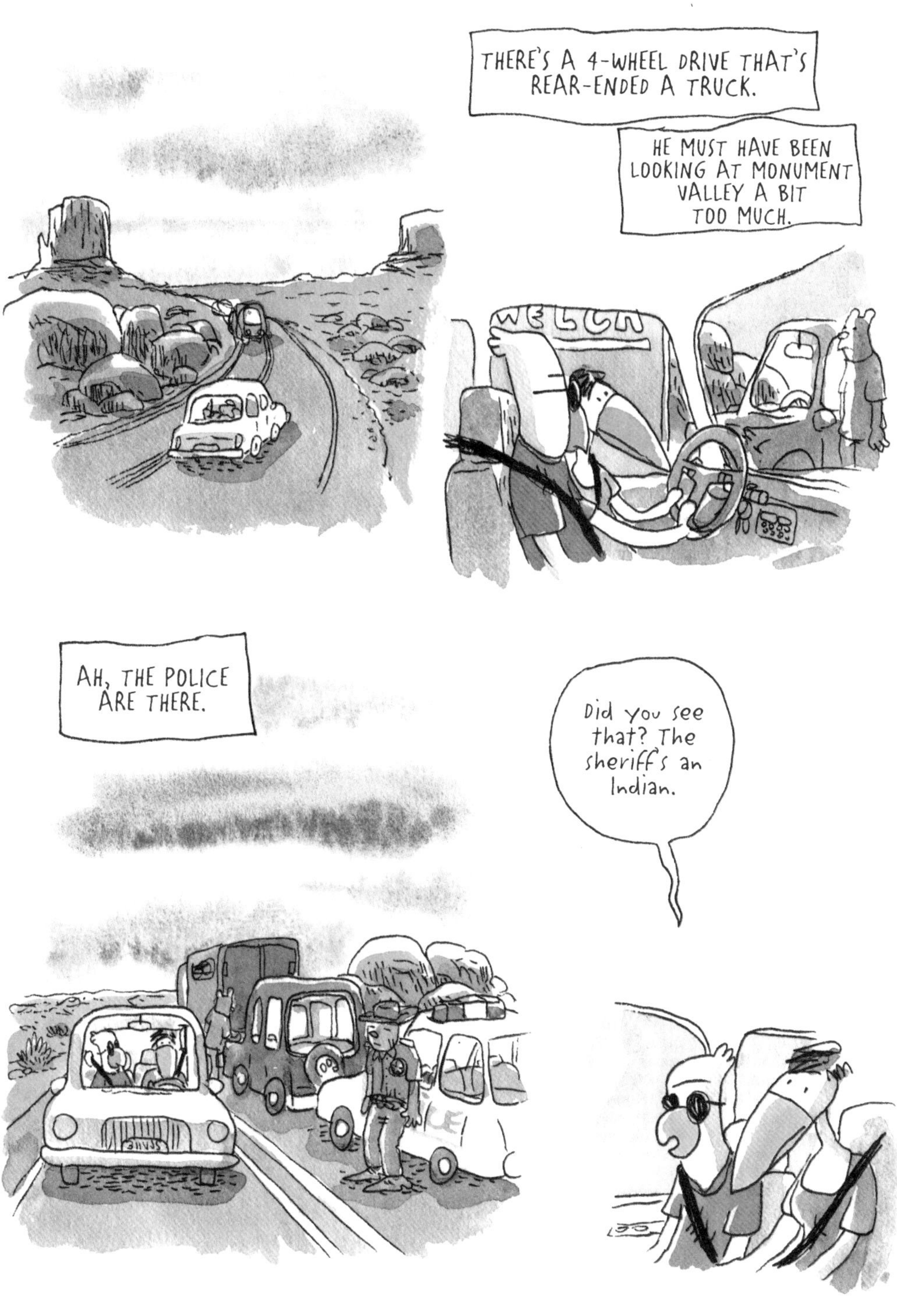
THERE'S A 4-WHEEL DRIVE THAT'S REAR-ENDED A TRUCK.
HE MUST HAVE BEEN LOOKING AT MONUMENT VALLEY A BIT TOO MUCH.
AH, THE POLICE ARE THERE.
Did you see that? The sheriff's an Indian.

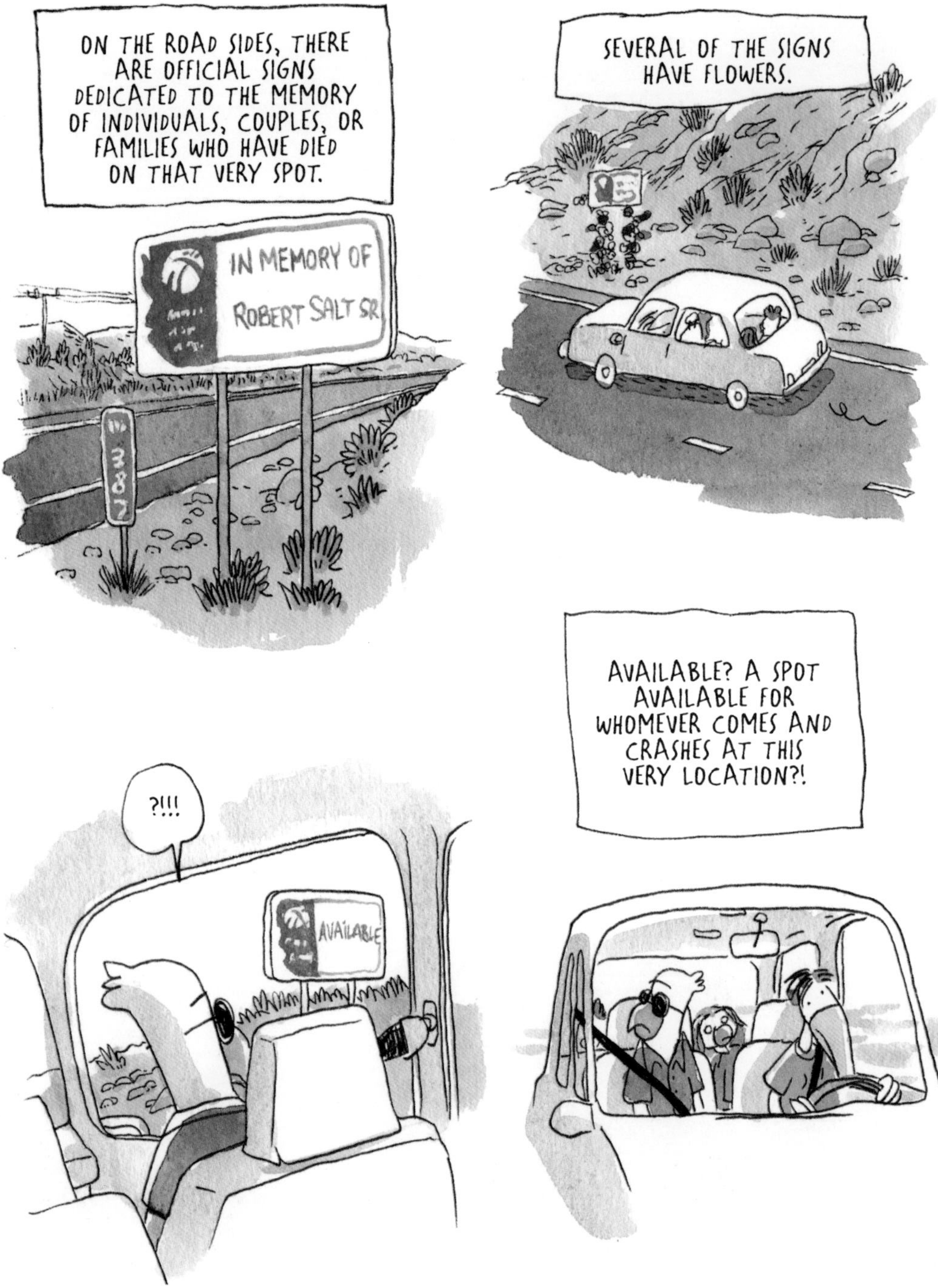
ON THE ROAD SIDES, THERE ARE OFFICIAL SIGNS DEDICATED TO THE MEMORY OF INDIVIDUALS, COUPLES, OR FAMILIES WHO HAVE DIED ON THAT VERY SPOT.
IN MEMORY OF
ROBERT SALT SR
SEVERAL OF THE SIGNS HAVE FLOWERS.
?!!!
AVAILABLE
AVAILABLE? A SPOT AVAILABLE FOR WHOMEVER COMES AND CRASHES AT THIS VERY LOCATION?!

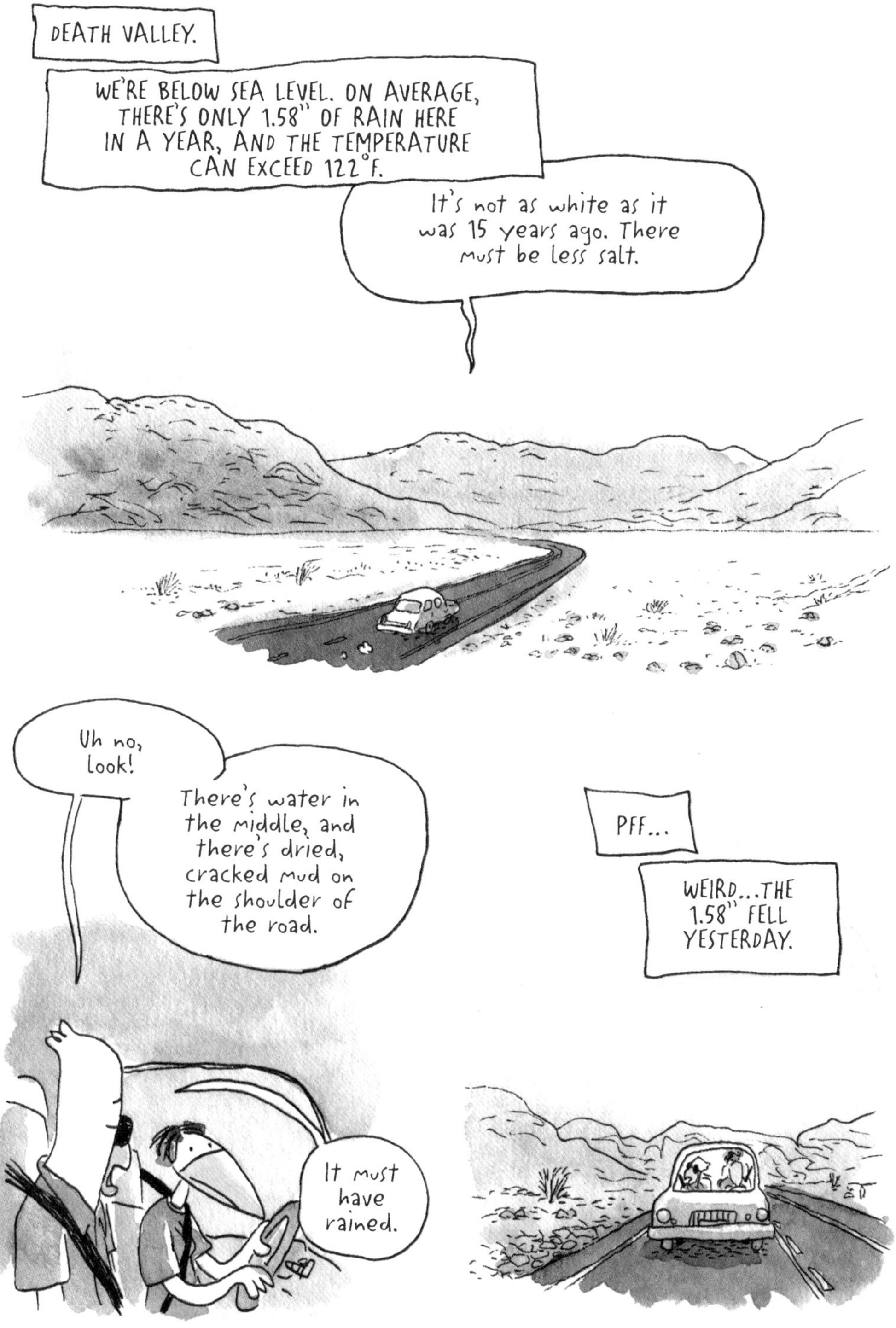
DEATH VALLEY.
WE'RE BELOW SEA LEVEL. ON AVERAGE, THERE'S ONLY 1.58" OF RAIN HERE IN A YEAR, AND THE TEMPERATURE CAN EXCEED 122°F.
It's not as white as it was 15 years ago. There must be less salt.
Uh no, look!
There's water in the middle, and there's dried, cracked mud on the shoulder of the road.
It must have rained.
PFF...
WEIRD...THE 1.58" FELL YESTERDAY.

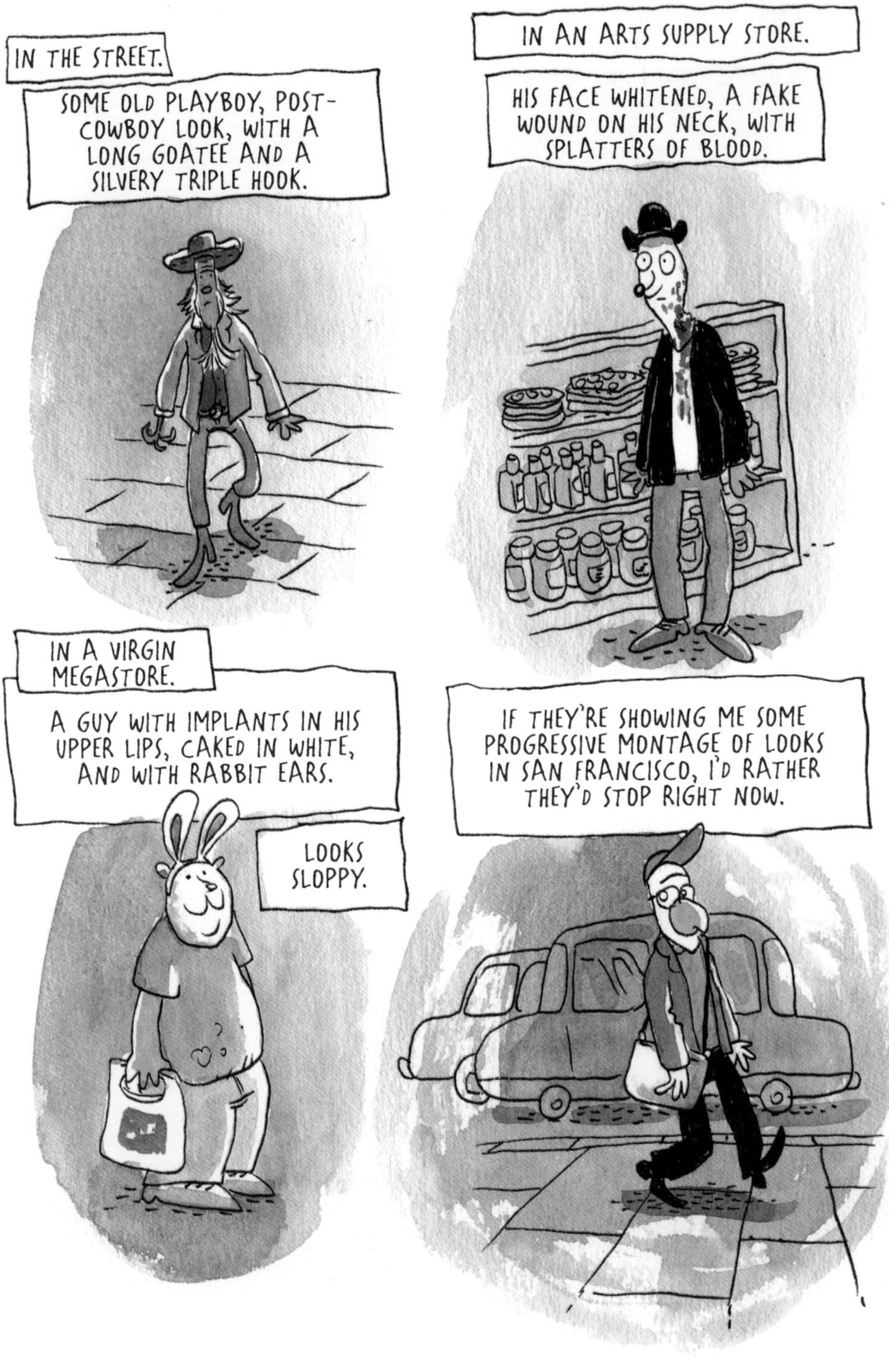
IN THE STREET.
SOME OLD PLAYBOY, POST-COWBOY LOOK, WITH A LONG GOATEE AND A SILVERY TRIPLE HOOK.
IN AN ARTS SUPPLY STORE.
HIS FACE WHITENED, A FAKE WOUND ON HIS NECK, WITH SPLATTERS OF BLOOD.
IN A VIRGIN MEGASTORE.
A GUY WITH IMPLANTS IN HIS UPPER LIPS, CAKED IN WHITE, AND WITH RABBIT EARS.
LOOKS SLOPPY.
IF THEY'RE SHOWING ME SOME PROGRESSIVE MONTAGE OF LOOKS IN SAN FRANCISCO, I'D RATHER THEY'D STOP RIGHT NOW.

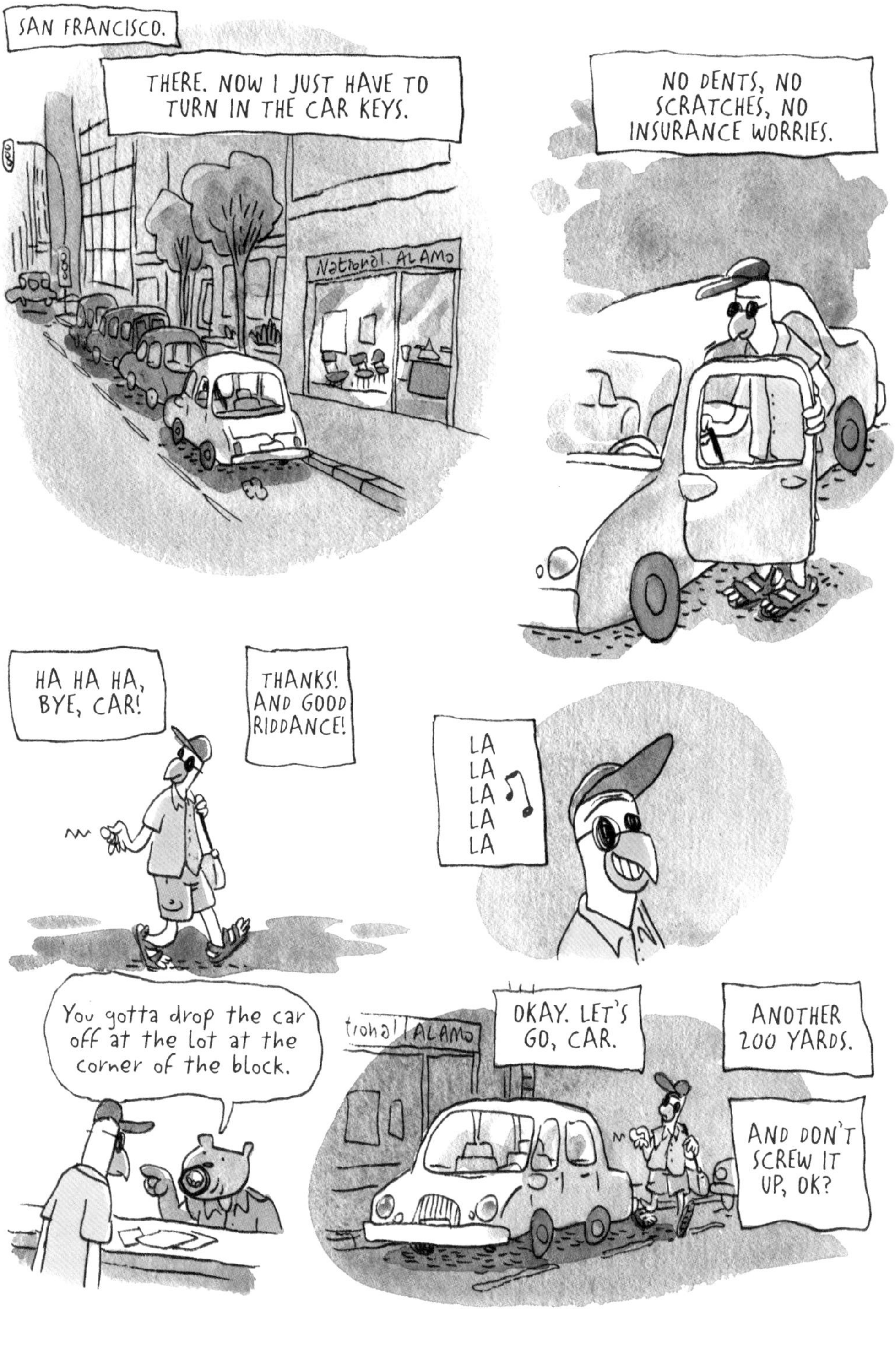
SAN FRANCISCO.
THERE. NOW I JUST HAVE TO TURN IN THE CAR KEYS.
National. ALAMO
NO DENTS, NO SCRATCHES, NO INSURANCE WORRIES.
HA HA HA, BYE, CAR!
THANKS! AND GOOD RIDDANCE!
LA LA LA LA LA
You gotta drop the car off at the lot at the corner of the block.
OKAY. LET'S GO, CAR.
ANOTHER 200 YARDS.
AND DON'T SCREW IT UP, OK?

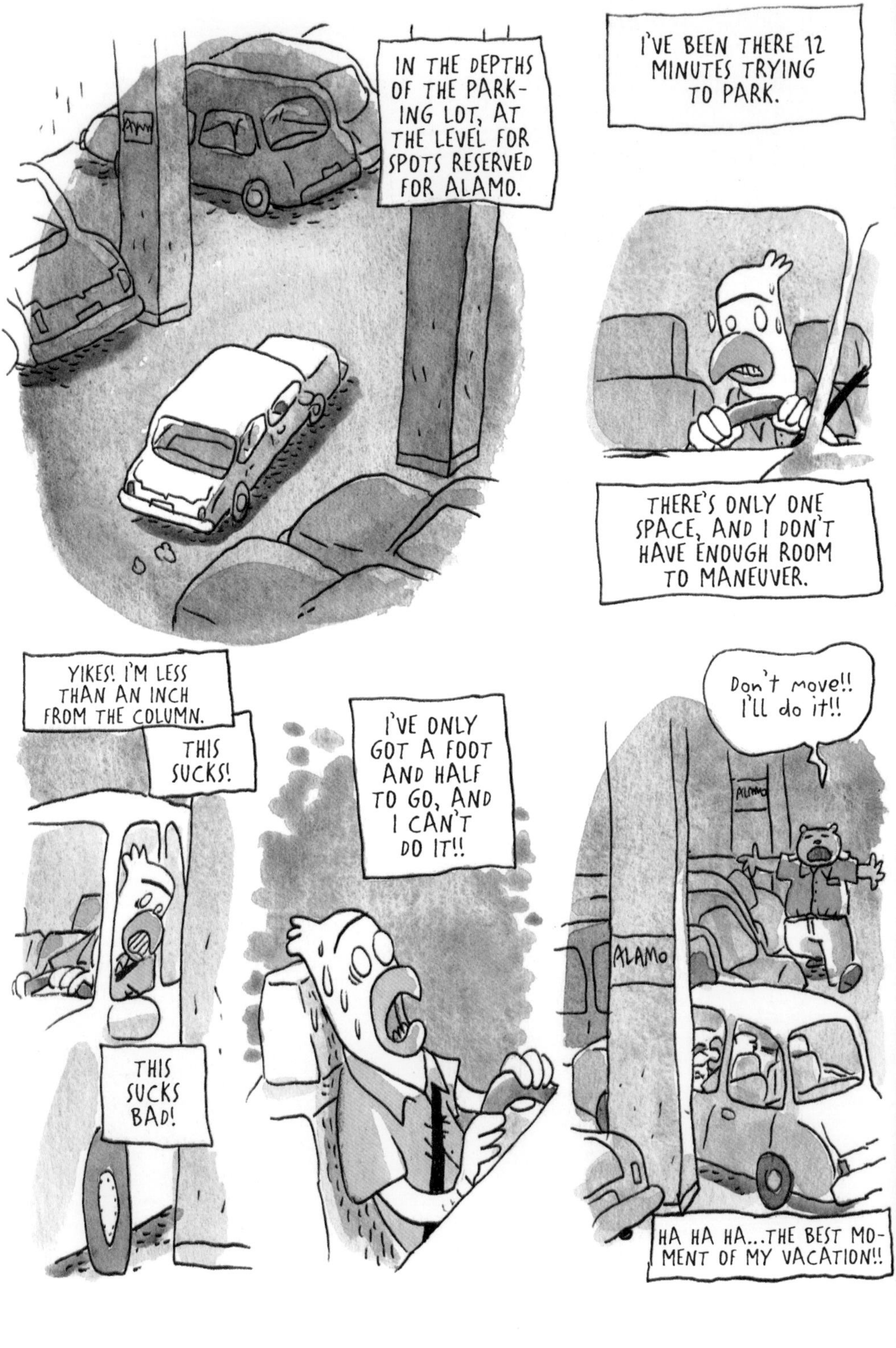
IN THE DEPTHS OF THE PARKING LOT, AT THE LEVEL FOR SPOTS RESERVED FOR ALAMO.
I'VE BEEN THERE 12 MINUTES TRYING TO PARK.
THERE'S ONLY ONE SPACE, AND I DON'T HAVE ENOUGH ROOM TO MANEUVER.
YIKES! I'M LESS THAN AN INCH FROM THE COLUMN.
THIS SUCKS!
THIS SUCKS BAD!
I'VE ONLY GOT A FOOT AND HALF TO GO, AND I CAN'T DO IT!!
Don't move!! I'll do it!!
ALAMO
HA HA HA...THE BEST MOMENT OF MY VACATION!!

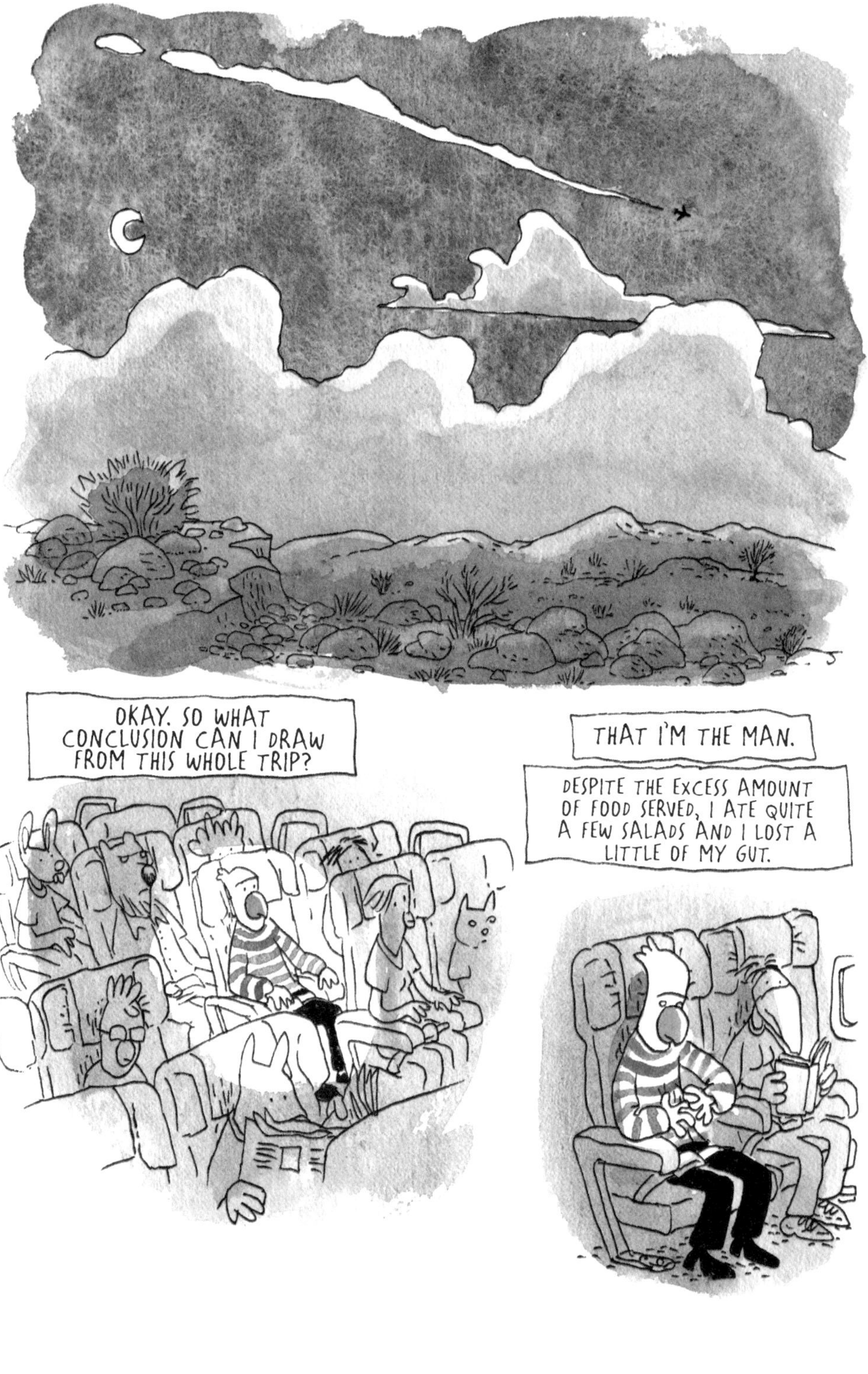
OKAY. SO WHAT CONCLUSION CAN I DRAW FROM THIS WHOLE TRIP?
THAT I'M THE MAN.
DESPITE THE EXCESS AMOUNT OF FOOD SERVED, I ATE QUITE A FEW SALADS AND I LOST A LITTLE OF MY GUT.

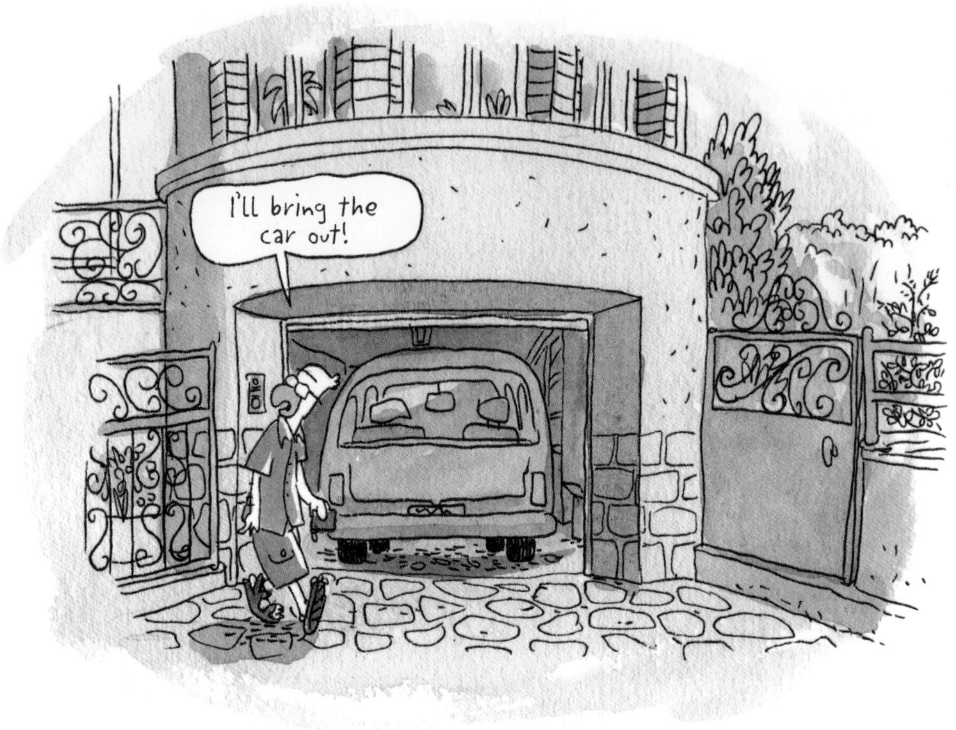
I'll bring the car out!

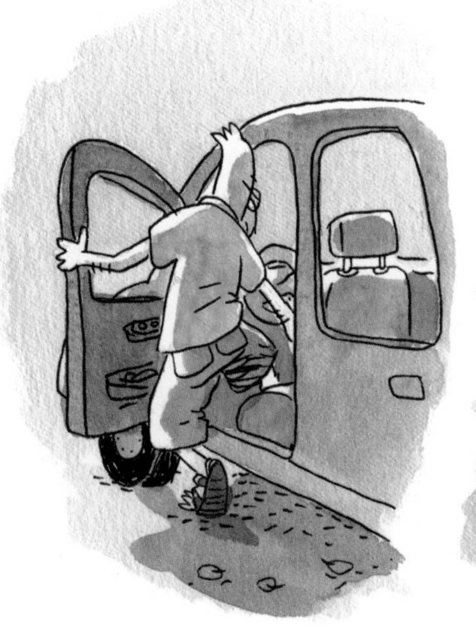

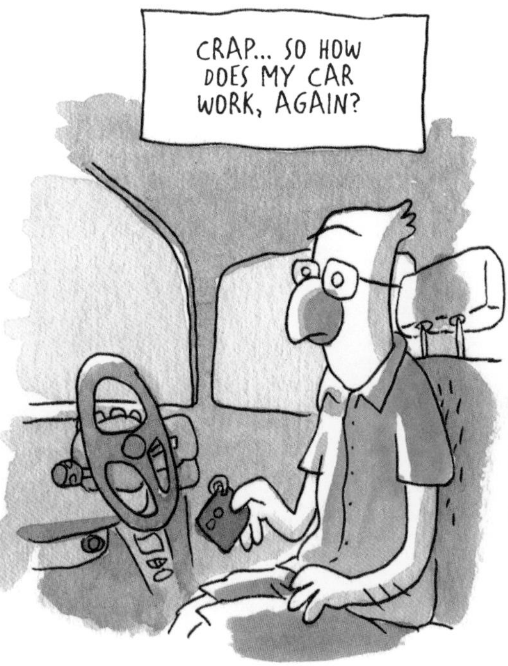
CRAP... SO HOW DOES MY CAR WORK, AGAIN?

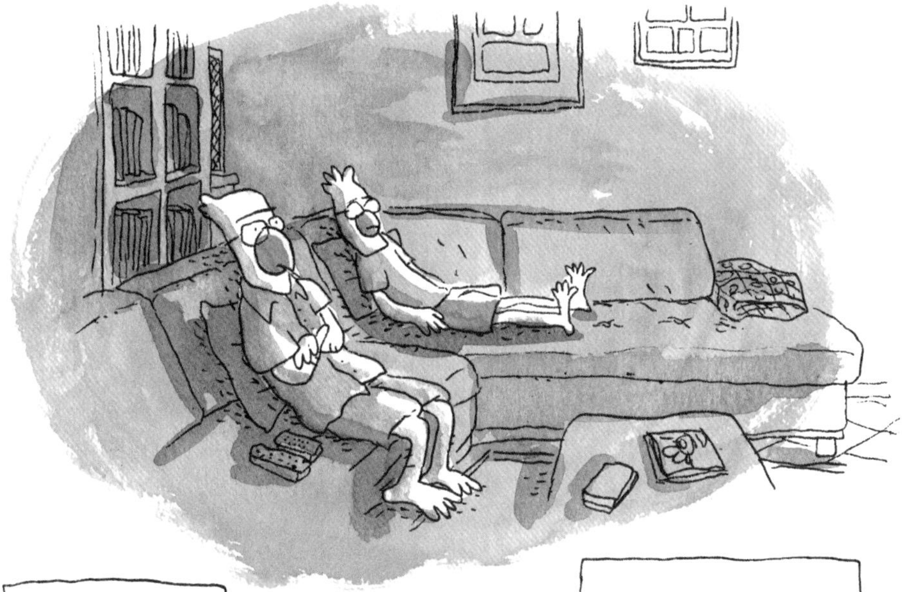

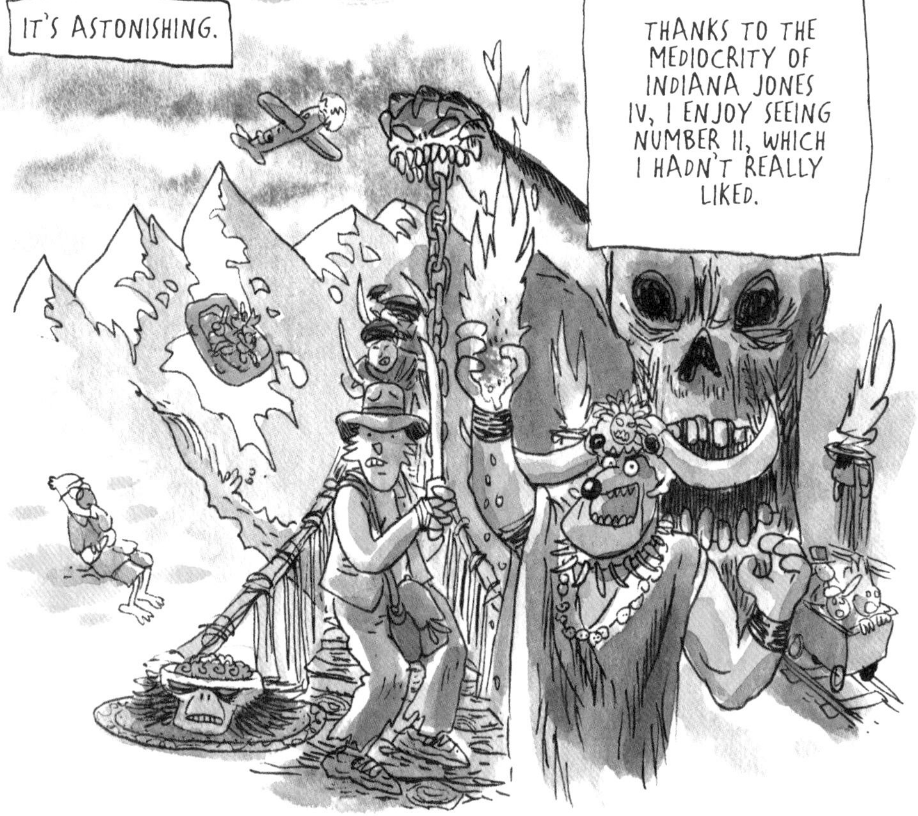
IT'S ASTONISHING.
THANKS TO THE MEDIOCRITY OF INDIANA JONES IV, I ENJOY SEEING NUMBER II, WHICH I HADN'T REALLY LIKED.

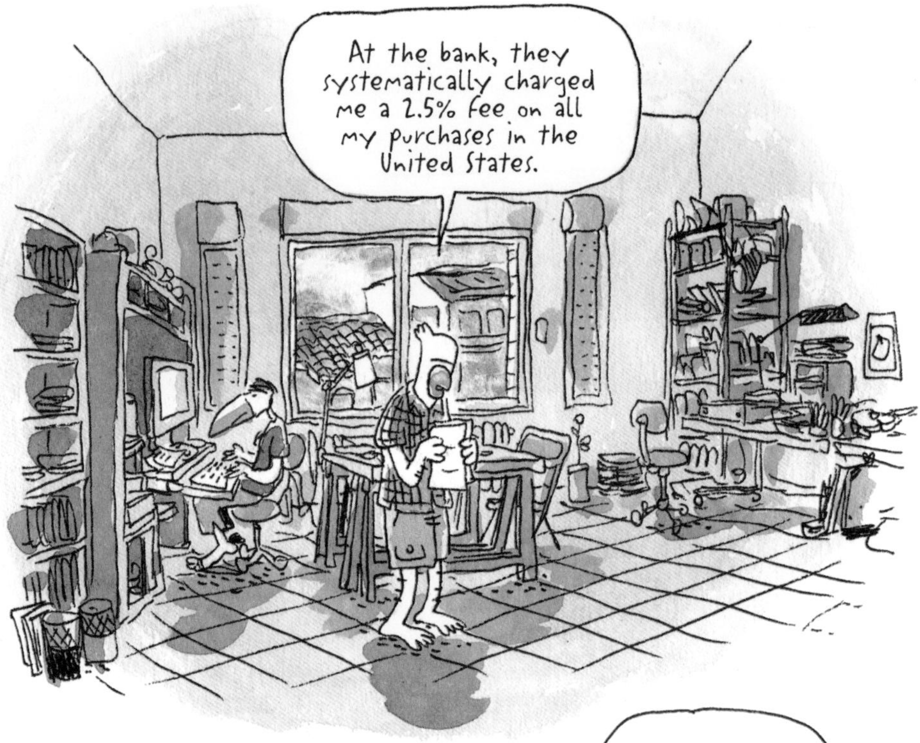
At the bank, they systematically charged me a 2.5% fee on all my purchases in the United States.

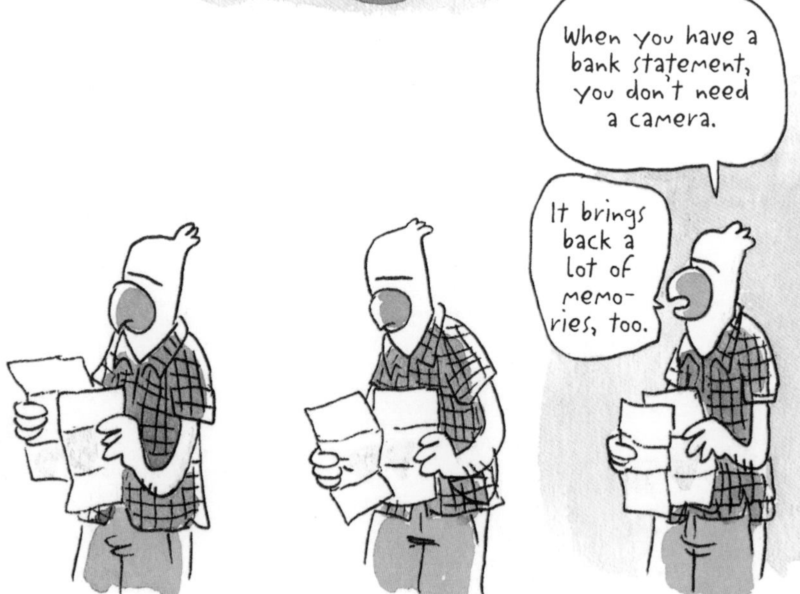
When you have a bank statement, you don't need a camera.
It brings back a lot of memo-ries, too.

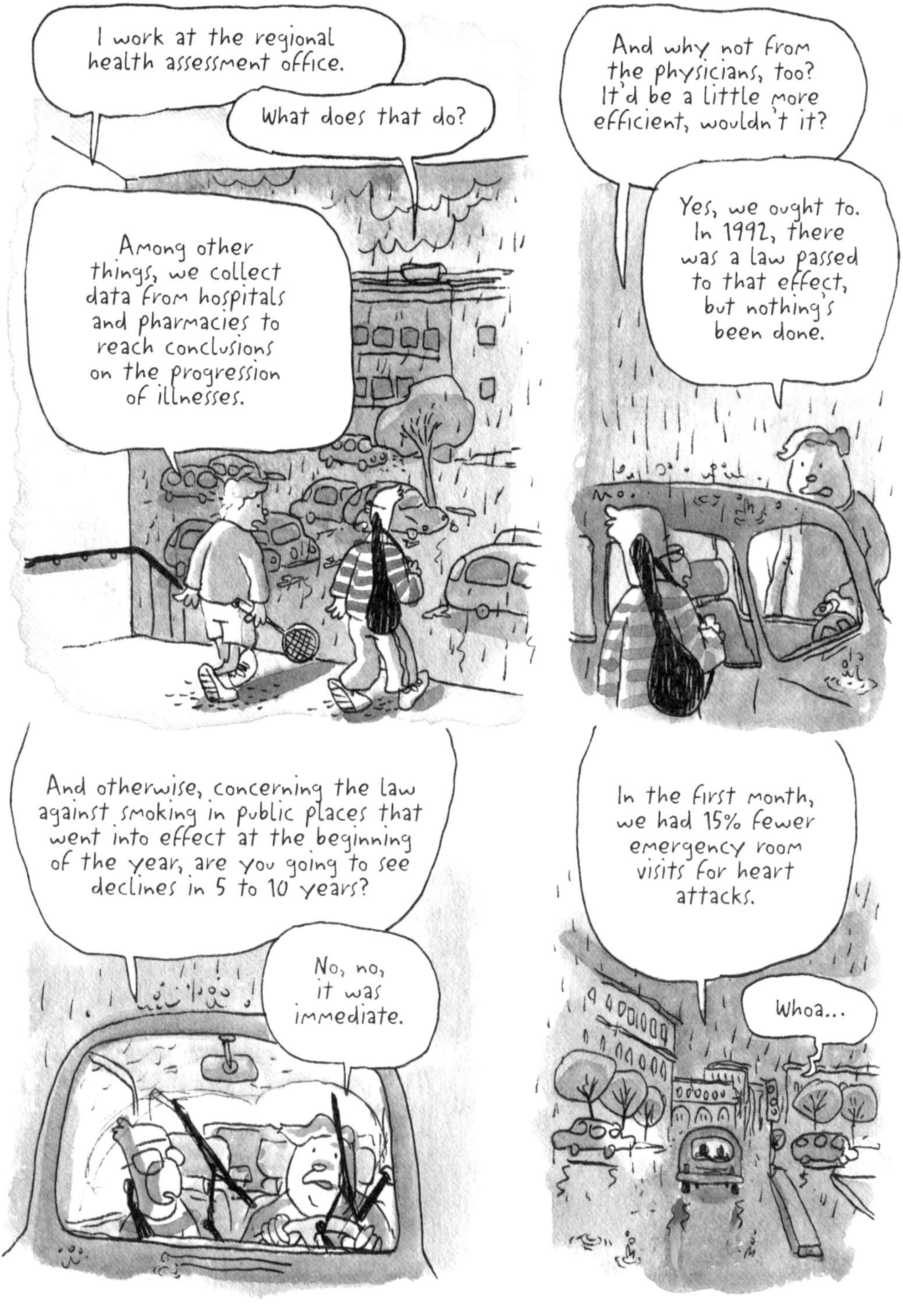
I work at the regional health assessment office.
What does that do?
Among other things, we collect data from hospitals and pharmacies to reach conclusions on the progression of illnesses.
And why not from the physicians, too? It'd be a little more efficient, wouldn't it?
Yes, we ought to. In 1992, there was a law passed to that effect, but nothing's been done.
And otherwise, concerning the law against smoking in public places that went into effect at the beginning of the year, are you going to see declines in 5 to 10 years?
No, no, it was immediate.
In the first month, we had 15% fewer emergency room visits for heart attacks.
Whoa...

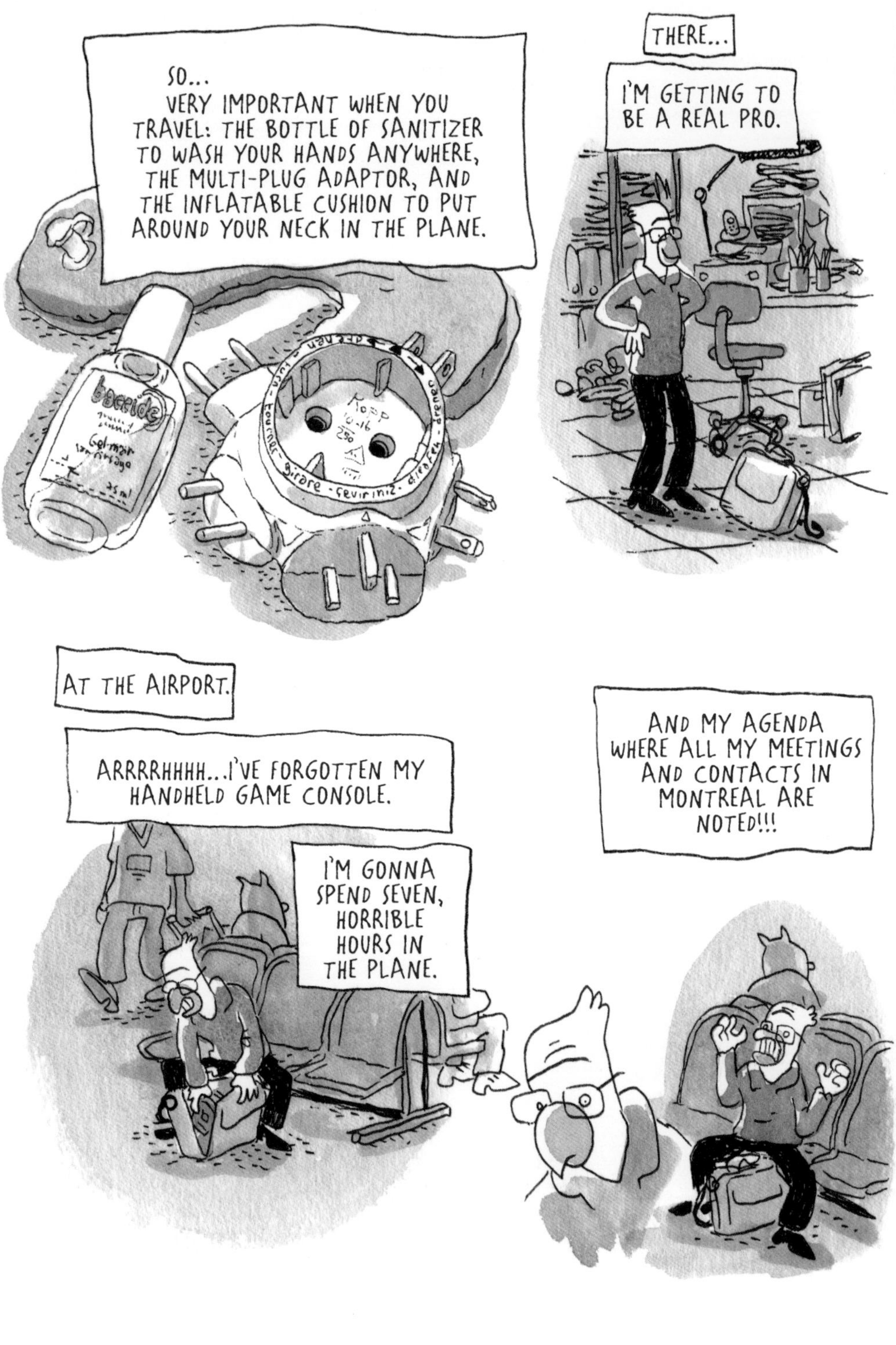
SO...
VERY IMPORTANT WHEN YOU TRAVEL: THE BOTTLE OF SANITIZER TO WASH YOUR HANDS ANYWHERE, THE MULTI-PLUG ADAPTOR, AND THE INFLATABLE CUSHION TO PUT AROUND YOUR NECK IN THE PLANE.
THERE...
I'M GETTING TO BE A REAL PRO.
AT THE AIRPORT.
ARRRRHHHH...I'VE FORGOTTEN MY HANDHELD GAME CONSOLE.
I'M GONNA SPEND SEVEN, HORRIBLE HOURS IN THE PLANE.
AND MY AGENDA WHERE ALL MY MEETINGS AND CONTACTS IN MONTREAL ARE NOTED!!!

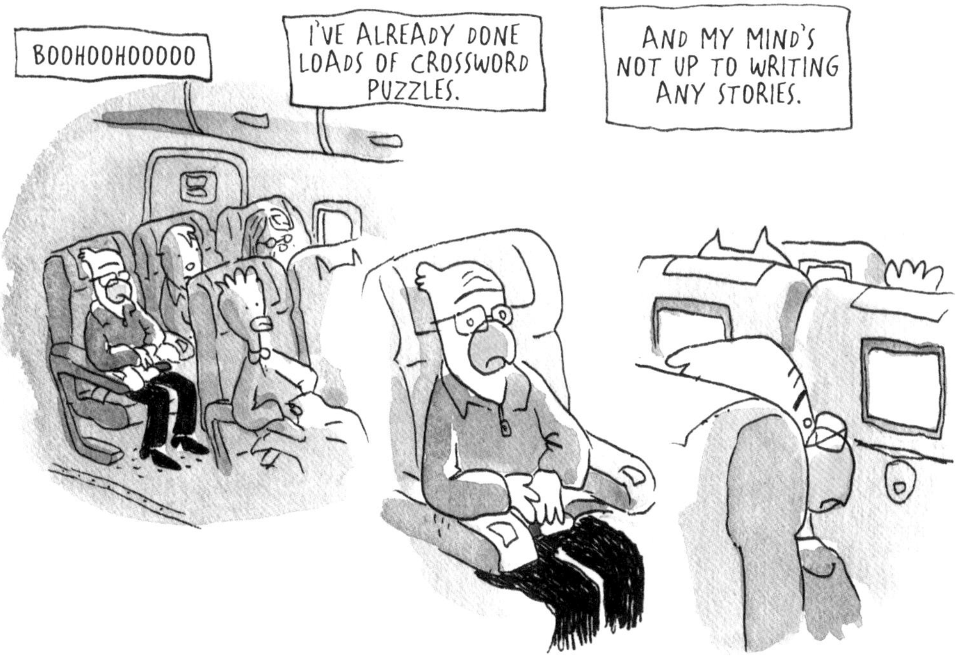
BOOHOOHOOOOO
I'VE ALREADY DONE LOADS OF CROSSWORD PUZZLES.
AND MY MIND'S NOT UP TO WRITING ANY STORIES.

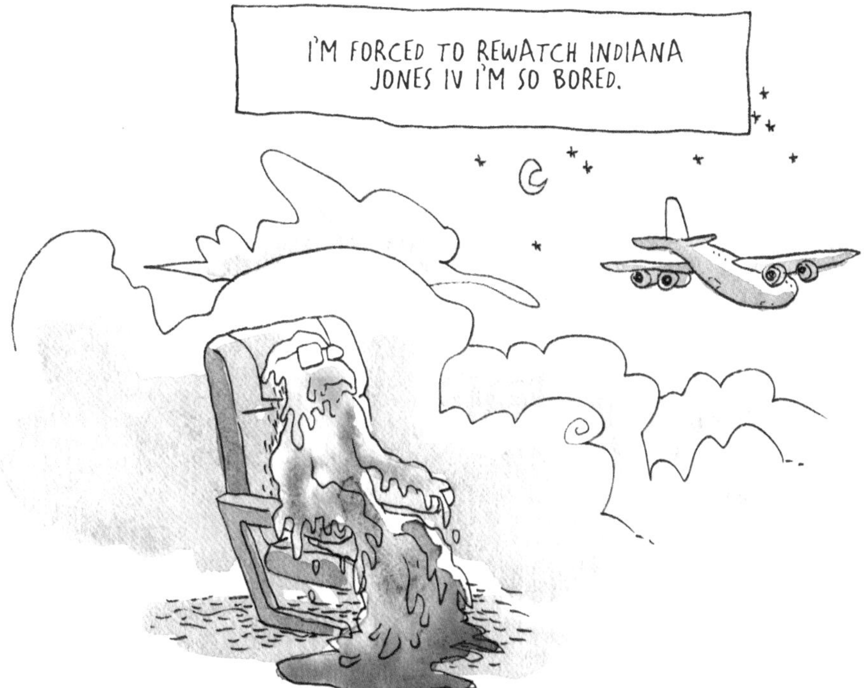
I'M FORCED TO REWATCH INDIANA JONES IV I'M SO BORED.

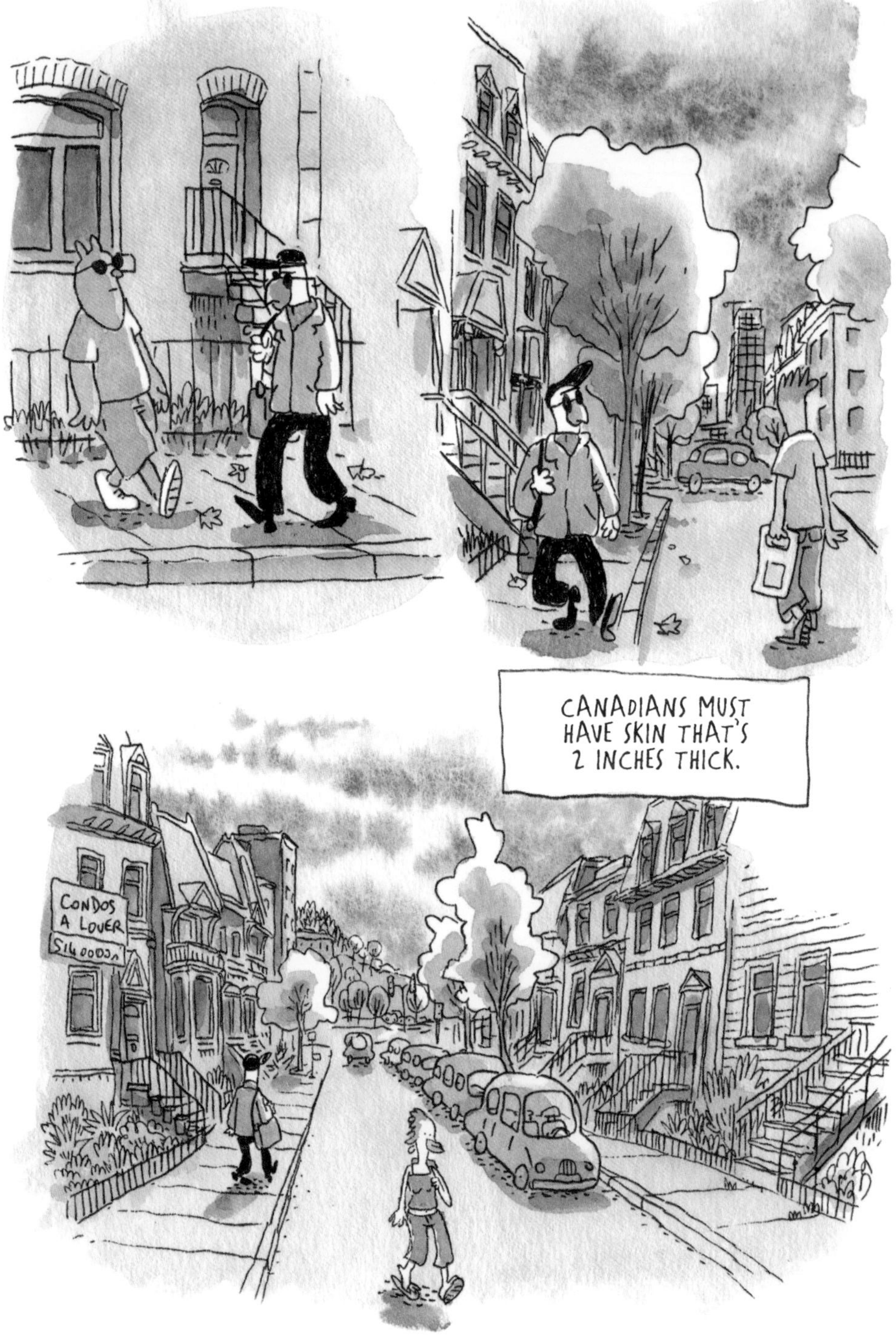
CANADIANS MUST HAVE SKIN THAT'S 2 INCHES THICK.
CONDOS A LOUER

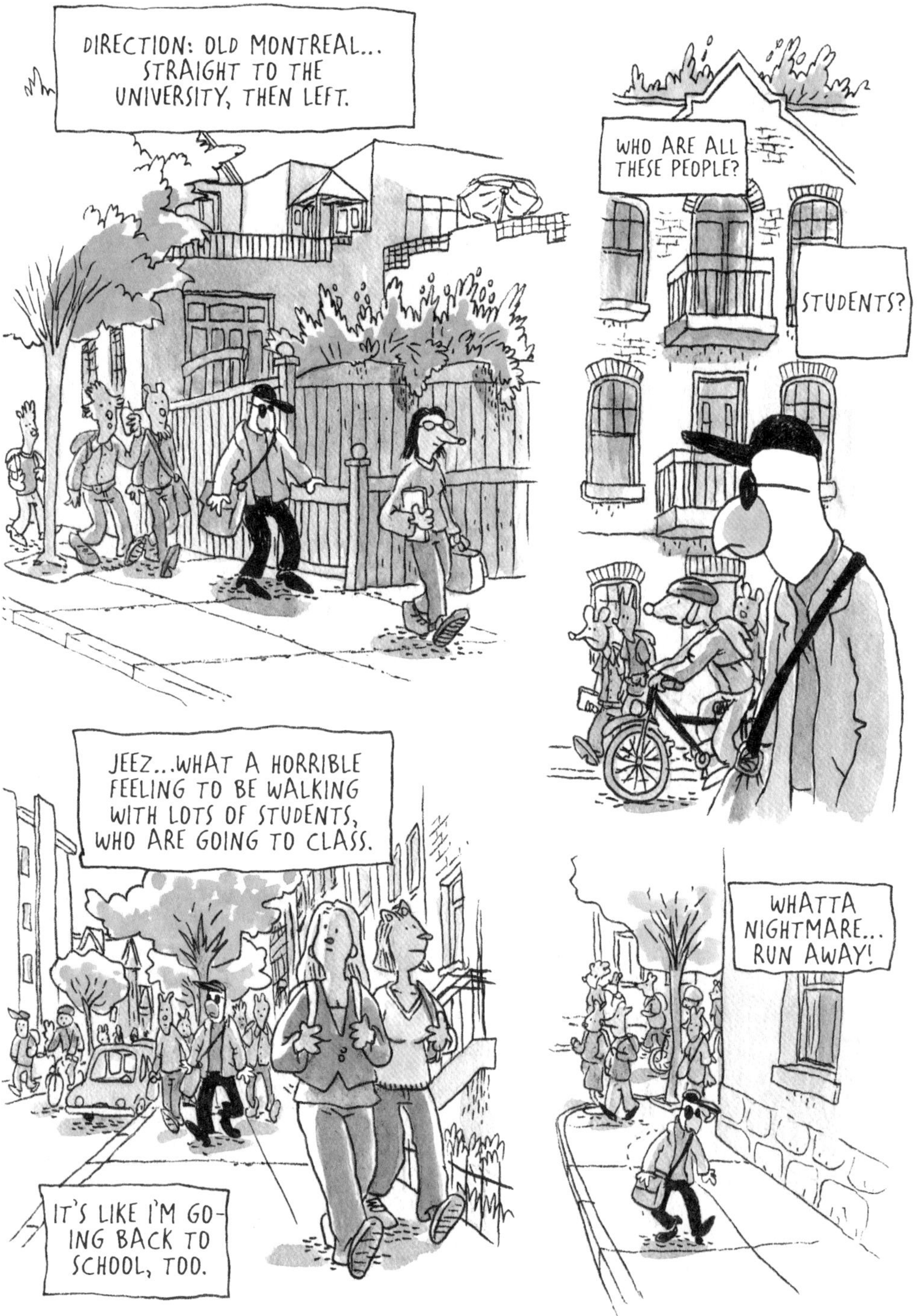
DIRECTION: OLD MONTREAL... STRAIGHT TO THE UNIVERSITY, THEN LEFT.
WHO ARE ALL THESE PEOPLE?
STUDENTS?
JEEZ...WHAT A HORRIBLE FEELING TO BE WALKING WITH LOTS OF STUDENTS, WHO ARE GOING TO CLASS.
IT'S LIKE I'M GO-ING BACK TO SCHOOL, TOO.
WHATTA NIGHTMARE... RUN AWAY!

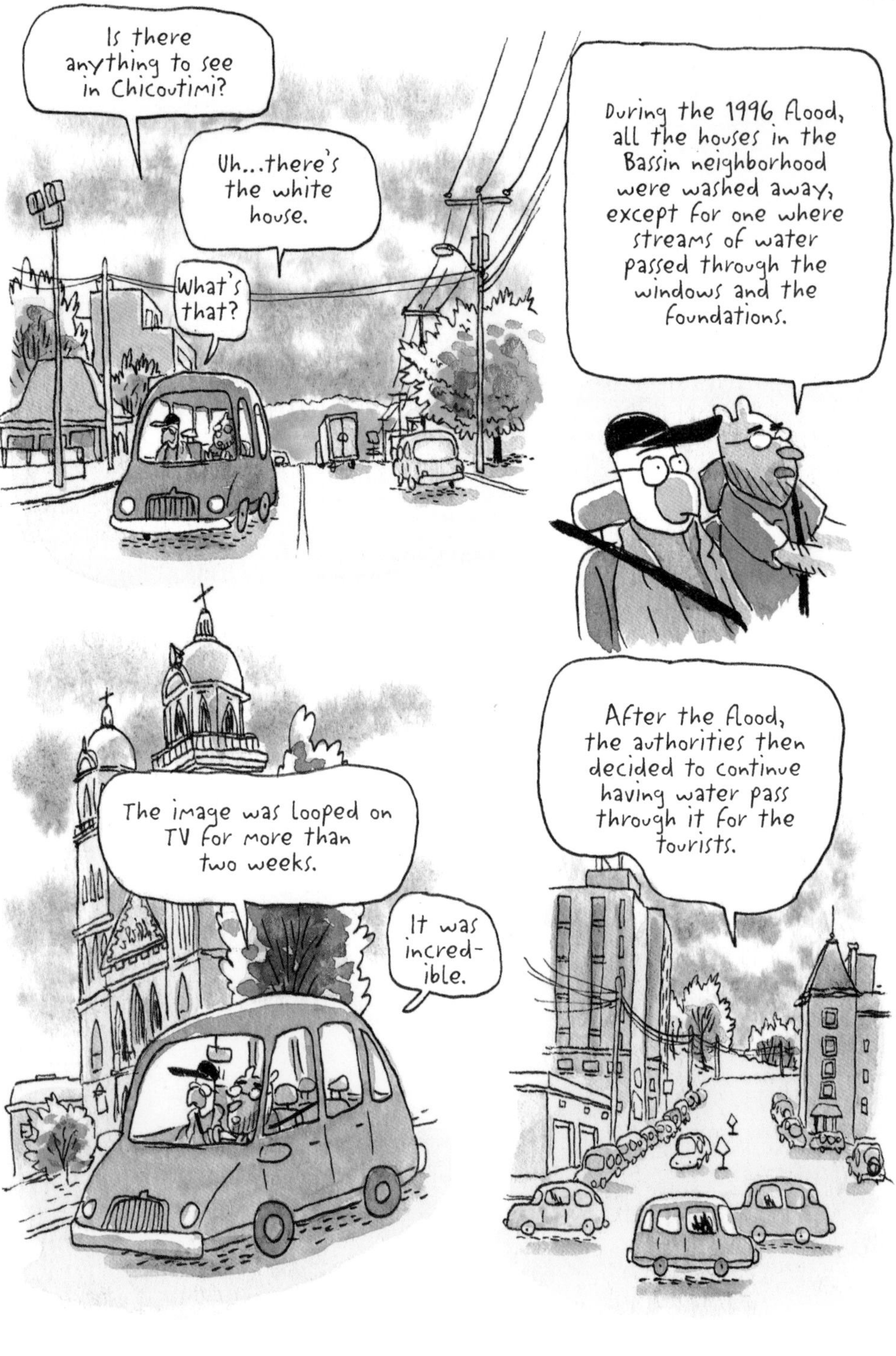
Is there anything to see in Chicoutimi?
Uh...there's the white house.
What's that?
During the 1996 flood, all the houses in the Bassin neighborhood were washed away, except for one where streams of water passed through the windows and the foundations.
The image was looped on TV for more than two weeks.
It was incred-ible.
After the flood, the authorities then decided to continue having water pass through it for the tourists.

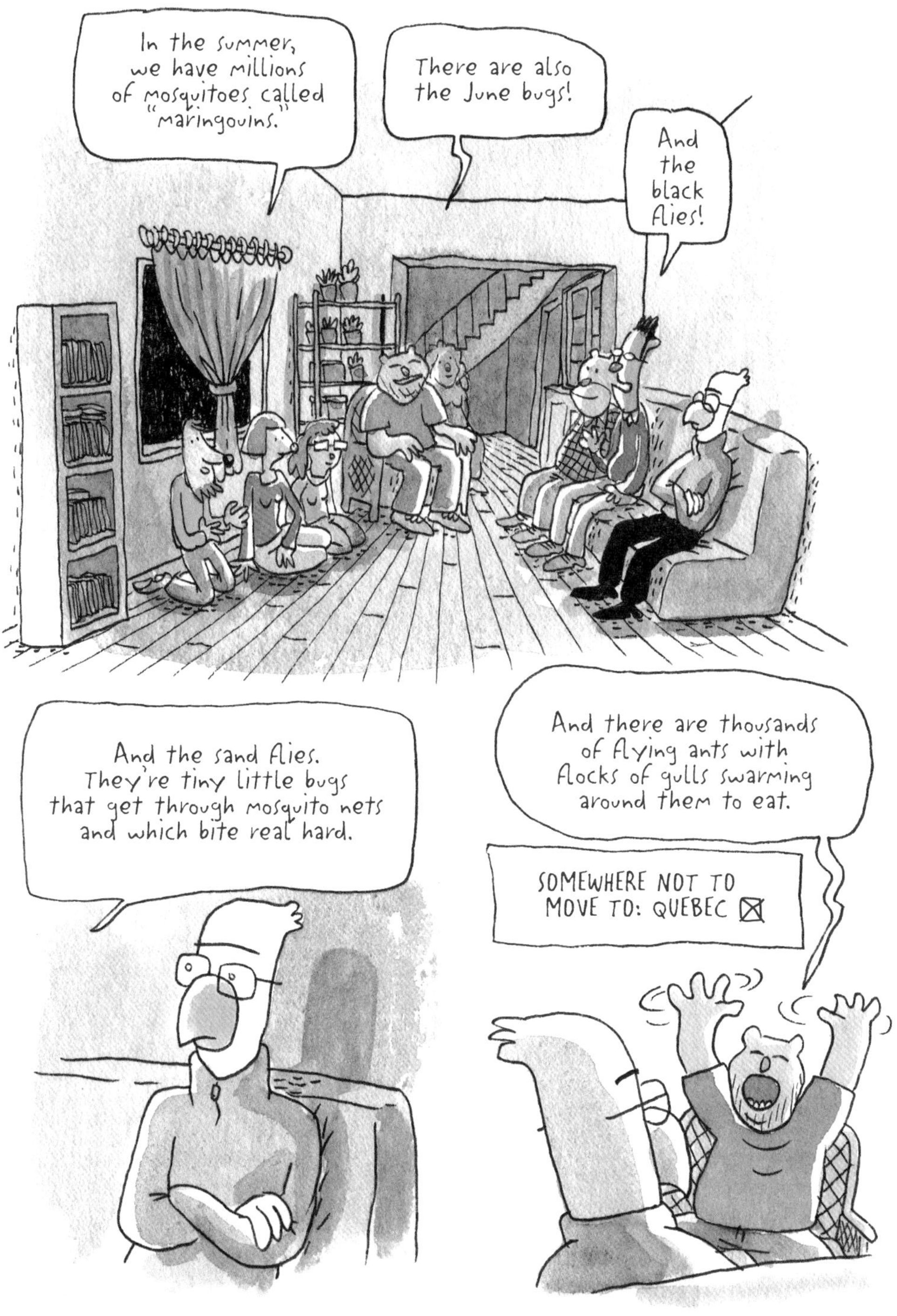
In the summer, we have millions of mosquitoes called "maringouins."
There are also the June bugs!
And the black flies!
And the sand flies. They're tiny little bugs that get through mosquito nets and which bite real hard.
And there are thousands of flying ants with flocks of gulls swarming around them to eat.
SOMEWHERE NOT TO MOVE TO: QUEBEC ☒

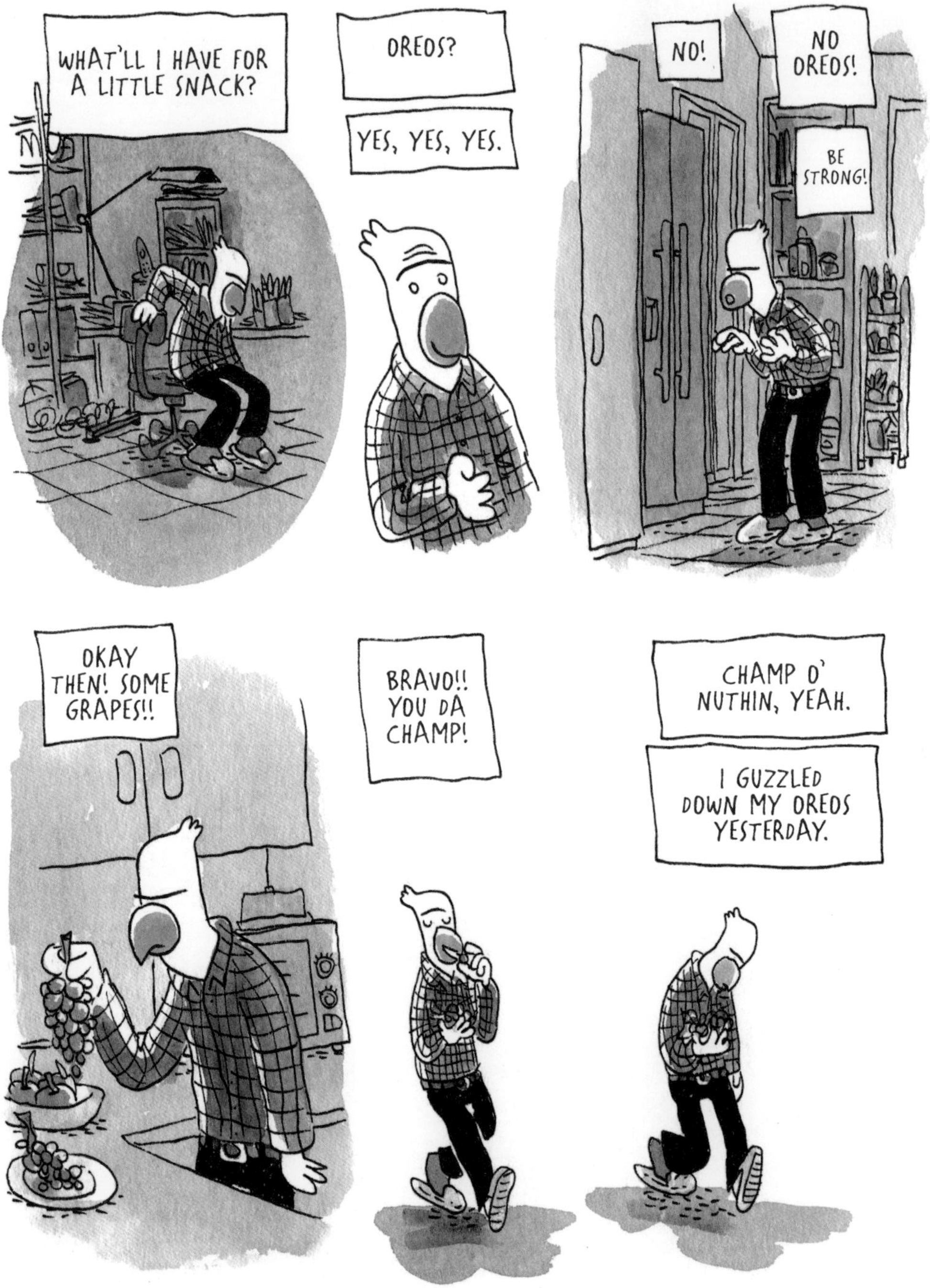

WHAT'LL I HAVE FOR A LITTLE SNACK?
OREOS?
YES, YES, YES.
NO!
NO OREOS!
BE STRONG!
OKAY THEN! SOME GRAPES!!
BRAVO!! YOU DA CHAMP!
CHAMP O' NUTHIN, YEAH.
I GUZZLED DOWN MY OREOS YESTERDAY.

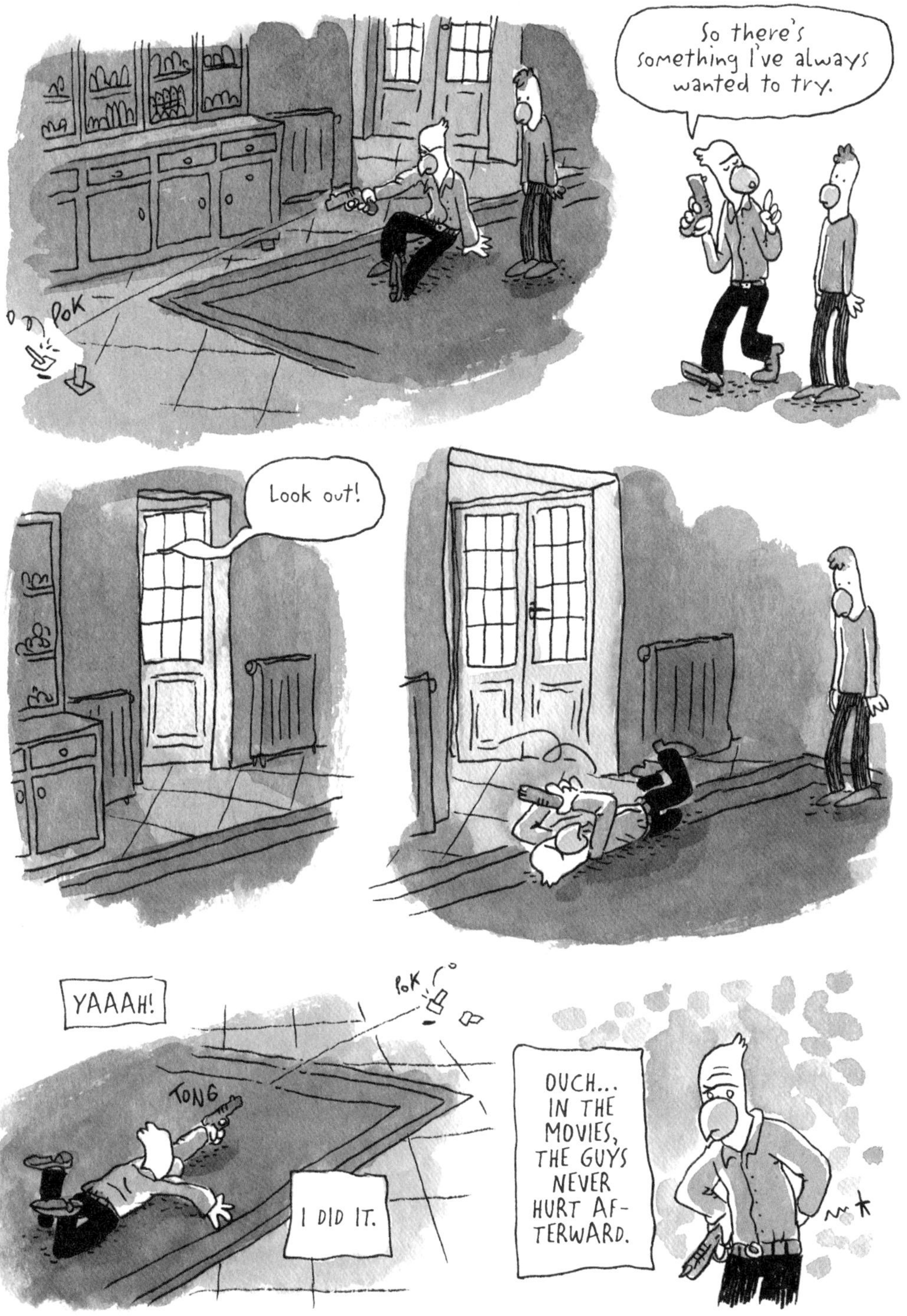
POK
So there's something I've always wanted to try.
Look out!
YAAAH!
POK
TONG
I DID IT.
OUCH... IN THE MOVIES, THE GUYS NEVER HURT AFTERWARD.

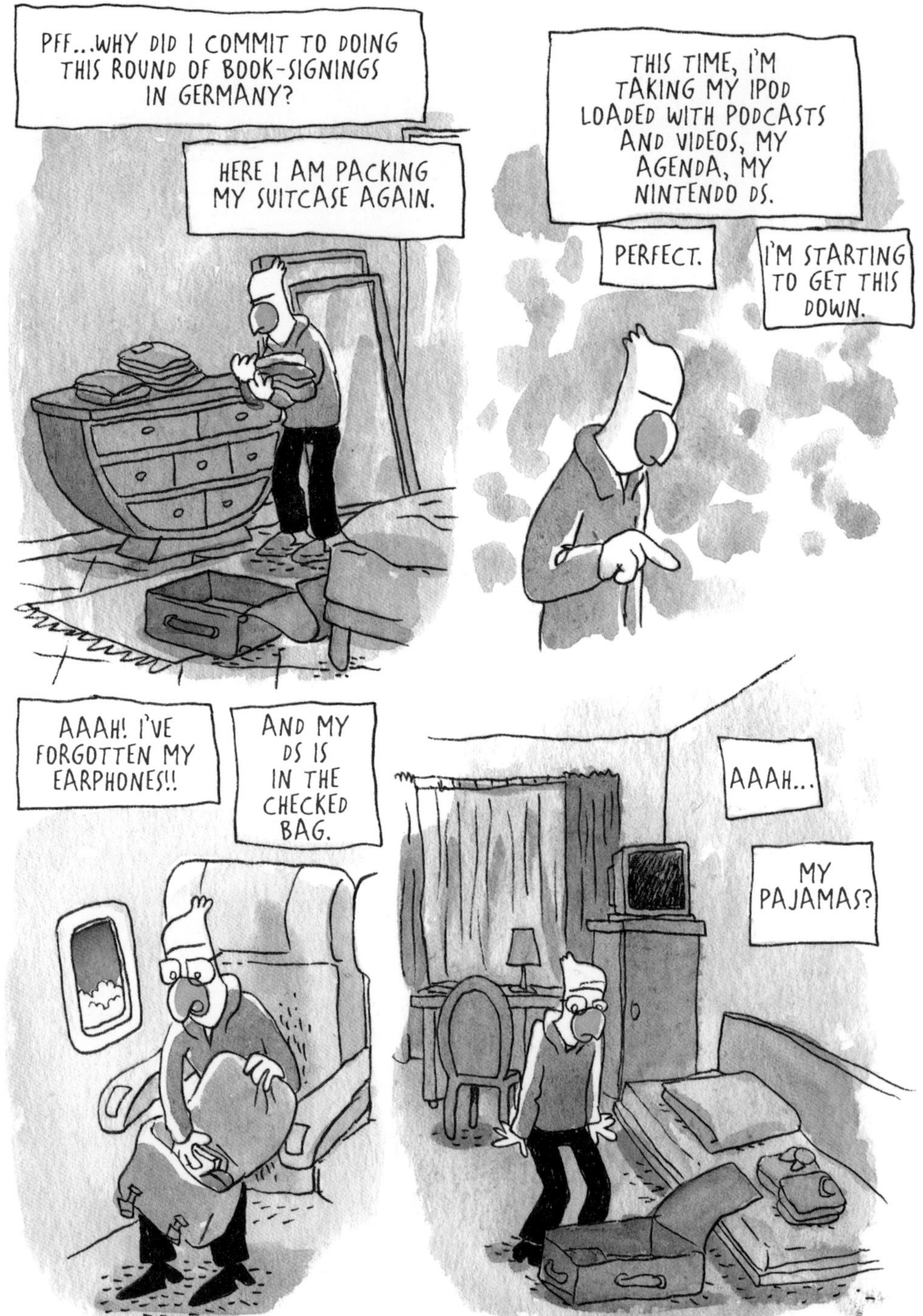

PFF...WHY DID I COMMIT TO DOING THIS ROUND OF BOOK-SIGNINGS IN GERMANY?
HERE I AM PACKING MY SUITCASE AGAIN.
THIS TIME, I'M TAKING MY IPOD LOADED WITH PODCASTS AND VIDEOS, MY AGENDA, MY NINTENDO DS.
PERFECT.
I'M STARTING TO GET THIS DOWN.
AAAH! I'VE FORGOTTEN MY EARPHONES!!
AND MY DS IS IN THE CHECKED BAG.
AAAH...
MY PAJAMAS?

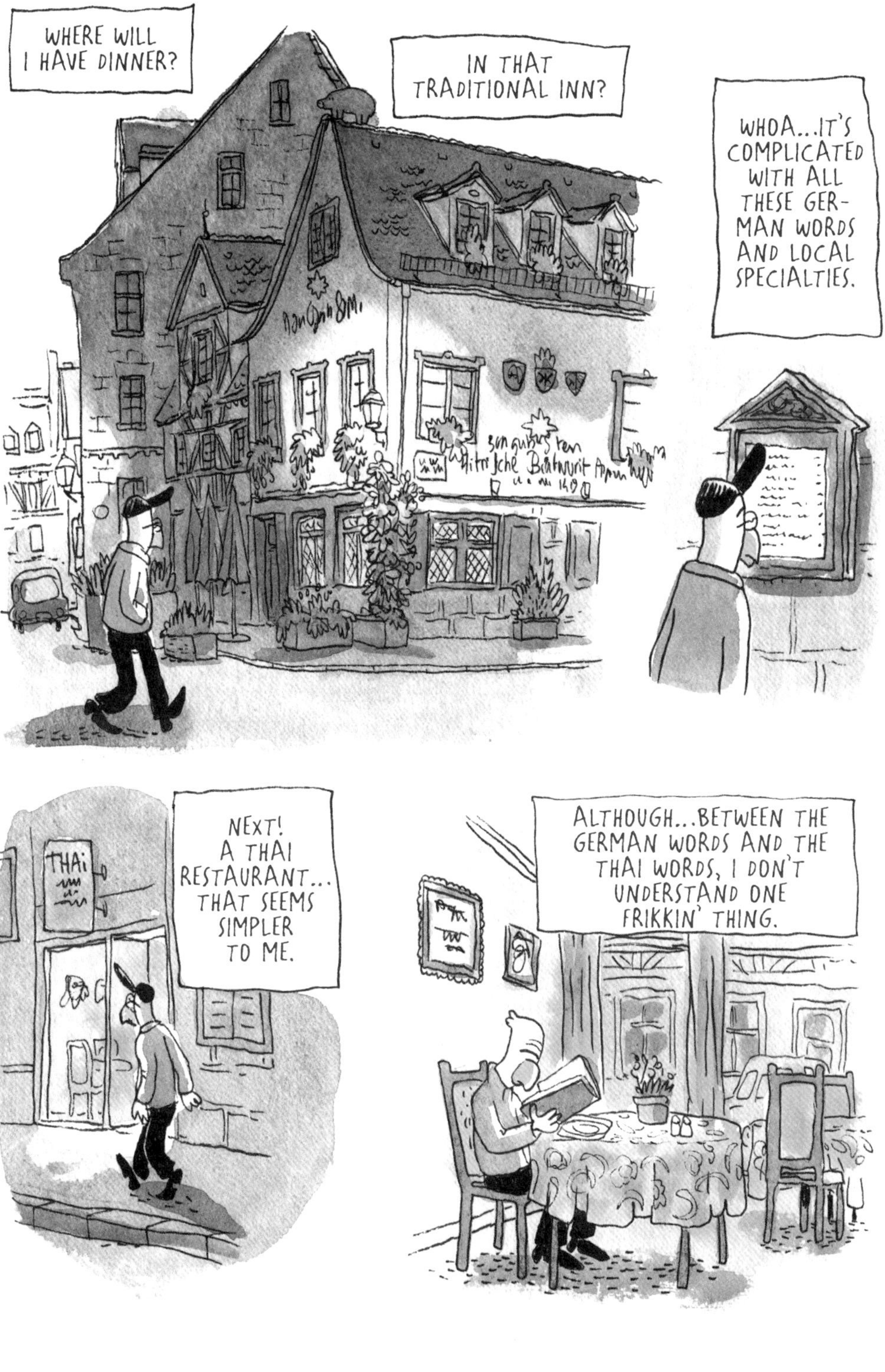
WHERE WILL I HAVE DINNER?
IN THAT TRADITIONAL INN?
WHOA...IT'S COMPLICATED WITH ALL THESE GER-MAN WORDS AND LOCAL SPECIALTIES.
THAi
NEXT! A THAI RESTAURANT... THAT SEEMS SIMPLER TO ME.
ALTHOUGH...BETWEEN THE GERMAN WORDS AND THE THAI WORDS, I DON'T UNDERSTAND ONE FRIKKIN' THING.

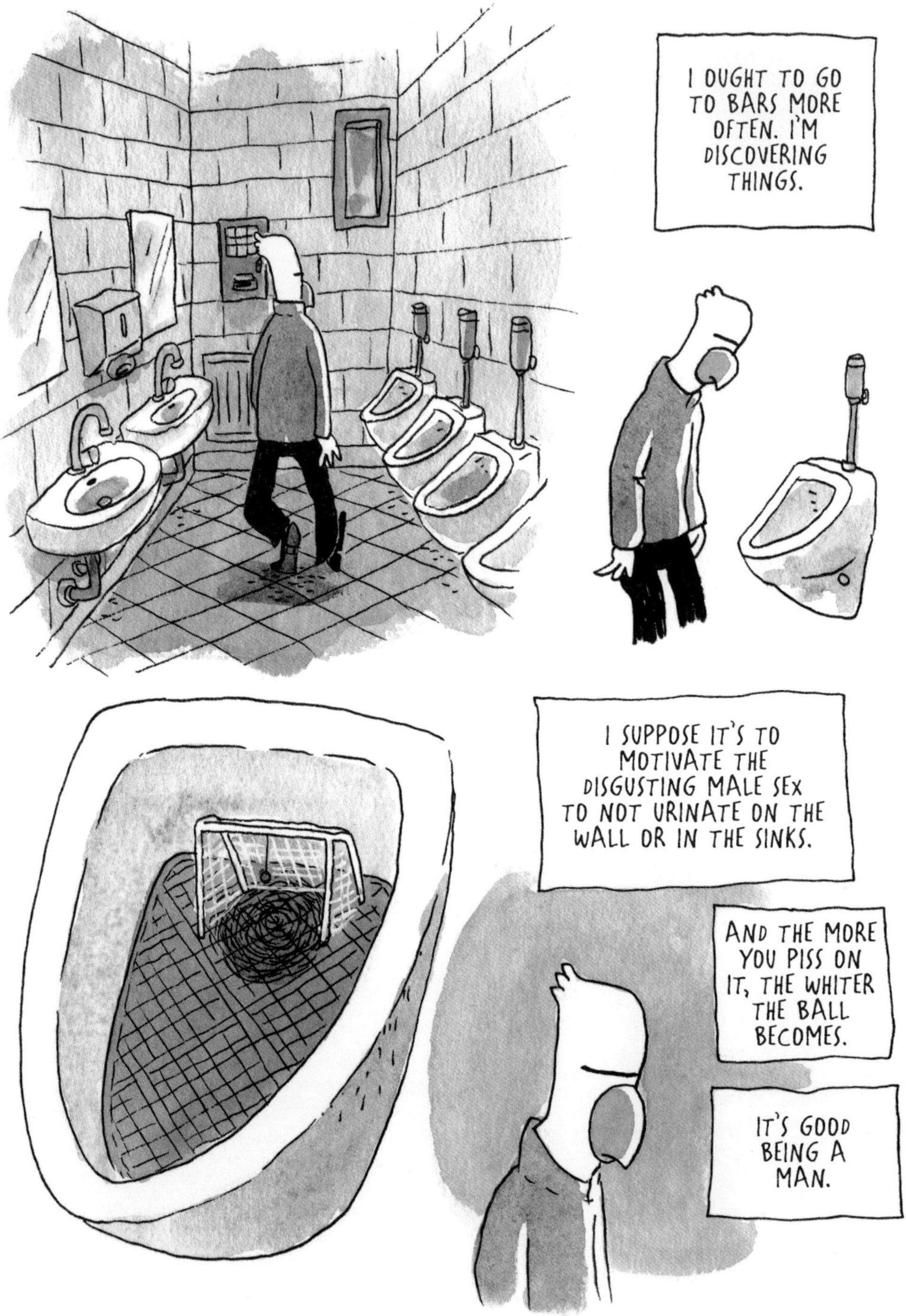
I OUGHT TO GO TO BARS MORE OFTEN. I'M DISCOVERING THINGS.
I SUPPOSE IT'S TO MOTIVATE THE DISGUSTING MALE SEX TO NOT URINATE ON THE WALL OR IN THE SINKS.
AND THE MORE YOU PISS ON IT, THE WHITER THE BALL BECOMES.
IT'S GOOD BEING A MAN.

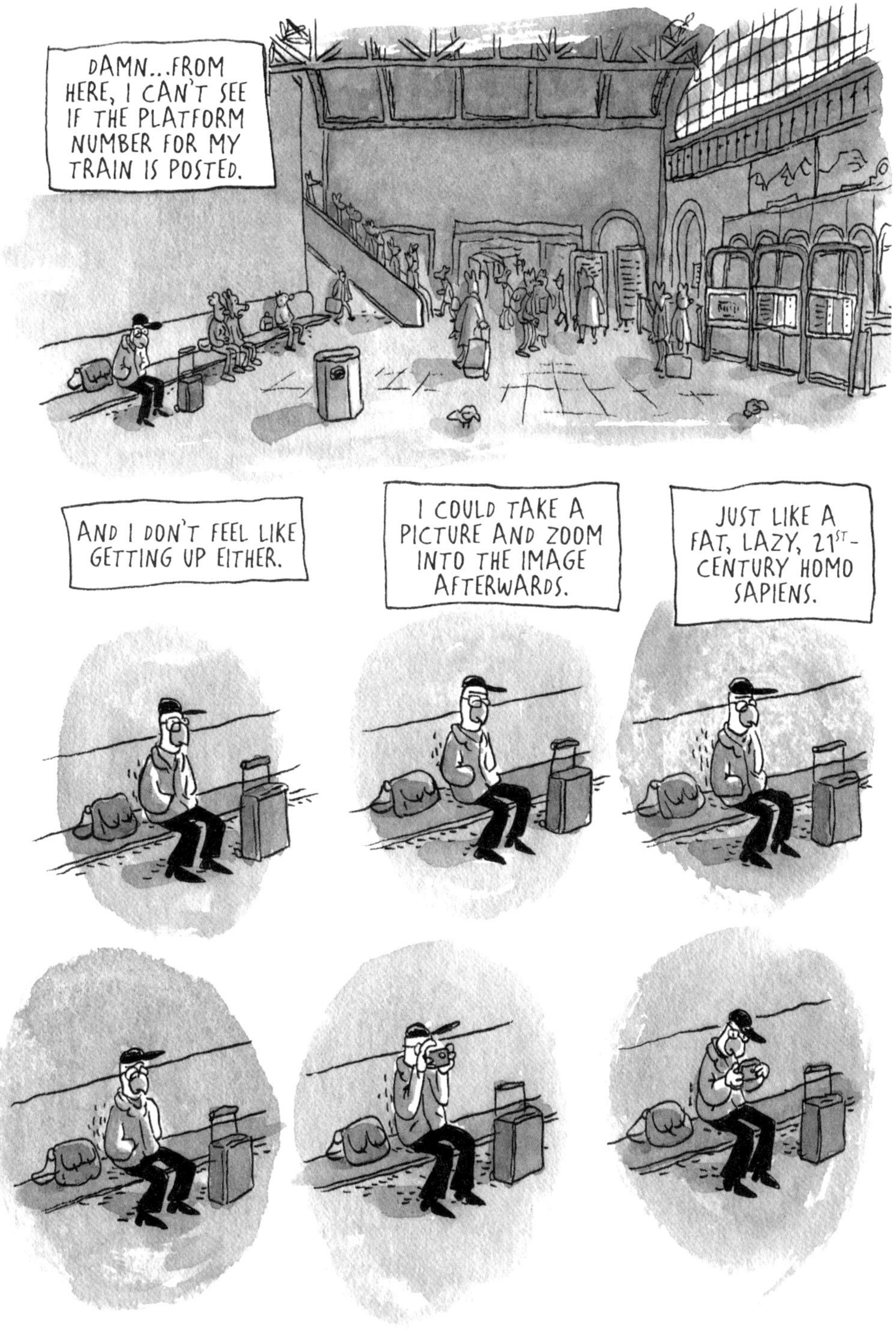
DAMN...FROM HERE, I CAN'T SEE IF THE PLATFORM NUMBER FOR MY TRAIN IS POSTED.
AND I DON'T FEEL LIKE GETTING UP EITHER.
I COULD TAKE A PICTURE AND ZOOM INTO THE IMAGE AFTERWARDS.
JUST LIKE A FAT, LAZY, 21ST-CENTURY HOMO SAPIENS.

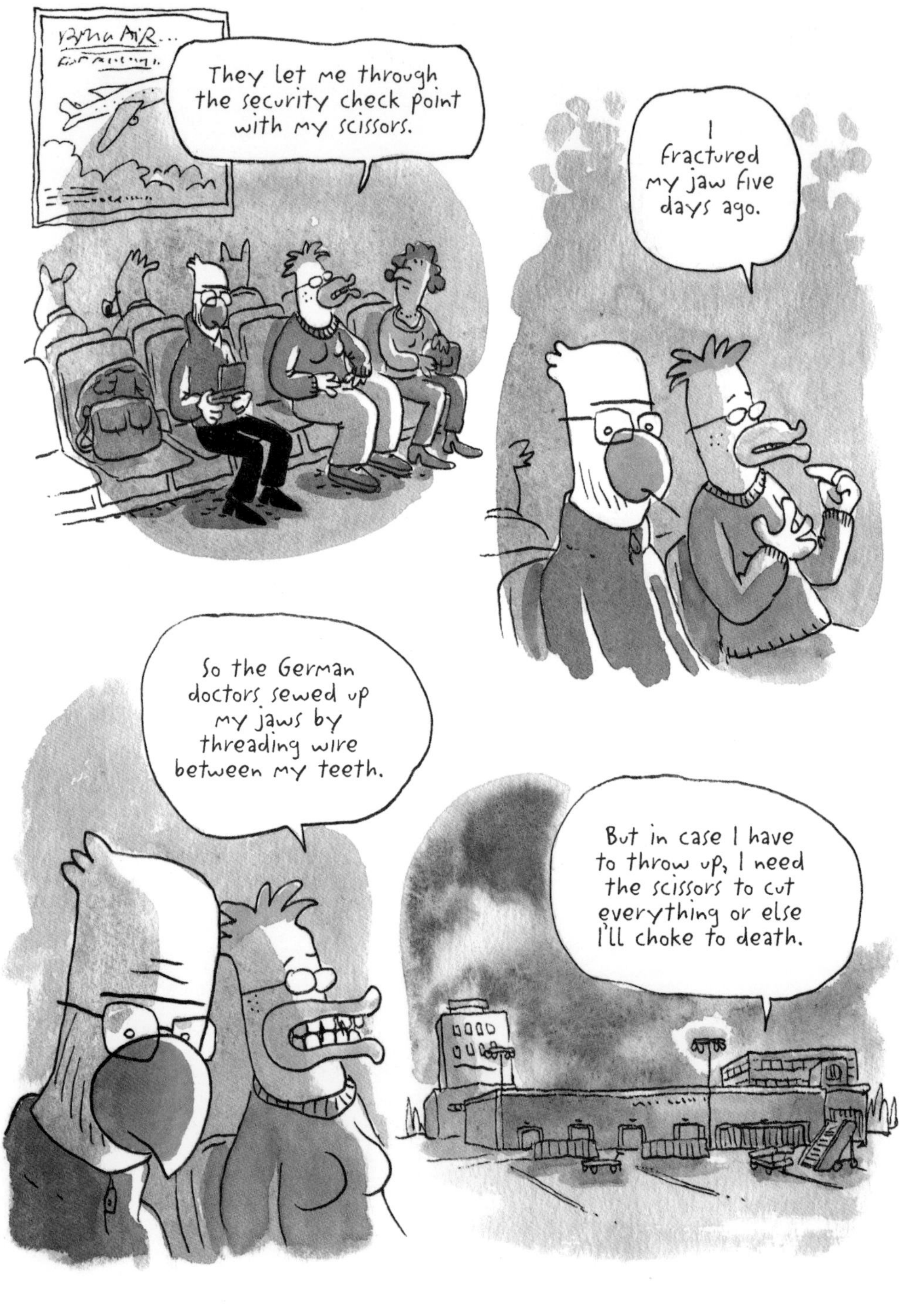
They let me through the security check point with my scissors.
I fractured my jaw five days ago.
So the German doctors sewed up my jaws by threading wire between my teeth.
But in case I have to throw up, I need the scissors to cut everything or else I'll choke to death.

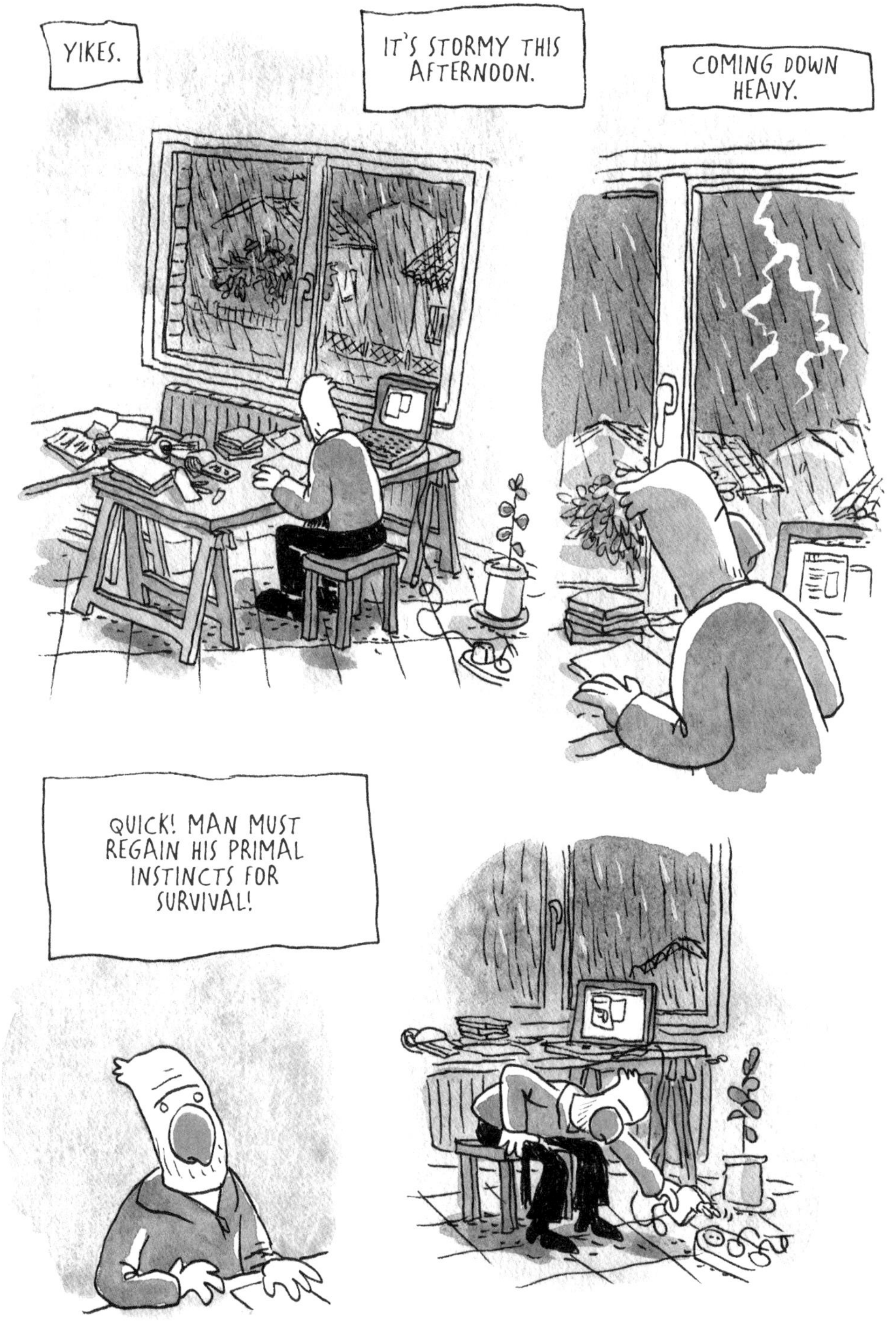
YIKES.
IT'S STORMY THIS AFTERNOON.
COMING DOWN HEAVY.
QUICK! MAN MUST REGAIN HIS PRIMAL INSTINCTS FOR SURVIVAL!

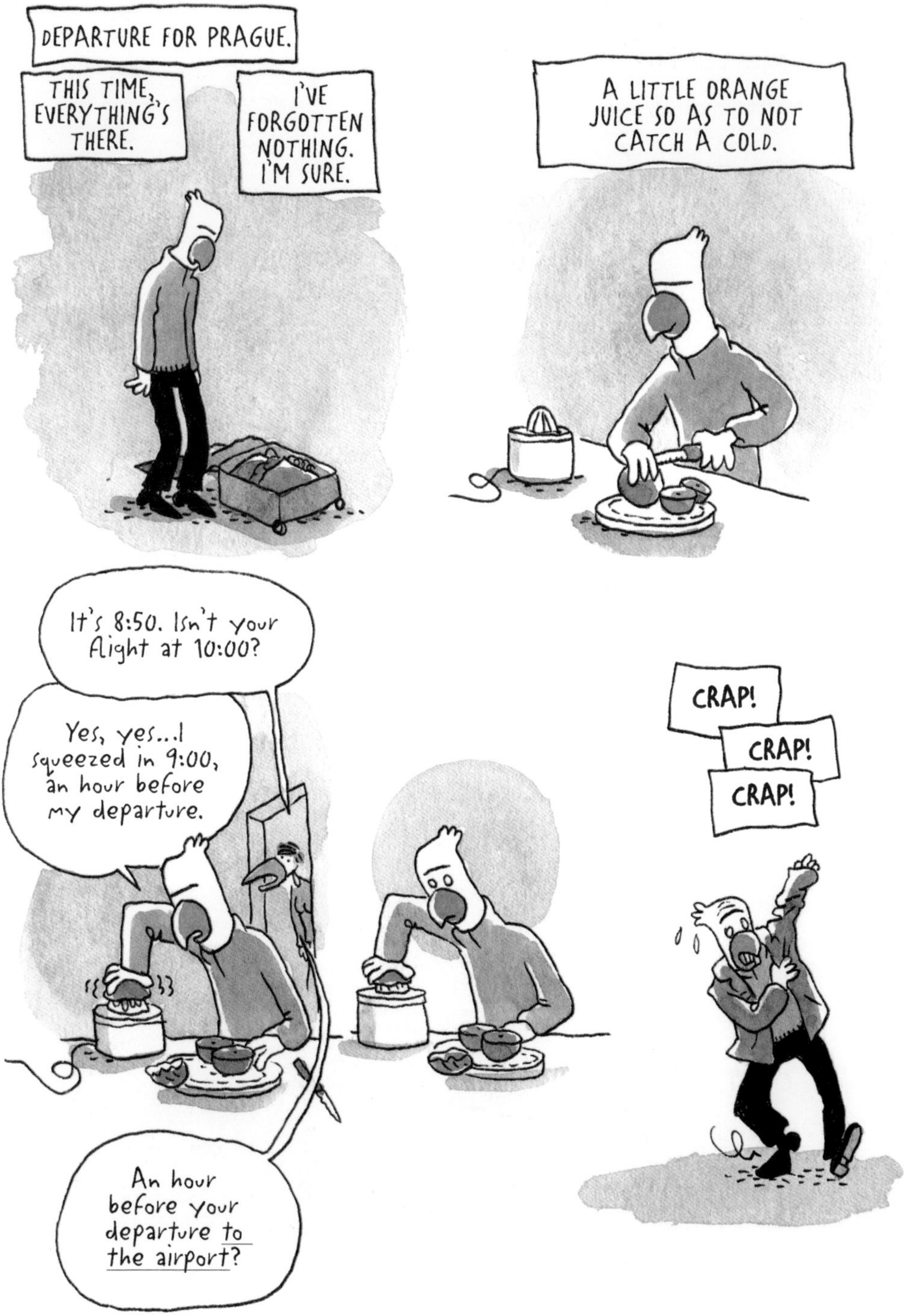
DEPARTURE FOR PRAGUE.
THIS TIME, EVERYTHING'S THERE.
I'VE FORGOTTEN NOTHING. I'M SURE.
A LITTLE ORANGE JUICE SO AS TO NOT CATCH A COLD.
It's 8:50. Isn't your flight at 10:00?
Yes, yes...I squeezed in 9:00, an hour before my departure.
An hour before your departure to the airport?
CRAP!
CRAP!
CRAP!

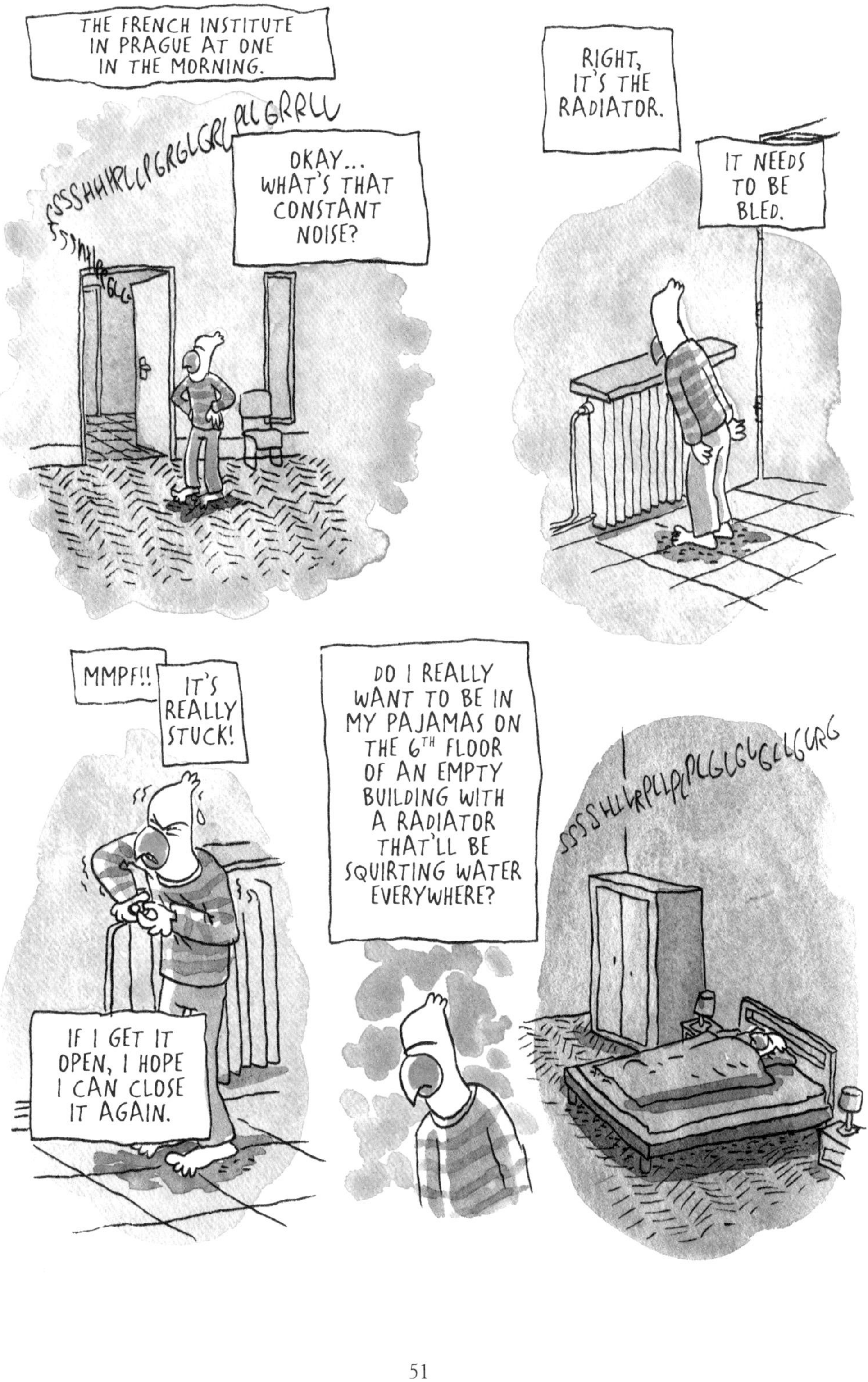
THE FRENCH INSTITUTE IN PRAGUE AT ONE IN THE MORNING.
OKAY... WHAT'S THAT CONSTANT NOISE?
RIGHT, IT'S THE RADIATOR.
IT NEEDS TO BE BLED.
MMPF!!
IT'S REALLY STUCK!
IF I GET IT OPEN, I HOPE I CAN CLOSE IT AGAIN.
DO I REALLY WANT TO BE IN MY PAJAMAS ON THE 6TH FLOOR OF AN EMPTY BUILDING WITH A RADIATOR THAT'LL BE SQUIRTING WATER EVERYWHERE?

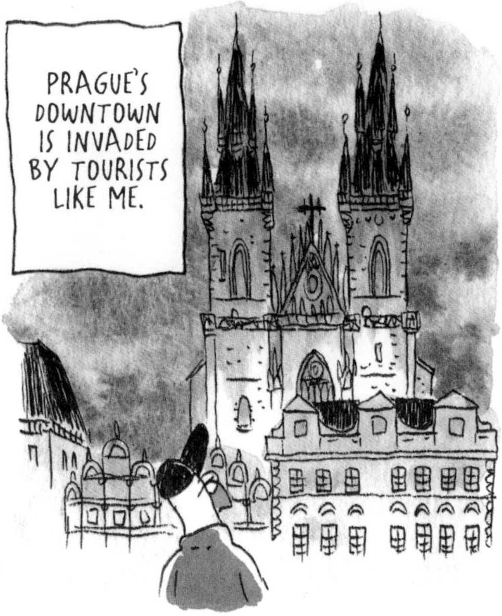
PRAGUE'S DOWNTOWN IS INVADED BY TOURISTS LIKE ME.

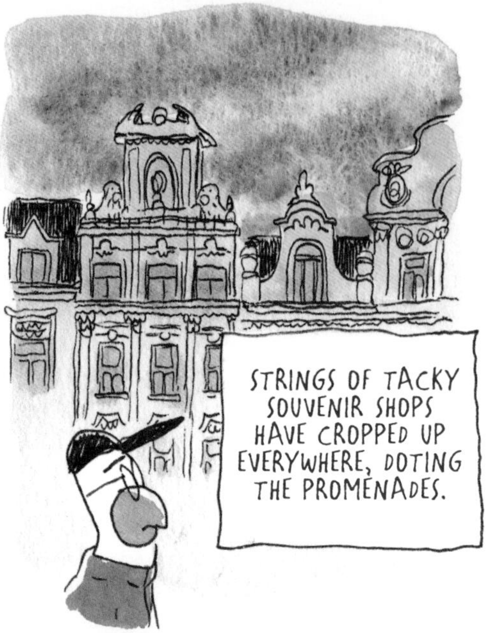
STRINGS OF TACKY SOUVENIR SHOPS HAVE CROPPED UP EVERYWHERE, DOTING THE PROMENADES.

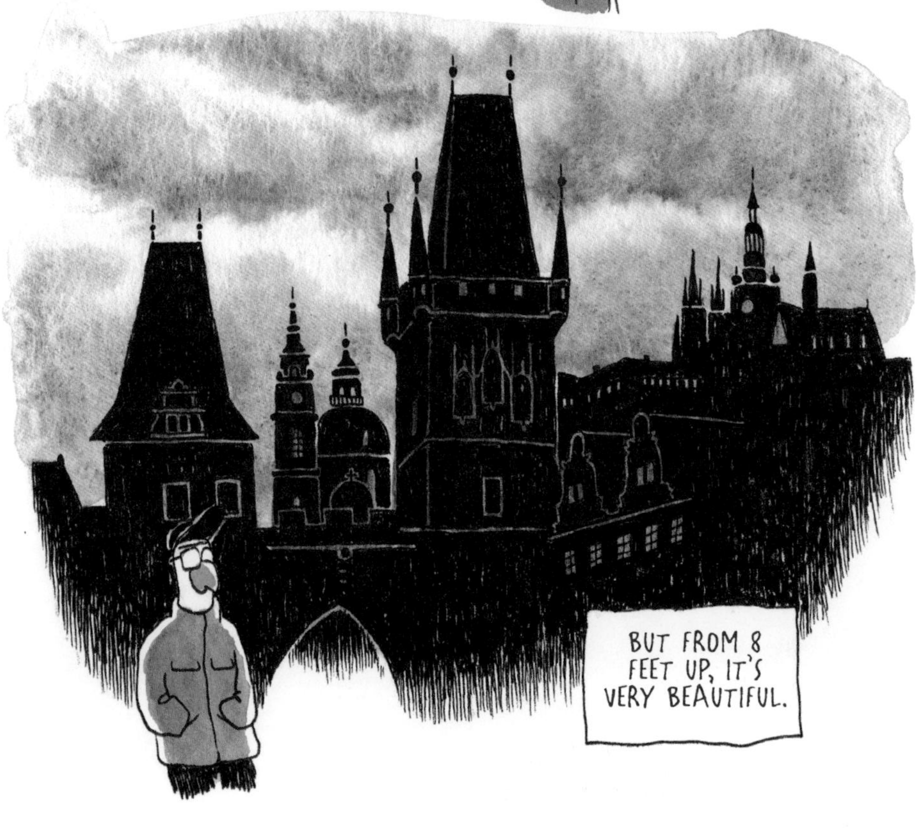
BUT FROM 8 FEET UP, IT'S VERY BEAUTIFUL.

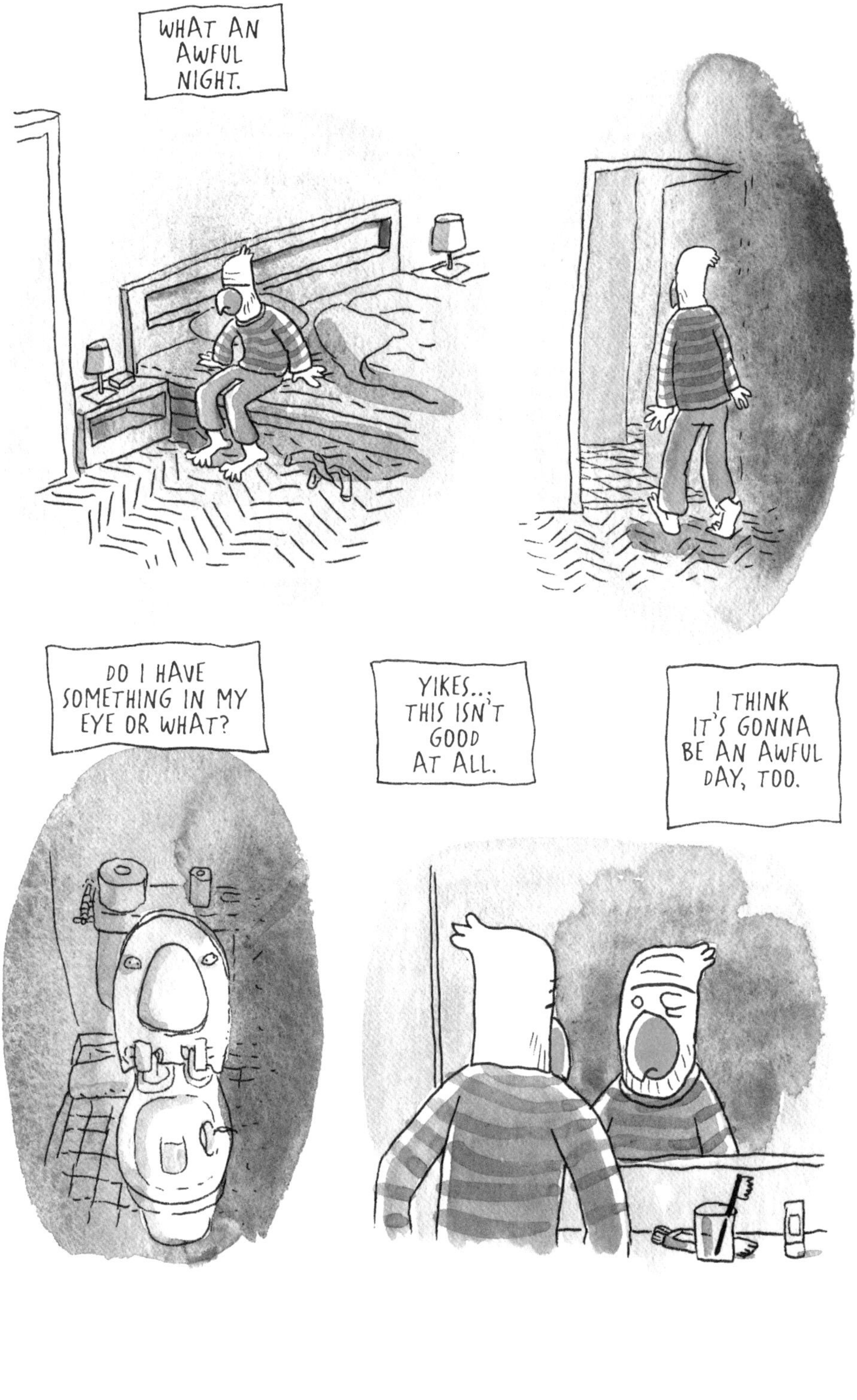
WHAT AN AWFUL NIGHT.
DO I HAVE SOMETHING IN MY EYE OR WHAT?
YIKES... THIS ISN'T GOOD AT ALL.
I THINK IT'S GONNA BE AN AWFUL DAY, TOO.

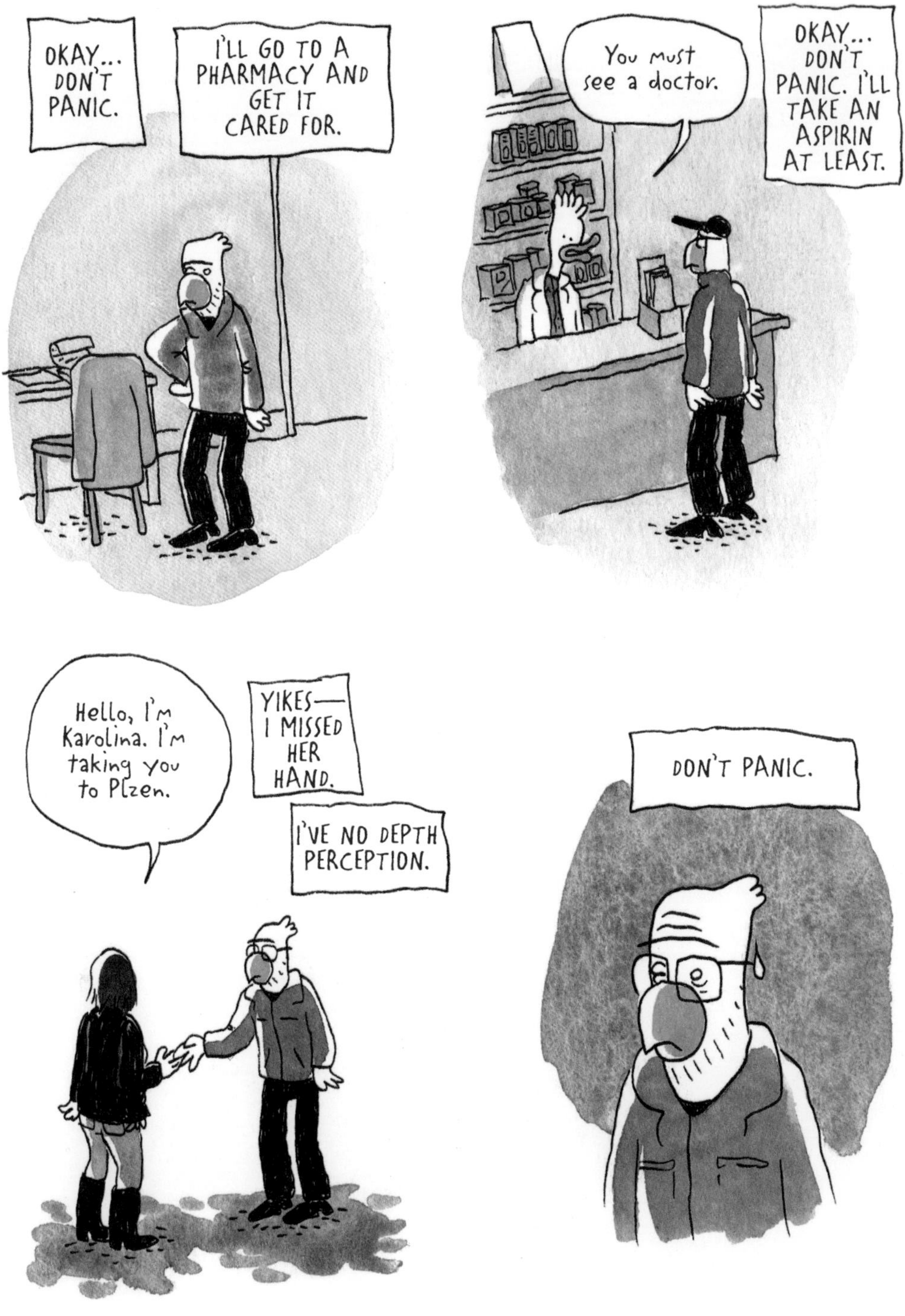
OKAY... DON'T PANIC.
I'LL GO TO A PHARMACY AND GET IT CARED FOR.
You must see a doctor.
OKAY... DON'T PANIC. I'LL TAKE AN ASPIRIN AT LEAST.
Hello, I'm Karolina. I'm taking you to Plzen.
YIKES— I MISSED HER HAND.
I'VE NO DEPTH PERCEPTION.
DON'T PANIC.

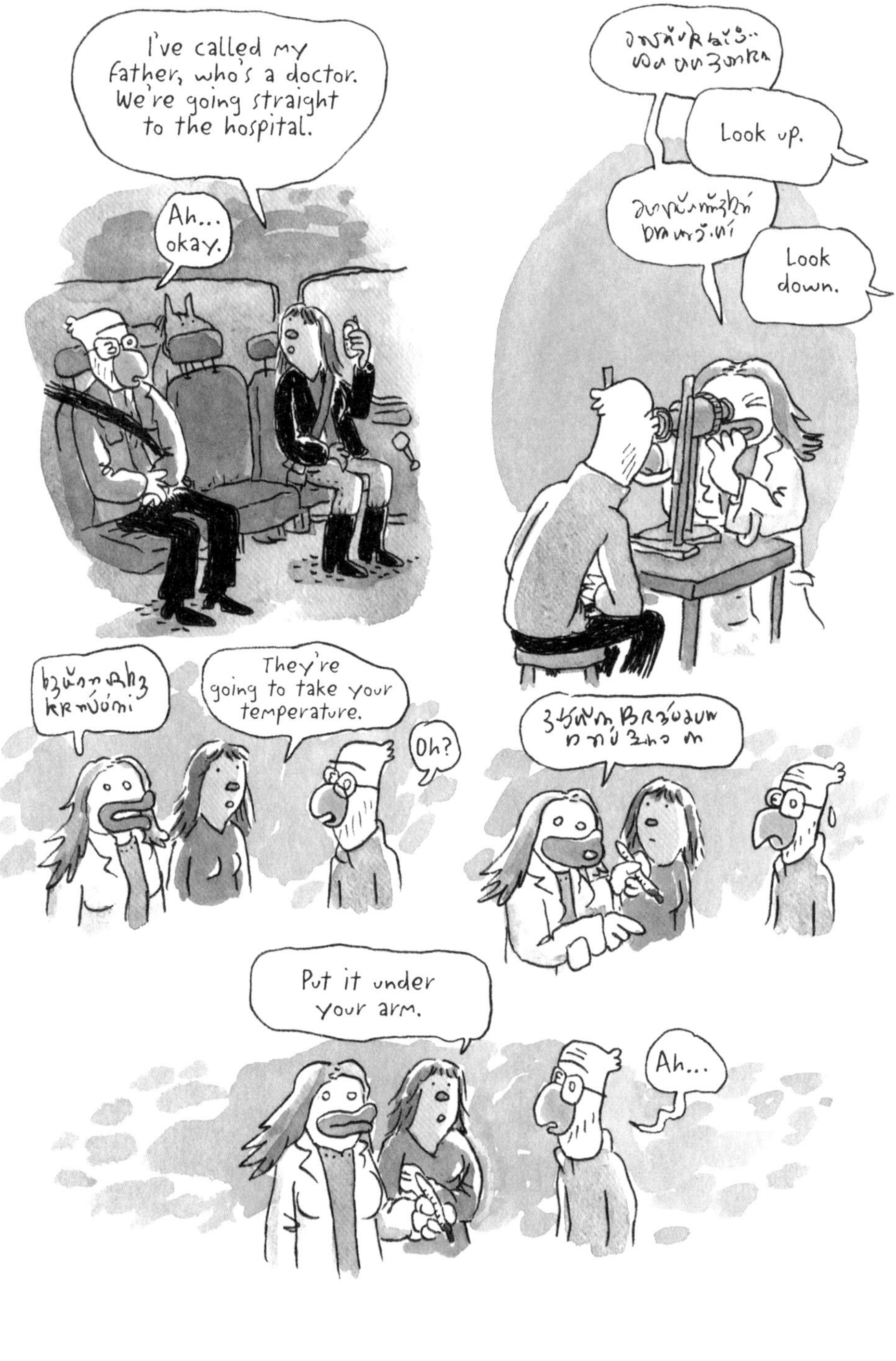
I've called my father, who's a doctor. We're going straight to the hospital.
Ah... okay.
Look up.
Look down.
They're going to take your temperature.
Oh?
Put it under your arm.
Ah...

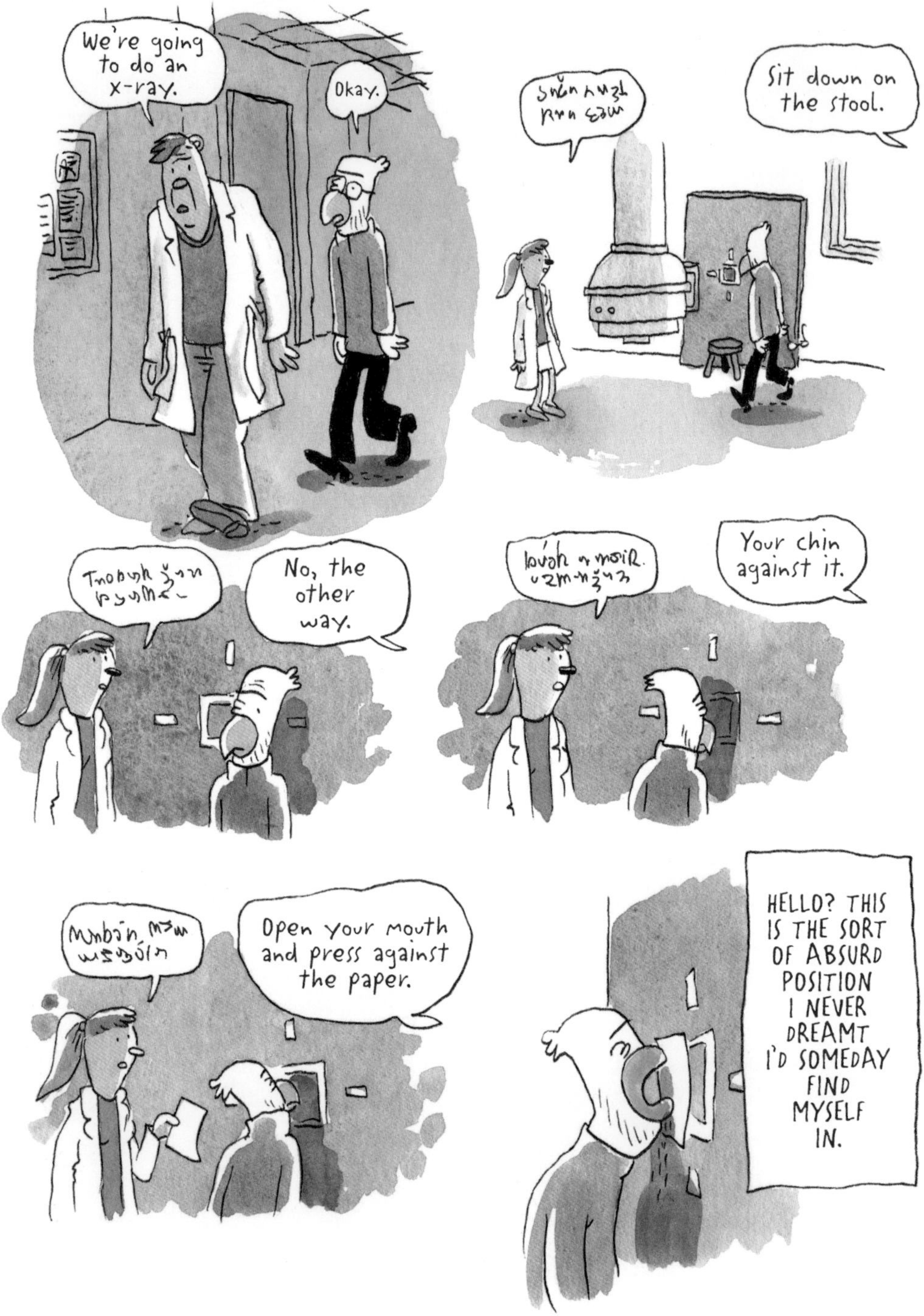
We're going to do an x-ray.
Okay.
Sit down on the stool.
No, the other way.
Your chin against it.
Open your mouth and press against the paper.
HELLO? THIS IS THE SORT OF ABSURD POSITION I NEVER DREAMT I'D SOMEDAY FIND MYSELF IN.

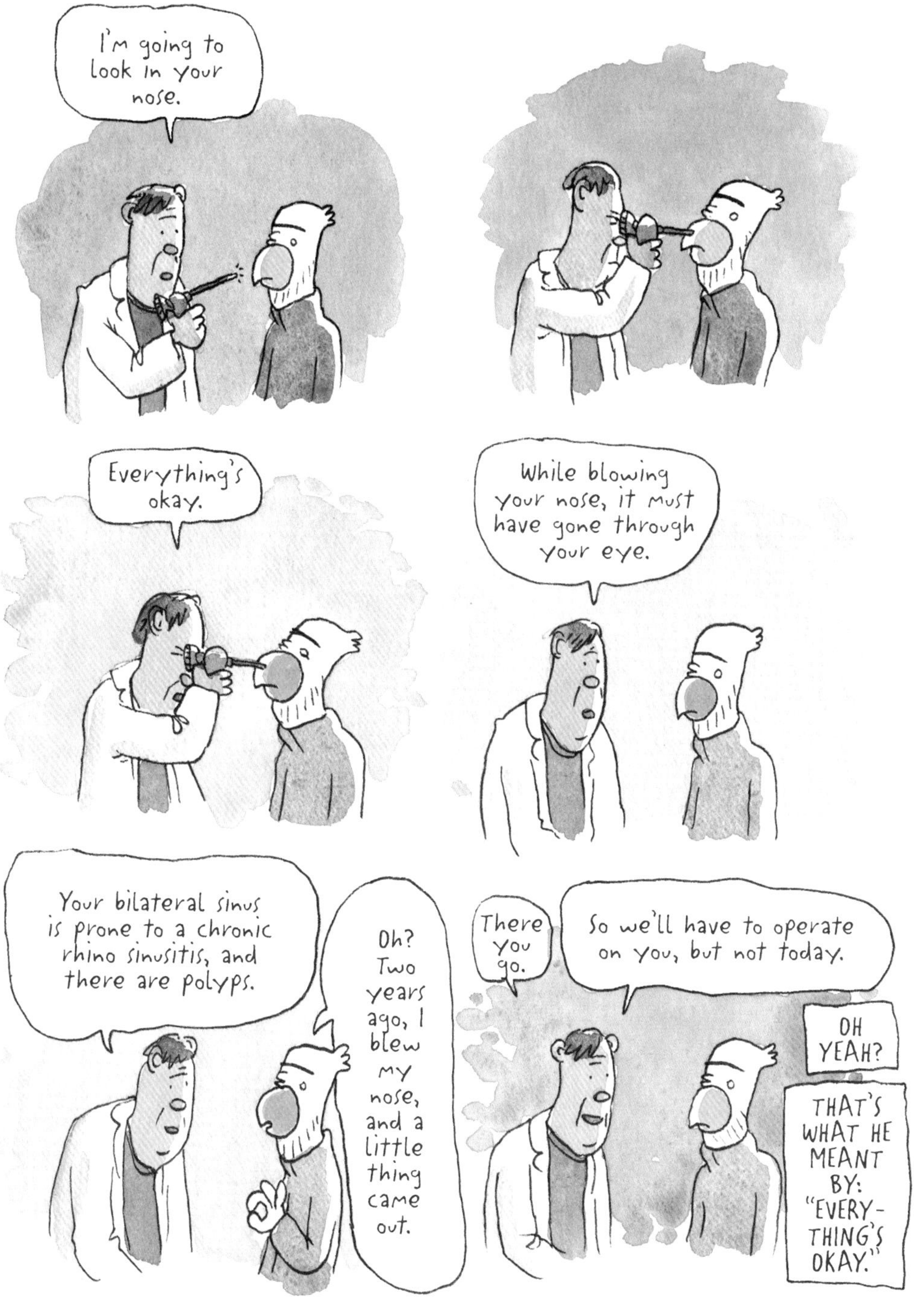
I'm going to look in your nose.
Everything's okay.
While blowing your nose, it must have gone through your eye.
Your bilateral sinus is prone to a chronic rhino sinusitis, and there are polyps.
Oh? Two years ago, I blew my nose, and a little thing came out.
There you go.
So we'll have to operate on you, but not today.
OH YEAH?
THAT'S WHAT HE MEANT BY: "EVERY-THING'S OKAY."

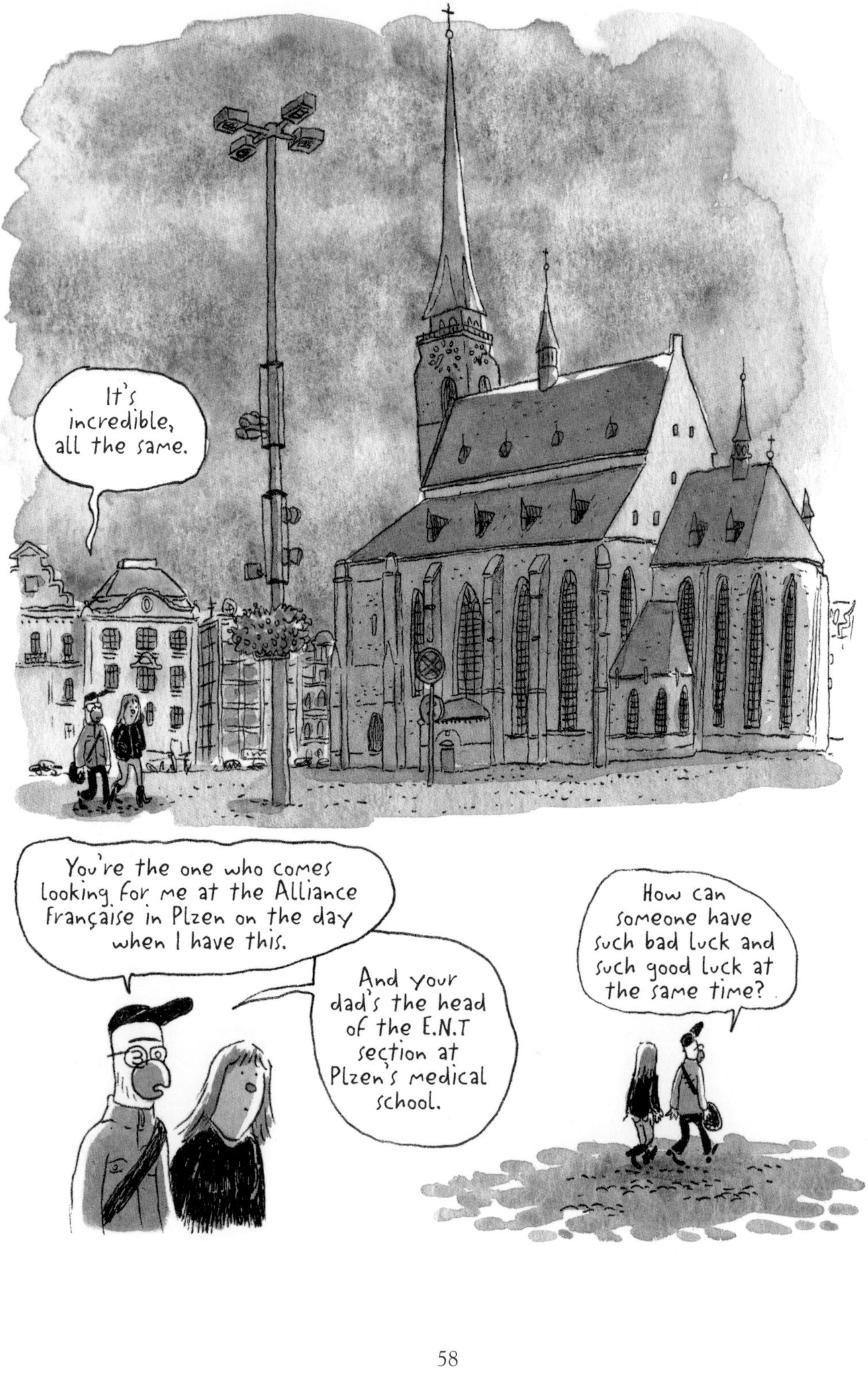
It's incredible, all the same.
You're the one who comes looking for me at the Alliance Française in Plzen on the day when I have this.
And your dad's the head of the E.N.T section at Plzen's medical school.
How can someone have such bad luck and such good luck at the same time?

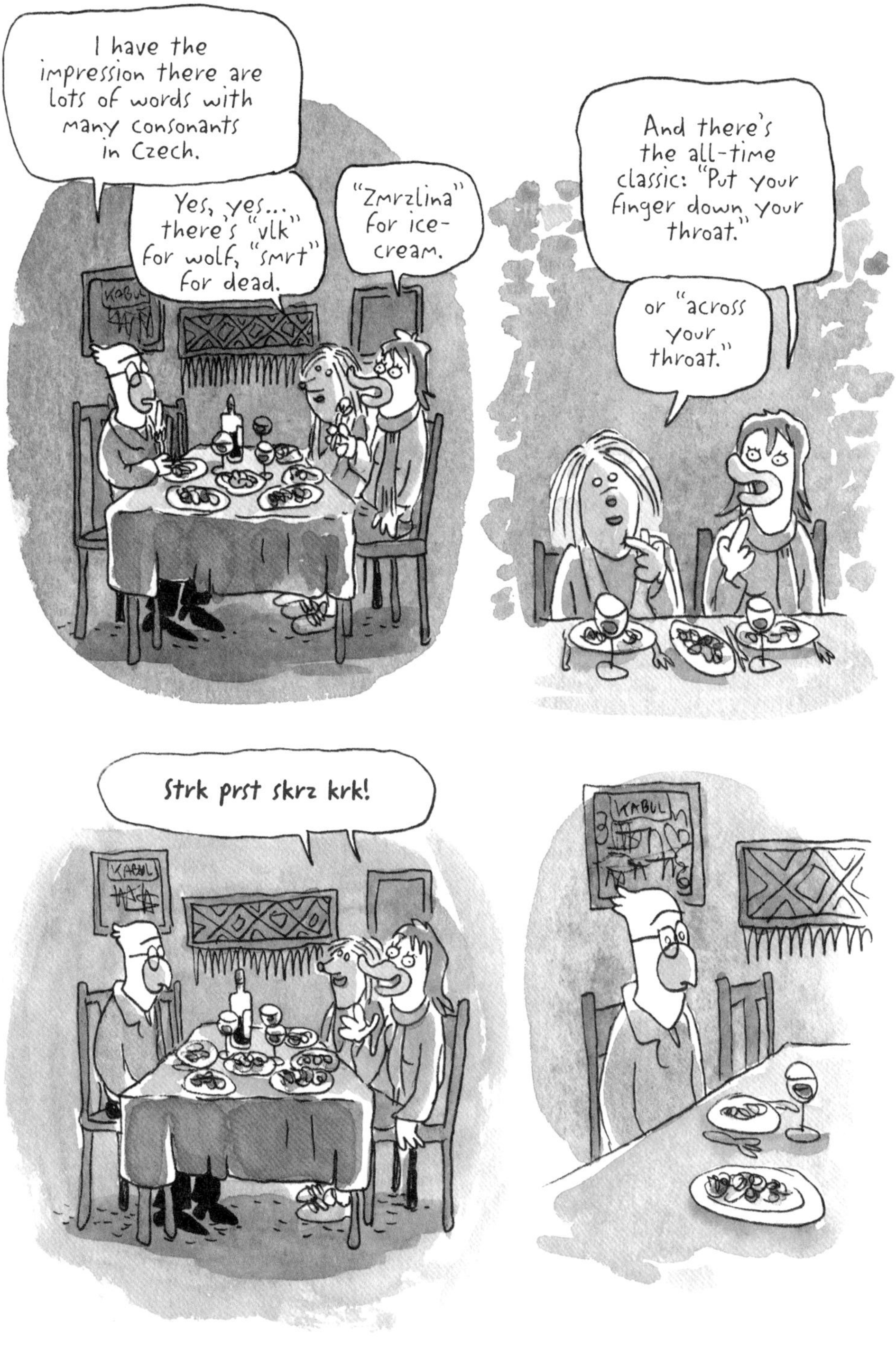
I have the impression there are lots of words with many consonants in Czech.
Yes, yes... there's "vlk" for wolf, "smrt" for dead.
"Zmrzlina" for ice-cream.
And there's the all-time classic: "Put your finger down your throat."
or "across your throat."
Strk prst skrz krk!
KABUL

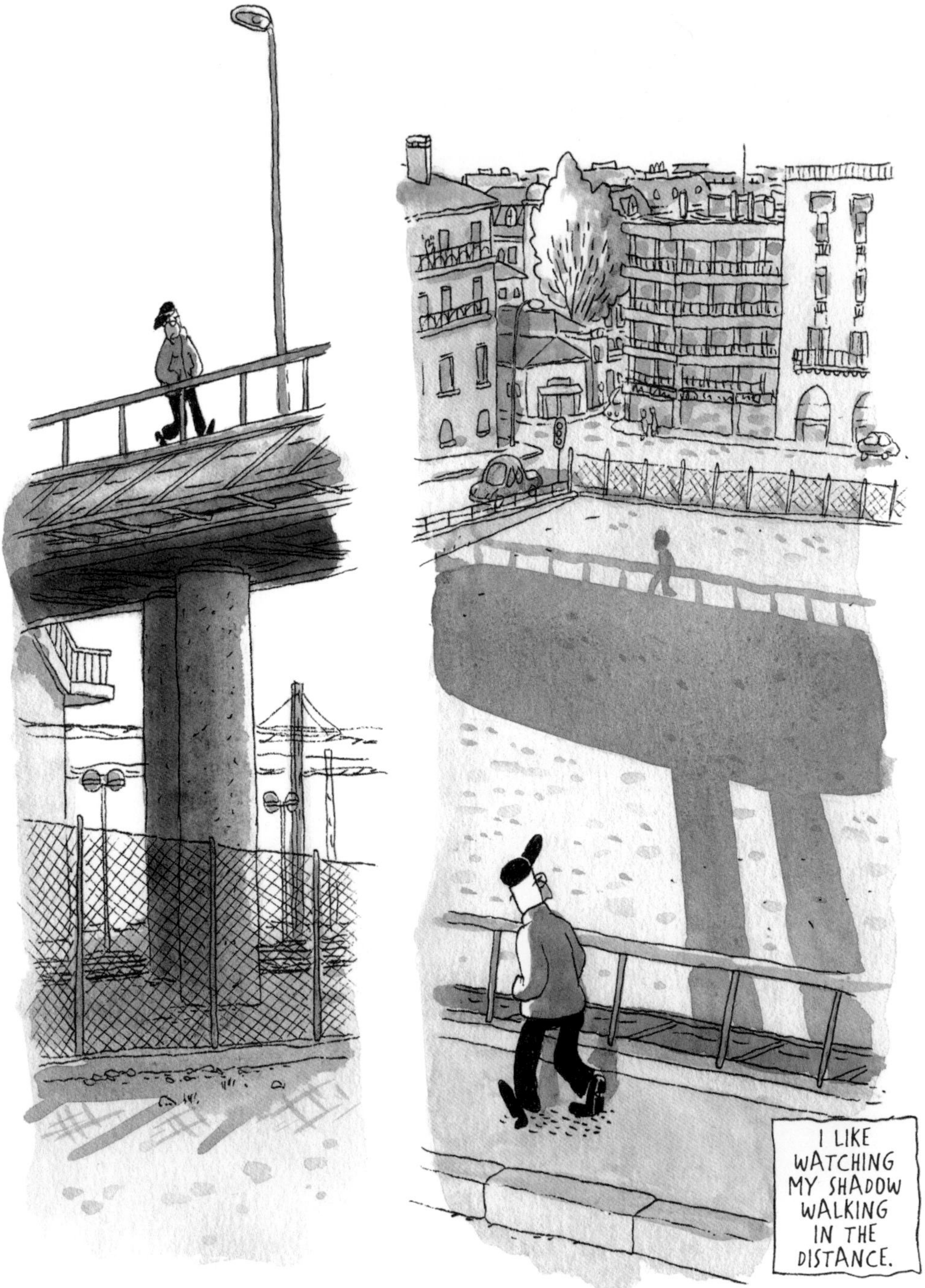
I LIKE WATCHING MY SHADOW WALKING IN THE DISTANCE.

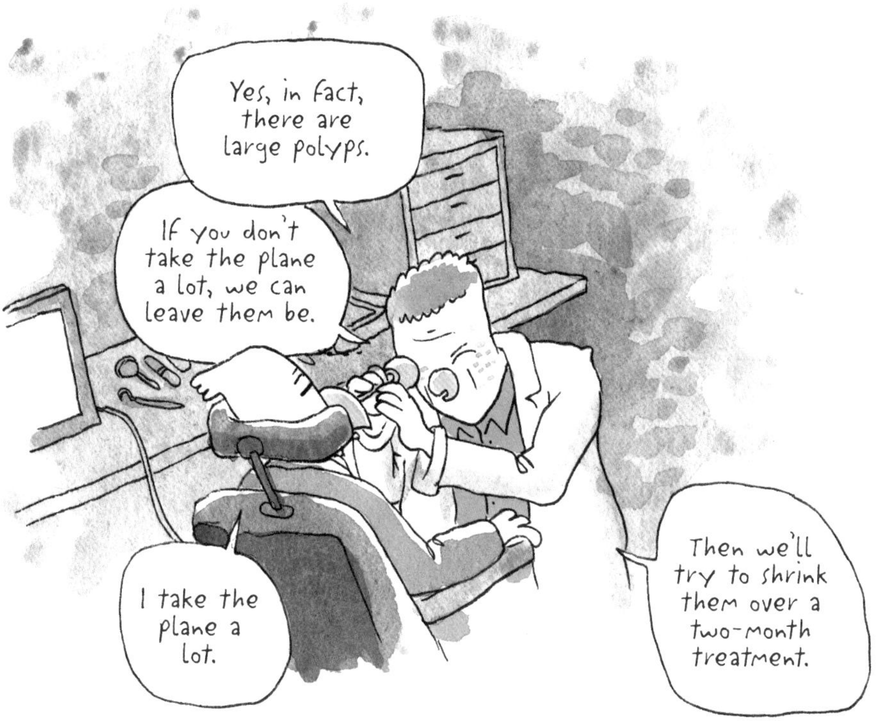
Yes, in fact, there are large polyps.
If you don't take the plane a lot, we can leave them be.
I take the plane a lot.
Then we'll try to shrink them over a two-month treatment.

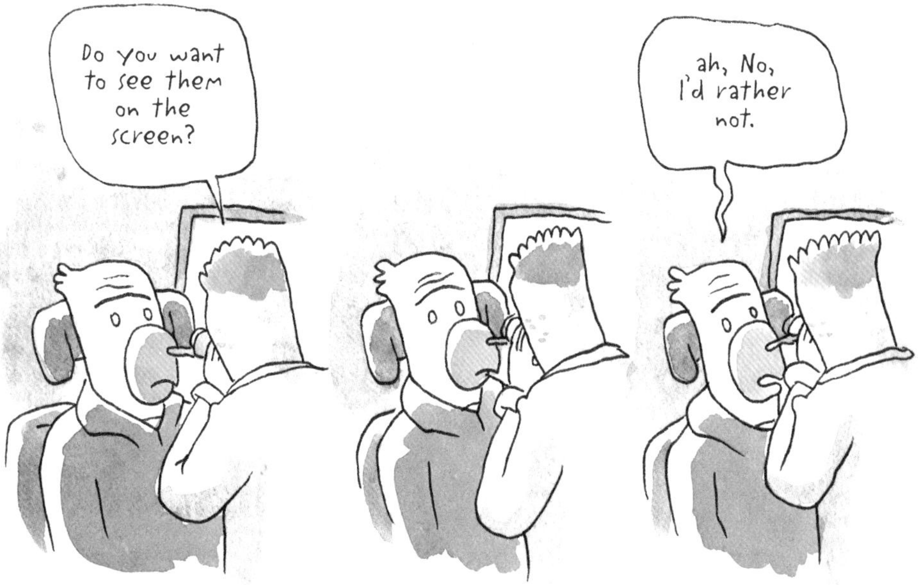
Do you want to see them on the screen?
ah, No, I'd rather not.

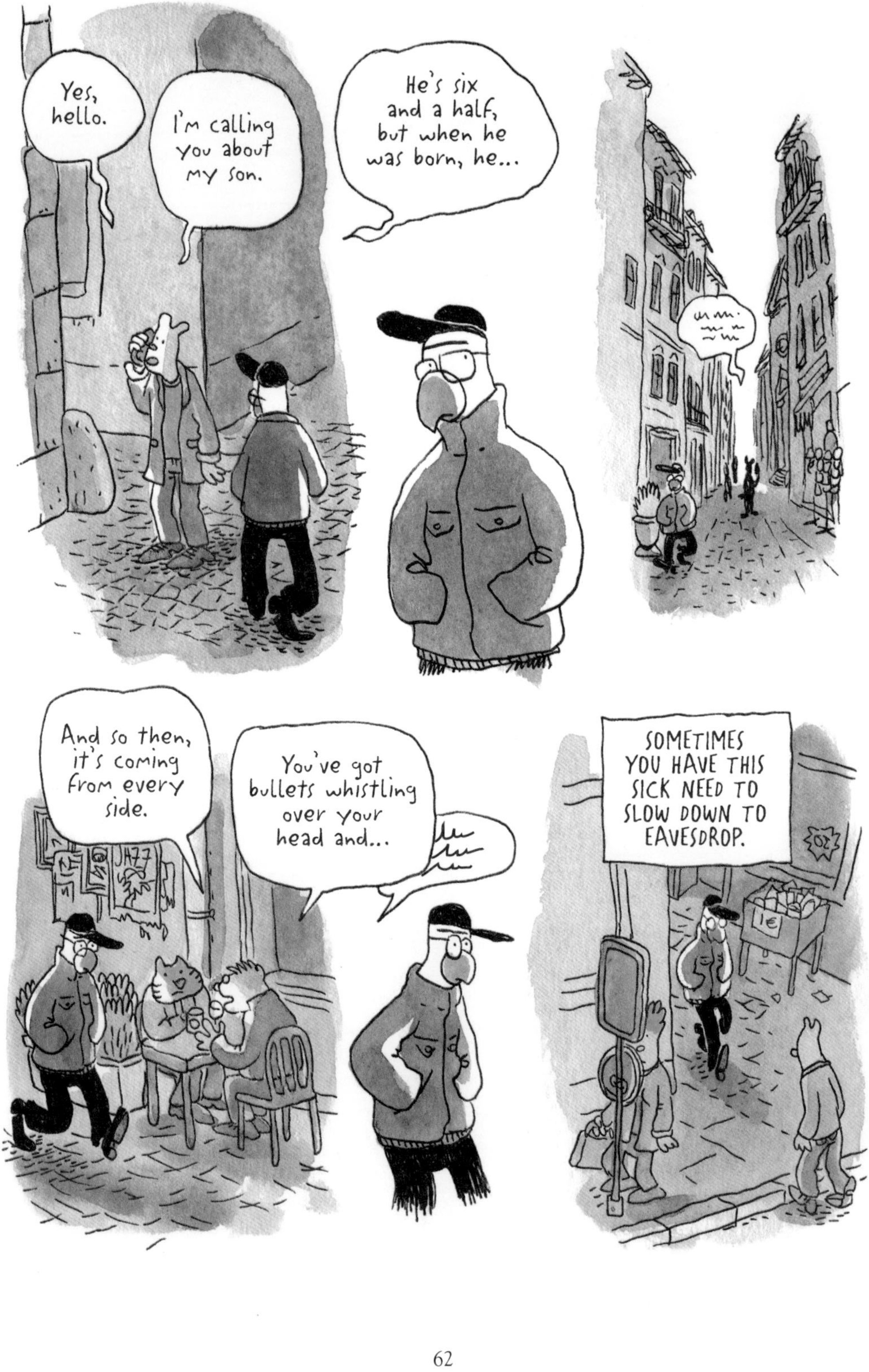
Yes, hello.
I'm calling you about my son.
He's six and a half, but when he was born, he...
And so then, it's coming from every side.
You've got bullets whistling over your head and...
SOMETIMES YOU HAVE THIS SICK NEED TO SLOW DOWN TO EAVESDROP.
1€

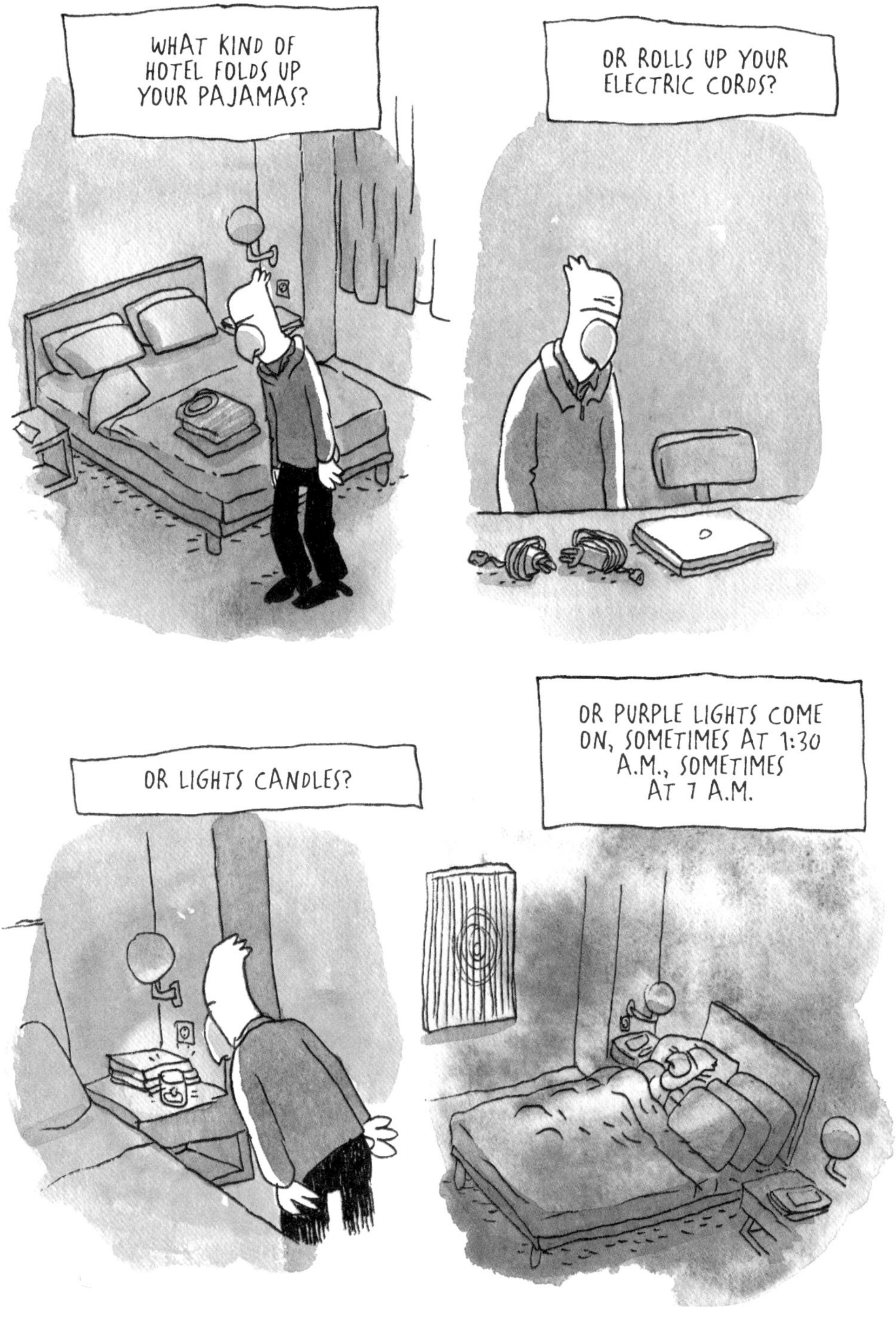
WHAT KIND OF HOTEL FOLDS UP YOUR PAJAMAS?
OR ROLLS UP YOUR ELECTRIC CORDS?
OR LIGHTS CANDLES?
OR PURPLE LIGHTS COME ON, SOMETIMES AT 1:30 A.M., SOMETIMES AT 7 A.M.

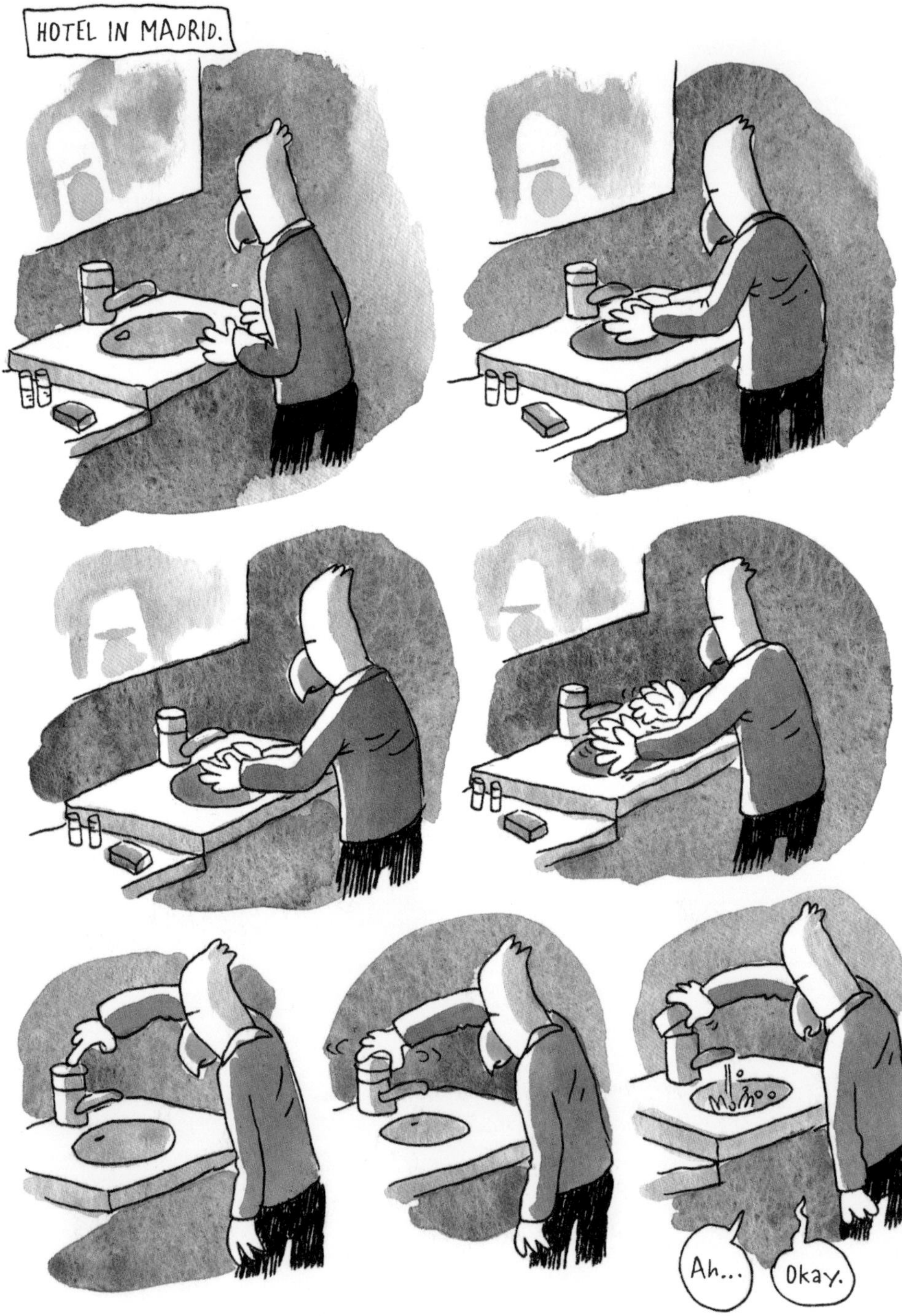
HOTEL IN MADRID.
Ah...
Okay.

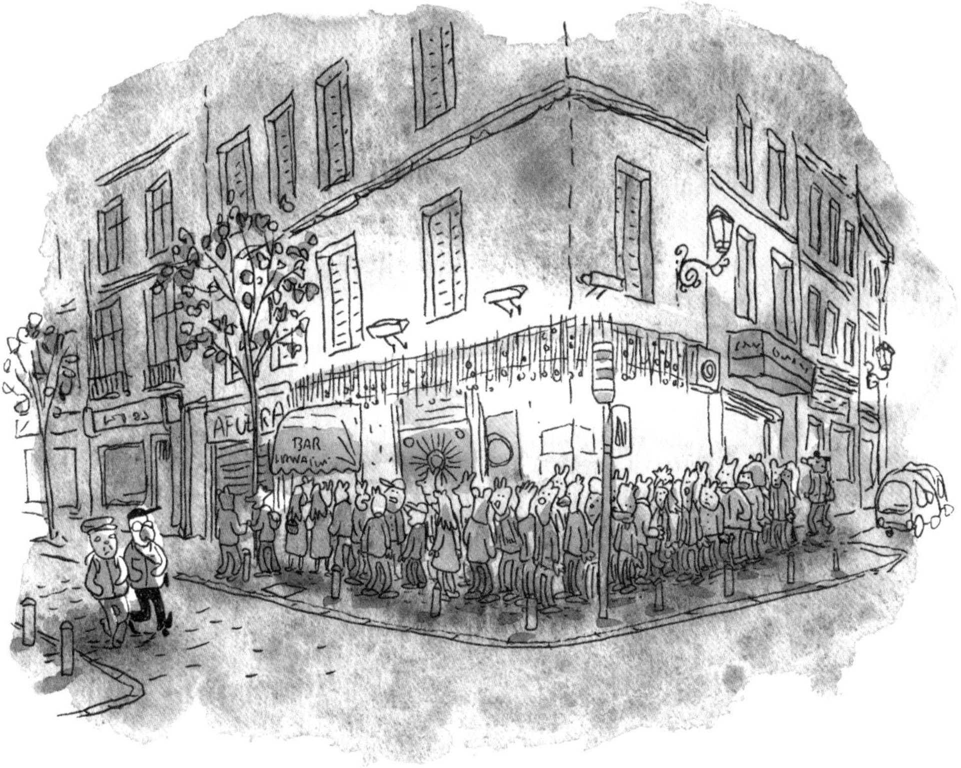
BAR

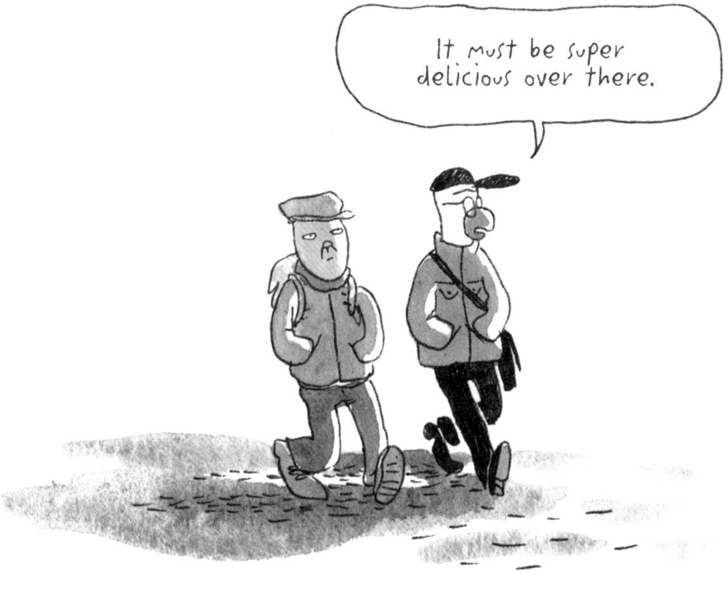
It must be super delicious over there.

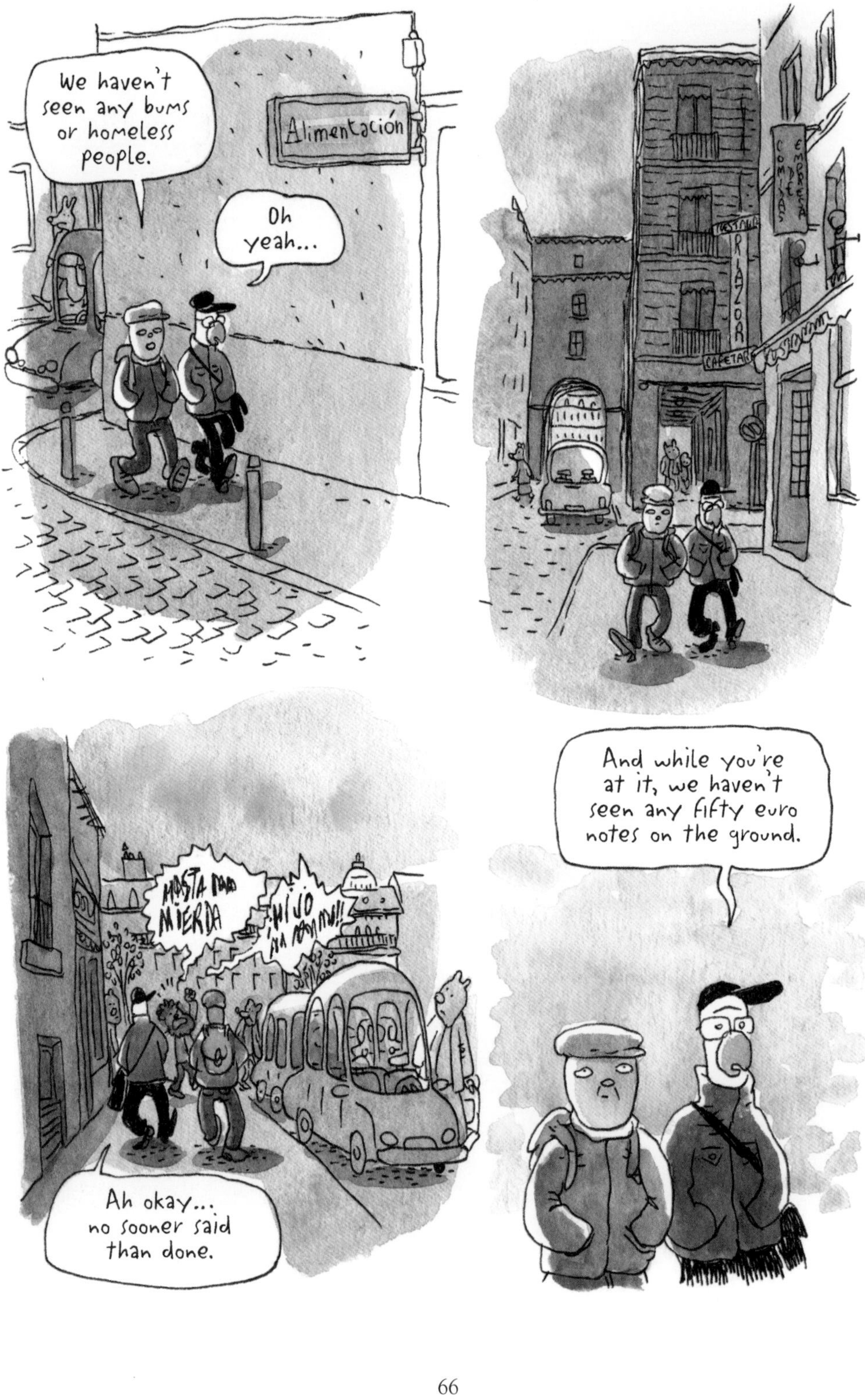
We haven't seen any bums or homeless people.
Alimentación
Oh yeah...
EMPRESA DE COMIDAS
RIAZOR
MIERDA
Ah okay... no sooner said than done.
And while you're at it, we haven't seen any fifty euro notes on the ground.

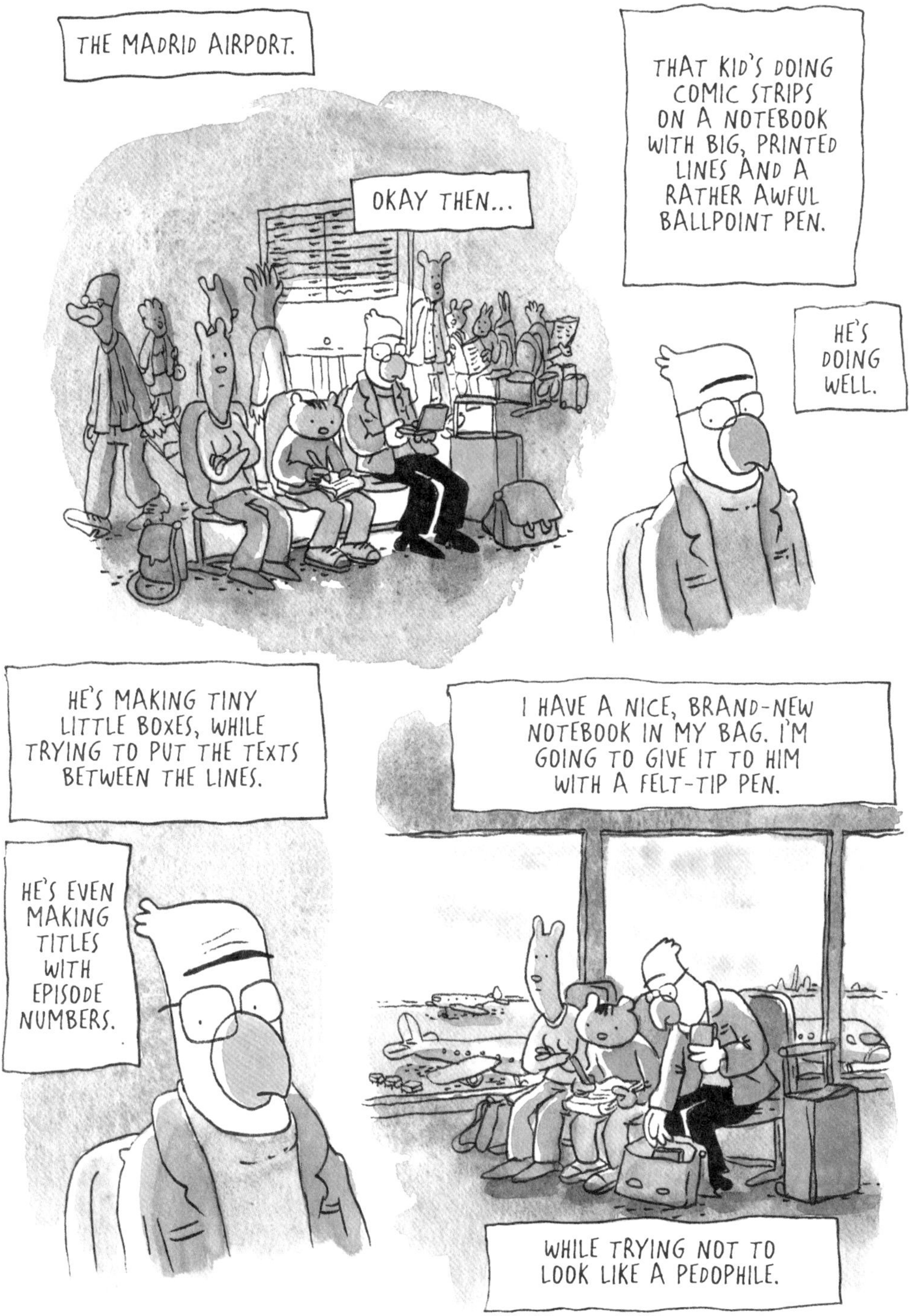
THE MADRID AIRPORT.
OKAY THEN...
THAT KID'S DOING COMIC STRIPS ON A NOTEBOOK WITH BIG, PRINTED LINES AND A RATHER AWFUL BALLPOINT PEN.
HE'S DOING WELL.
HE'S MAKING TINY LITTLE BOXES, WHILE TRYING TO PUT THE TEXTS BETWEEN THE LINES.
HE'S EVEN MAKING TITLES WITH EPISODE NUMBERS.
I HAVE A NICE, BRAND-NEW NOTEBOOK IN MY BAG. I'M GOING TO GIVE IT TO HIM WITH A FELT-TIP PEN.
WHILE TRYING NOT TO LOOK LIKE A PEDOPHILE.

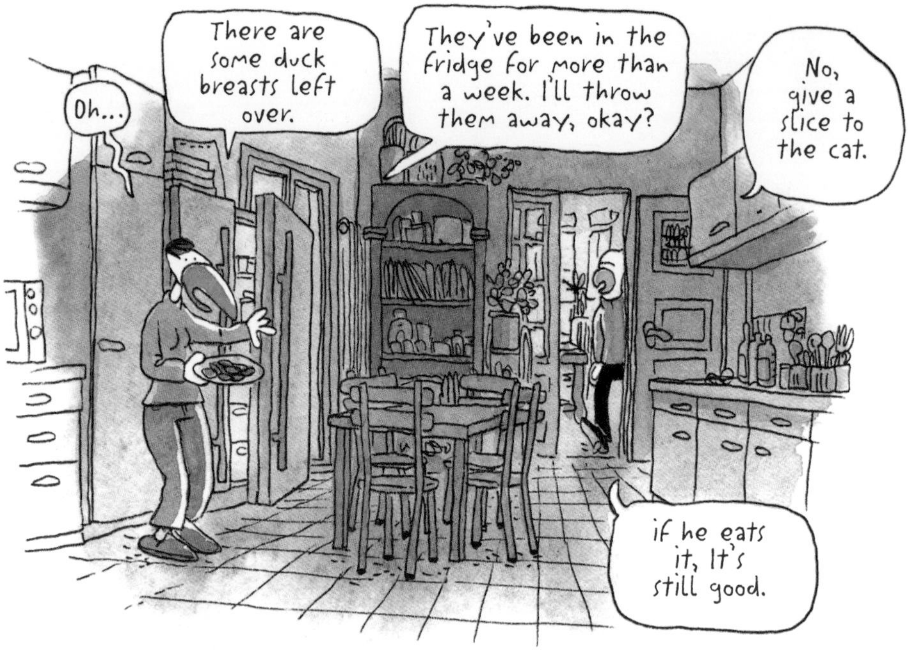
Oh...
There are some duck breasts left over.
They've been in the fridge for more than a week. I'll throw them away, okay?
No, give a slice to the cat.
if he eats it, It's still good.

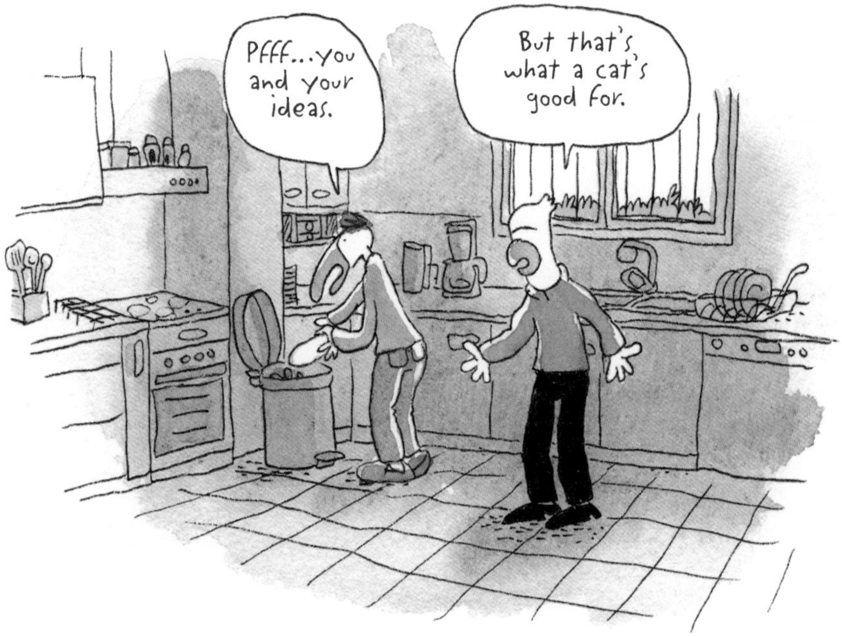
Pfff...you and your ideas.
But that's what a cat's good for.

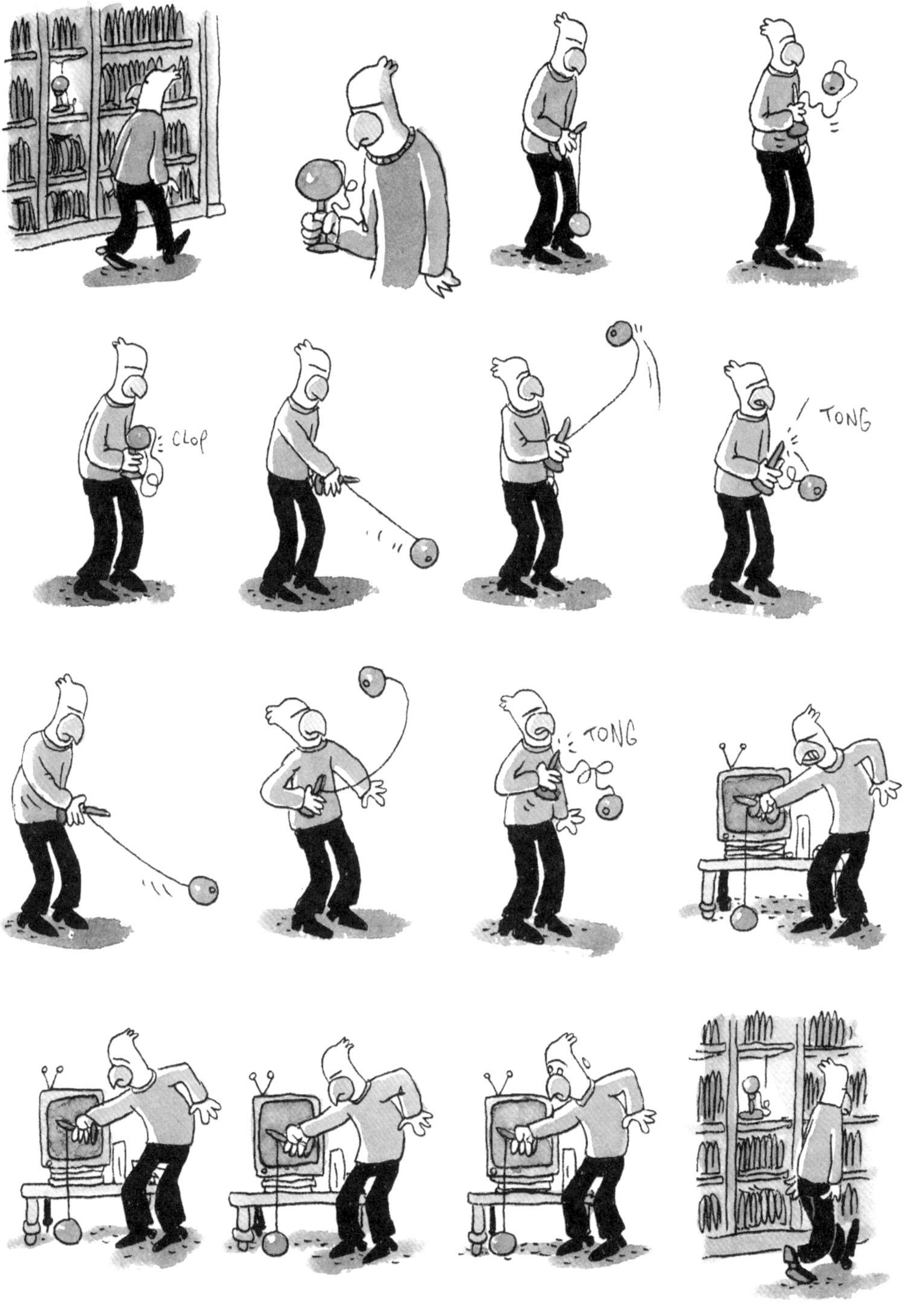
CLOP
TONG
TONG

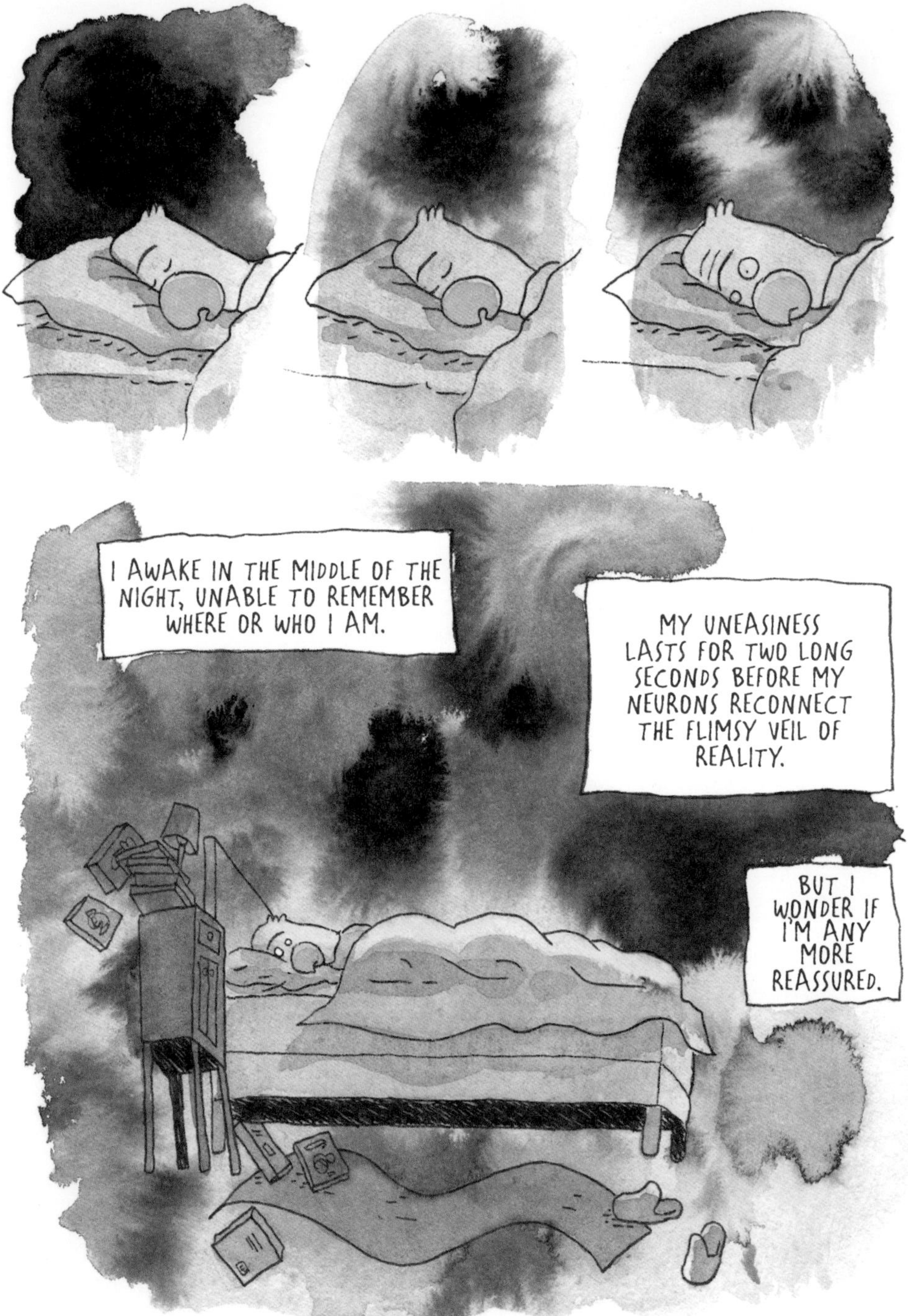

I AWAKE IN THE MIDDLE OF THE NIGHT, UNABLE TO REMEMBER WHERE OR WHO I AM.
MY UNEASINESS LASTS FOR TWO LONG SECONDS BEFORE MY NEURONS RECONNECT THE FLIMSY VEIL OF REALITY.
BUT I WONDER IF I'M ANY MORE REASSURED.

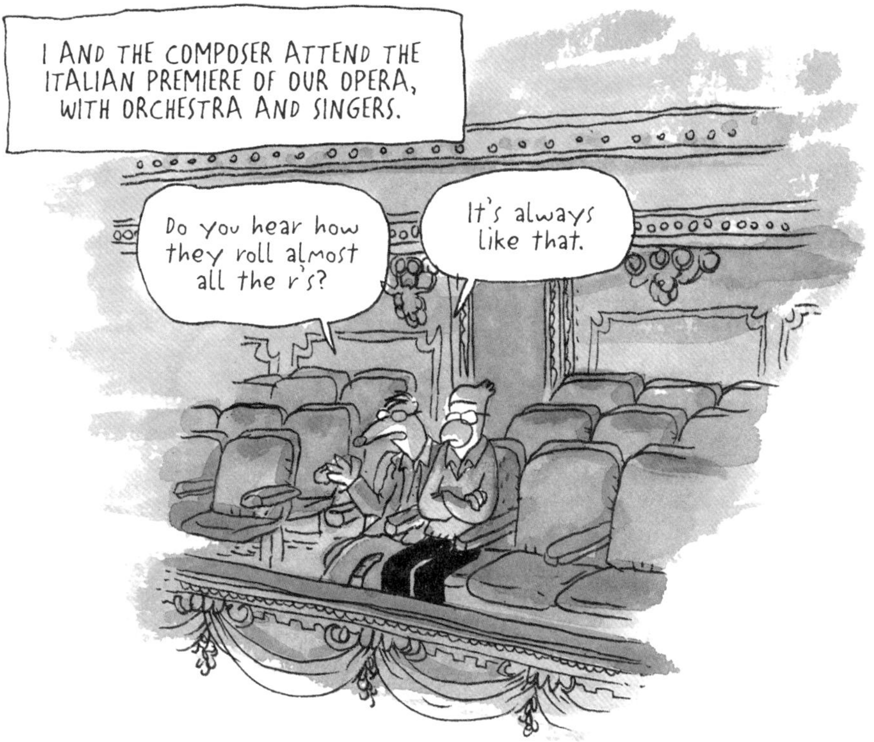
I AND THE COMPOSER ATTEND THE ITALIAN PREMIERE OF OUR OPERA, WITH ORCHESTRA AND SINGERS.
Do you hear how they roll almost all the r's?
It's always like that.

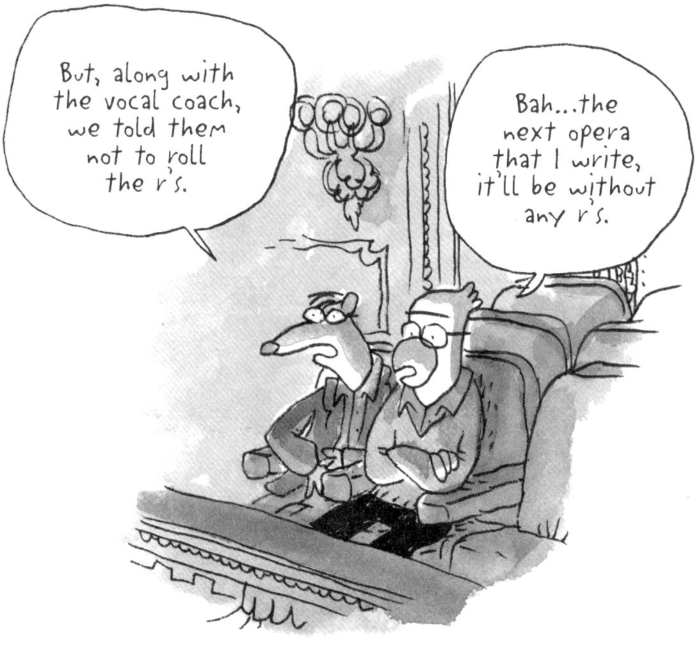
But, along with the vocal coach, we told them not to roll the r's.
Bah...the next opera that I write, it'll be without any r's.

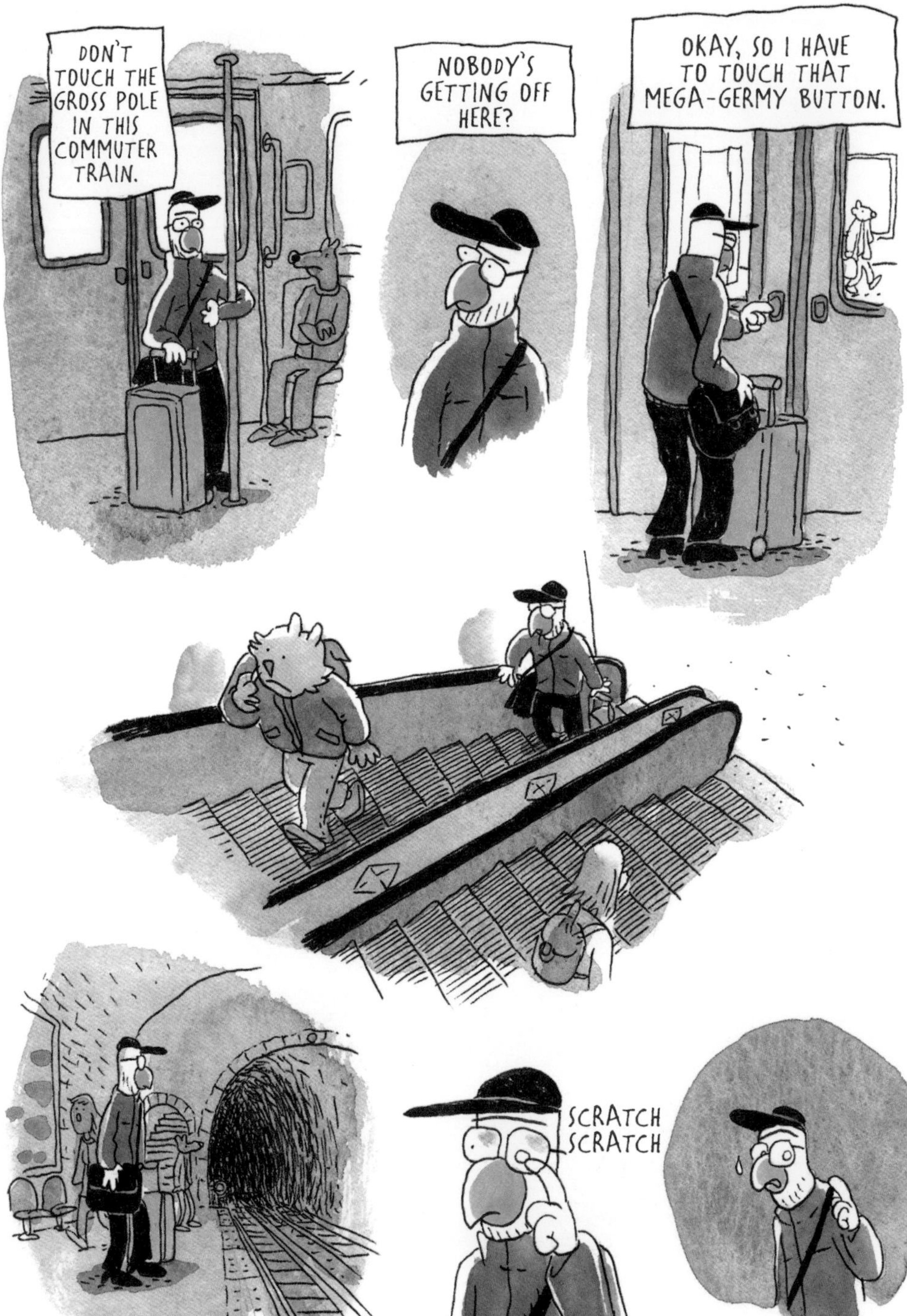
DON'T TOUCH THE GROSS POLE IN THIS COMMUTER TRAIN.
NOBODY'S GETTING OFF HERE?
OKAY, SO I HAVE TO TOUCH THAT MEGA-GERMY BUTTON.
SCRATCH SCRATCH

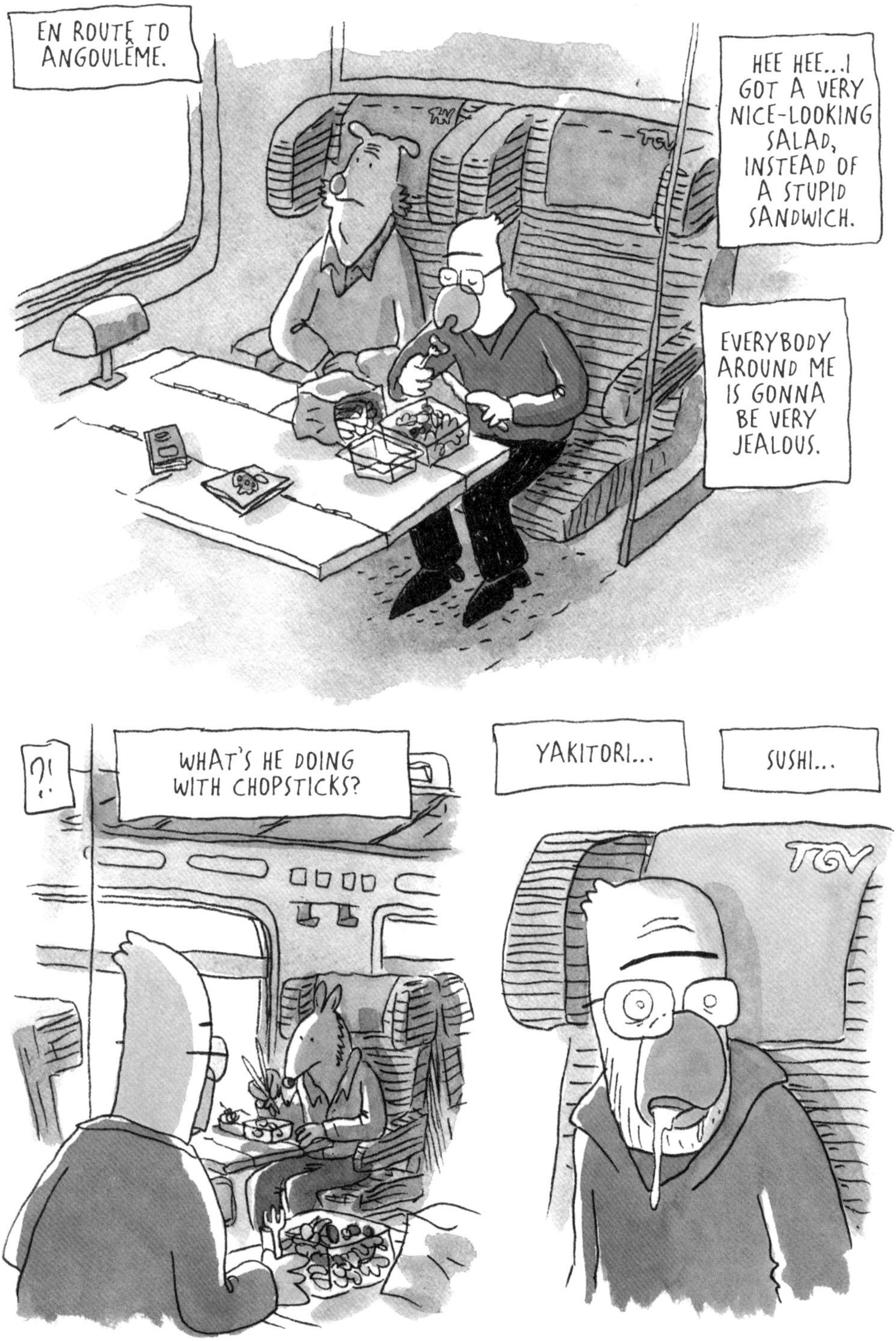
EN ROUTE TO ANGOULÊME.
HEE HEE...I GOT A VERY NICE-LOOKING SALAD, INSTEAD OF A STUPID SANDWICH.
EVERYBODY AROUND ME IS GONNA BE VERY JEALOUS.
?!
WHAT'S HE DOING WITH CHOPSTICKS?
YAKITORI...
SUSHI...
TGV

INTERESTING CONVERSATIONS IN THE WORLD OF COMICS.

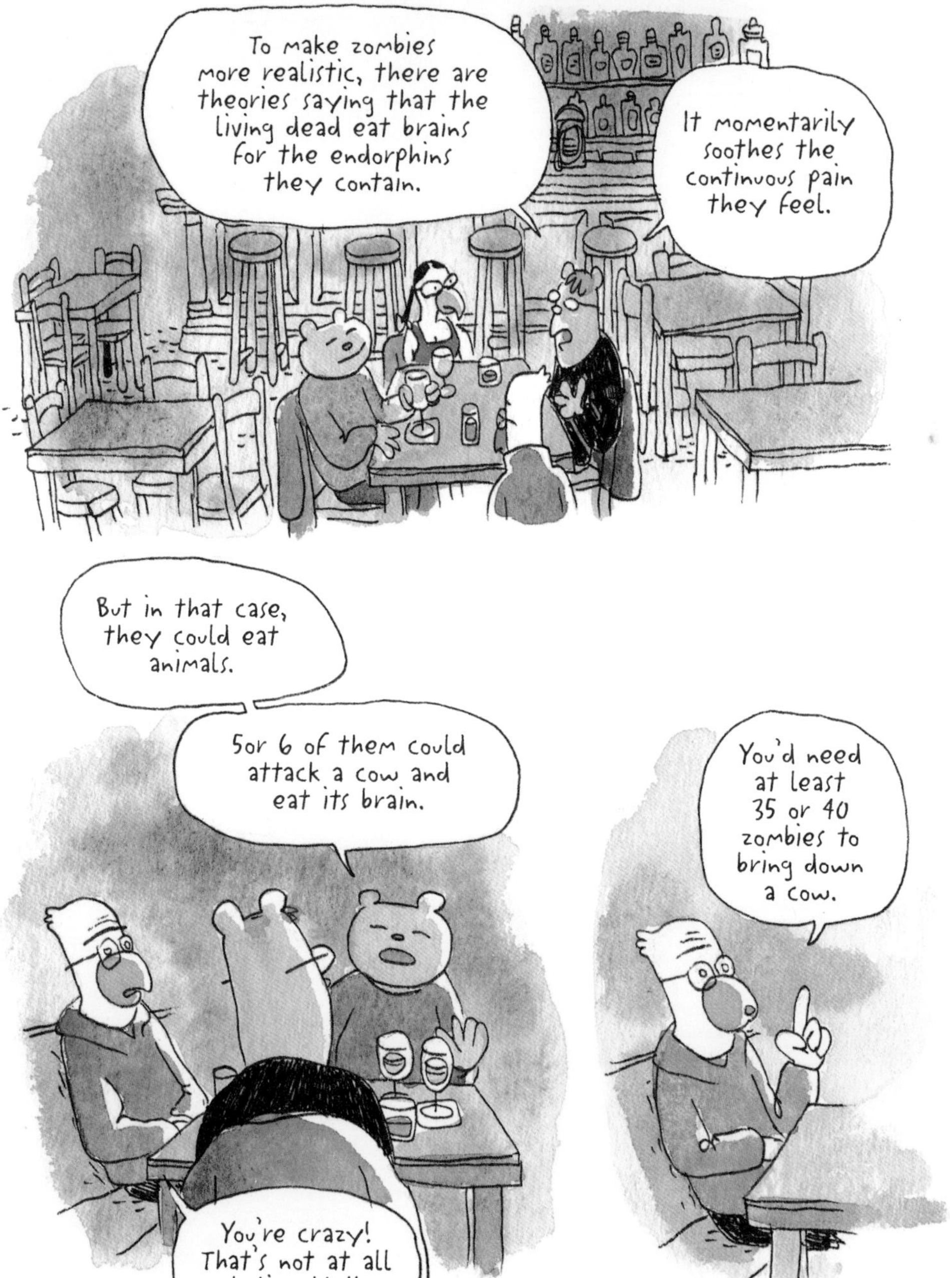
To make zombies more realistic, there are theories saying that the living dead eat brains for the endorphins they contain.
It momentarily soothes the continuous pain they feel.
But in that case, they could eat animals.
5or 6 of them could attack a cow and eat its brain.
You're crazy! That's not at all believable!!
You'd need at least 35 or 40 zombies to bring down a cow.

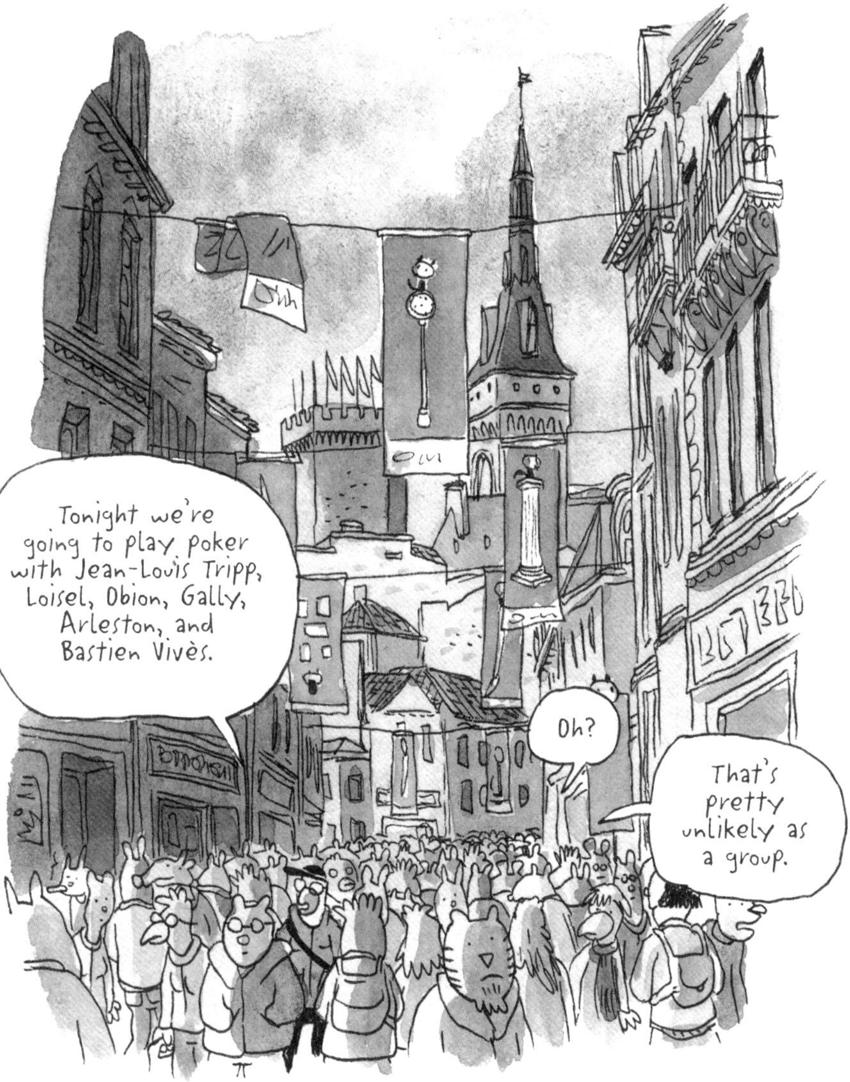
Tonight we're going to play poker with Jean-Louis Tripp, Loisel, Obion, Gally, Arleston, and Bastien Vivès.
Oh?
That's pretty unlikely as a group.

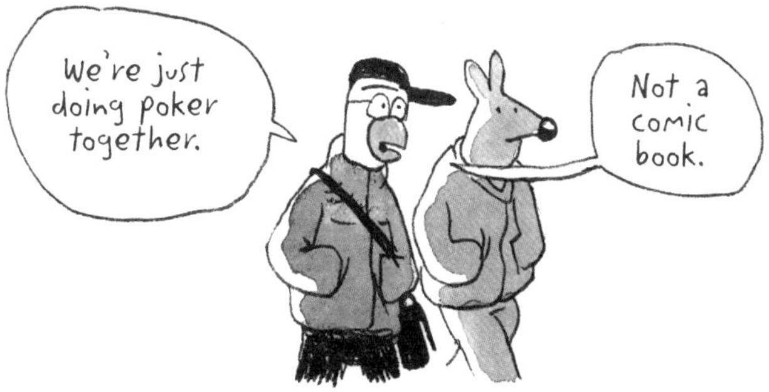
We're just doing poker together.
Not a comic book.

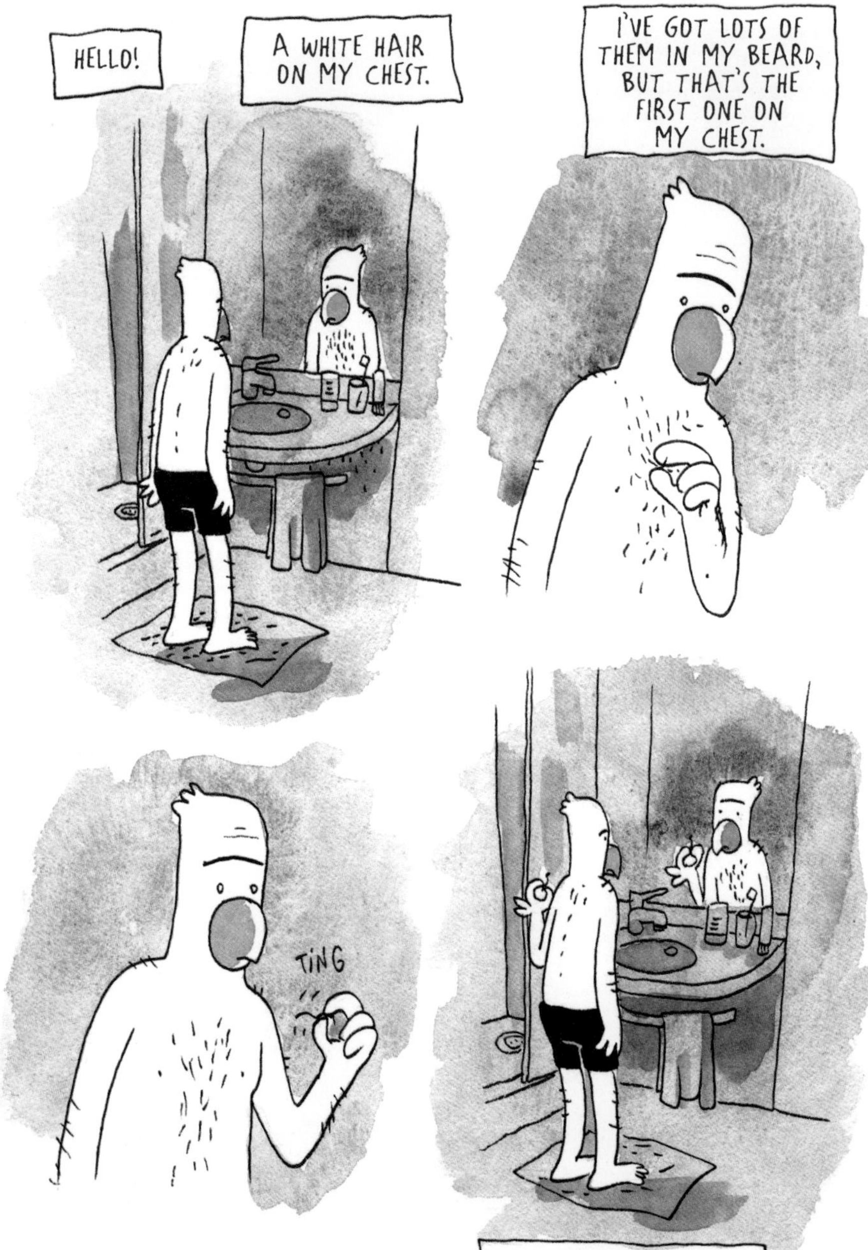
HELLO!
A WHITE HAIR ON MY CHEST.
I'VE GOT LOTS OF THEM IN MY BEARD, BUT THAT'S THE FIRST ONE ON MY CHEST.
TING
WHY DID I PLUCK IT OUT?

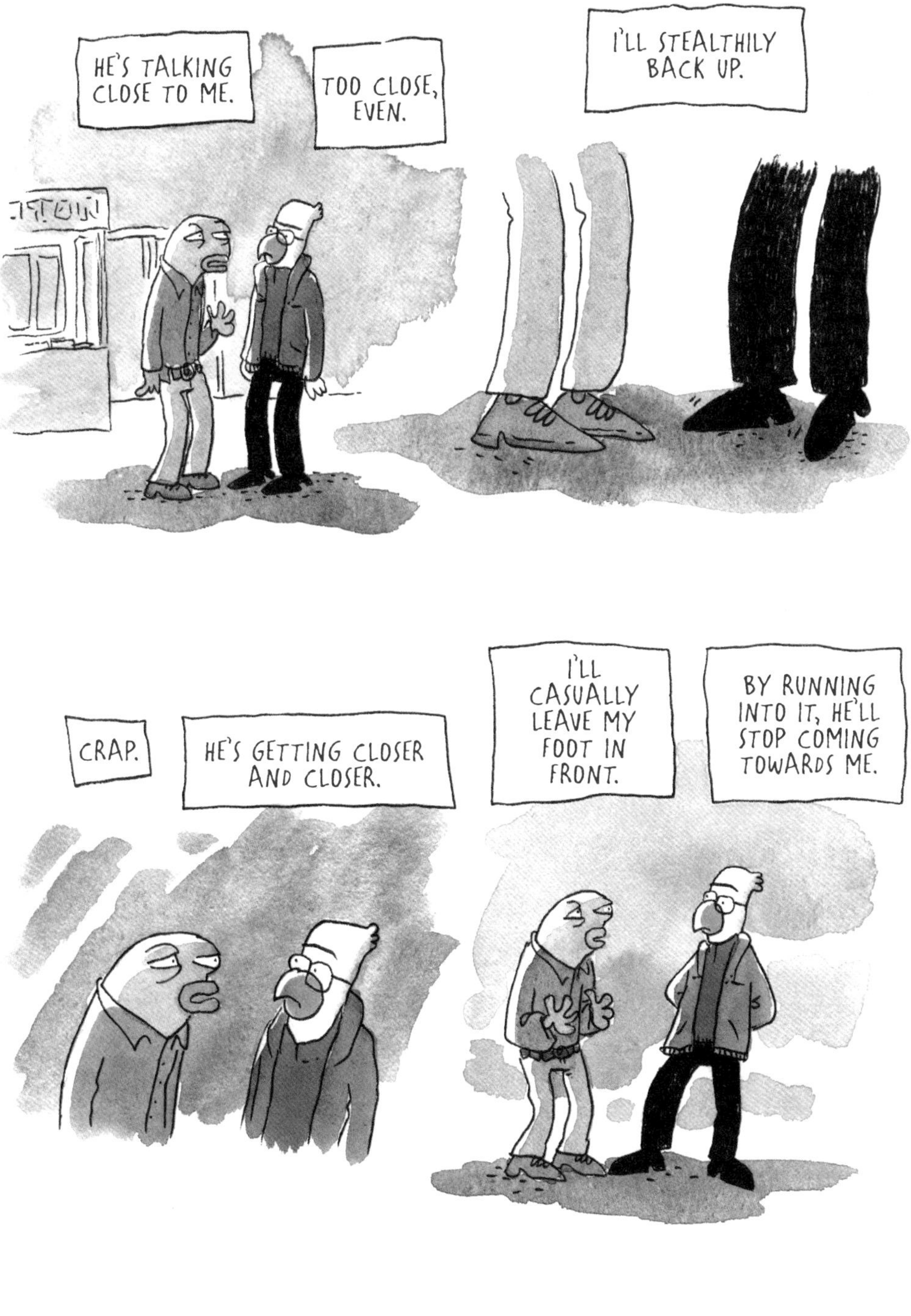
HE'S TALKING CLOSE TO ME.
TOO CLOSE, EVEN.
I'LL STEALTHILY BACK UP.
CRAP.
HE'S GETTING CLOSER AND CLOSER.
I'LL CASUALLY LEAVE MY FOOT IN FRONT.
BY RUNNING INTO IT, HE'LL STOP COMING TOWARDS ME.

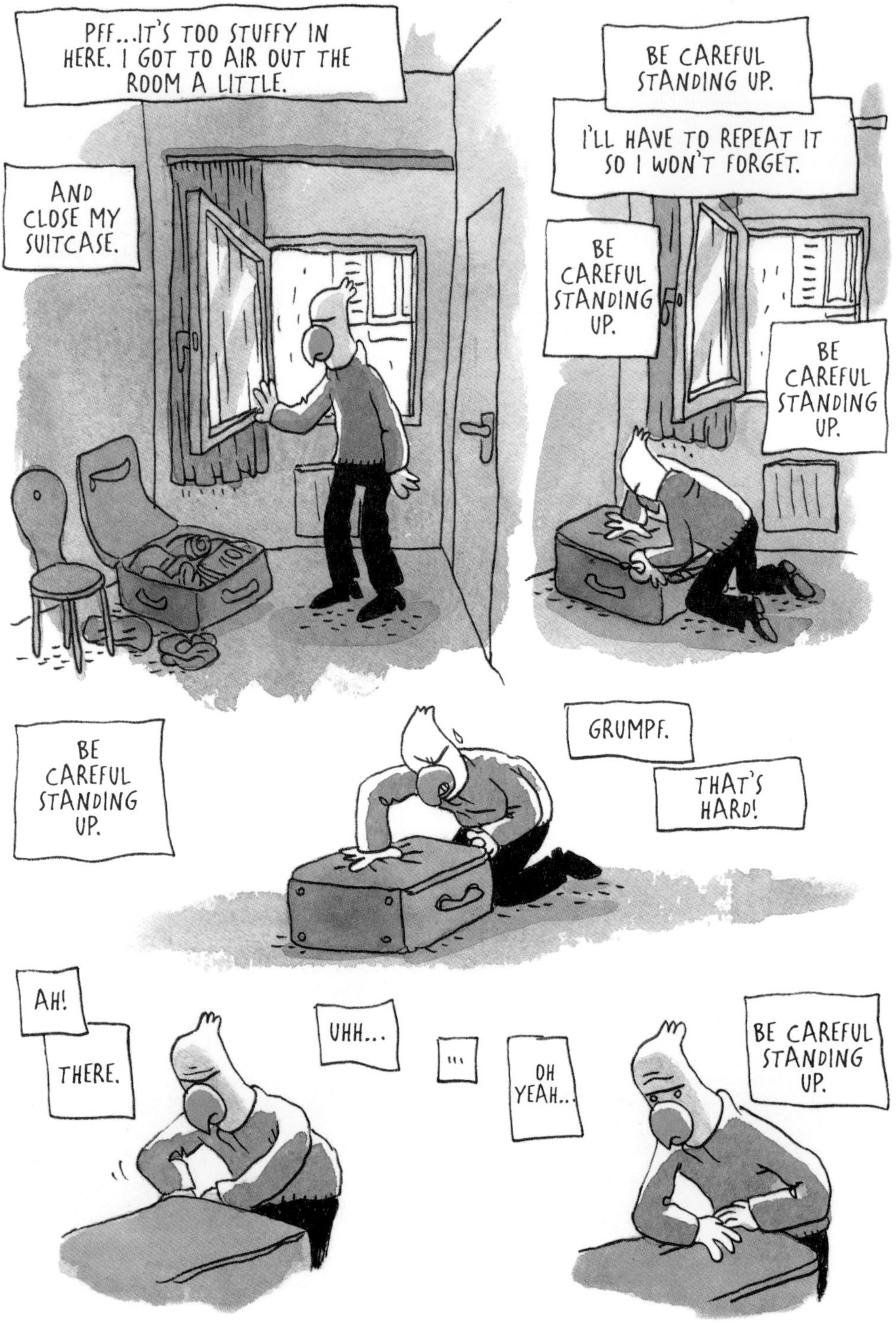
PFF...IT'S TOO STUFFY IN HERE. I GOT TO AIR OUT THE ROOM A LITTLE.
AND CLOSE MY SUITCASE.
BE CAREFUL STANDING UP.
I'LL HAVE TO REPEAT IT SO I WON'T FORGET.
BE CAREFUL STANDING UP.
BE CAREFUL STANDING UP.
BE CAREFUL STANDING UP.
GRUMPF.
THAT'S HARD!
AH!
THERE.
UHH...
...
OH YEAH...
BE CAREFUL STANDING UP.

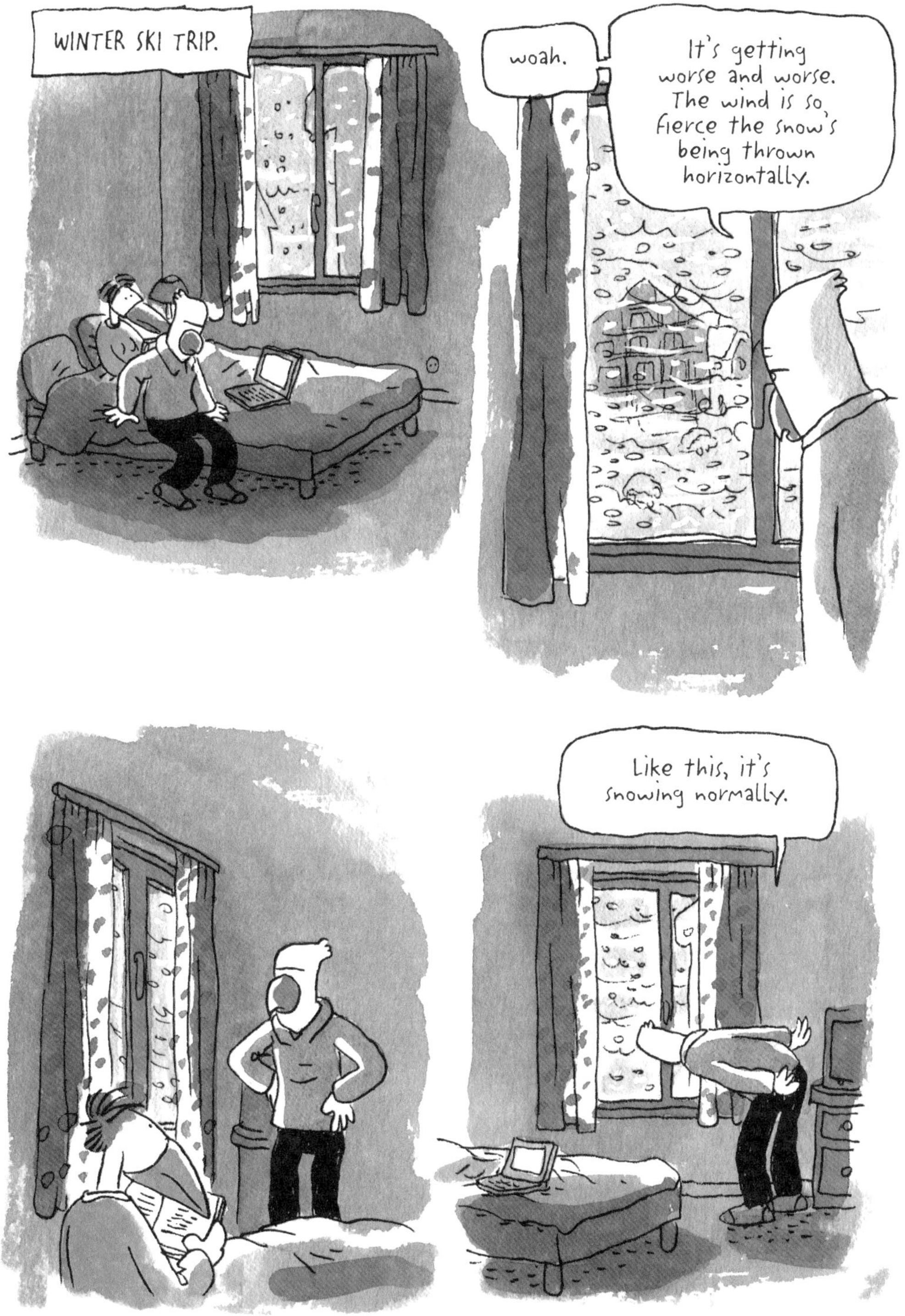
WINTER SKI TRIP.
woah.
It's getting worse and worse. The wind is so fierce the snow's being thrown horizontally.
Like this, it's snowing normally.

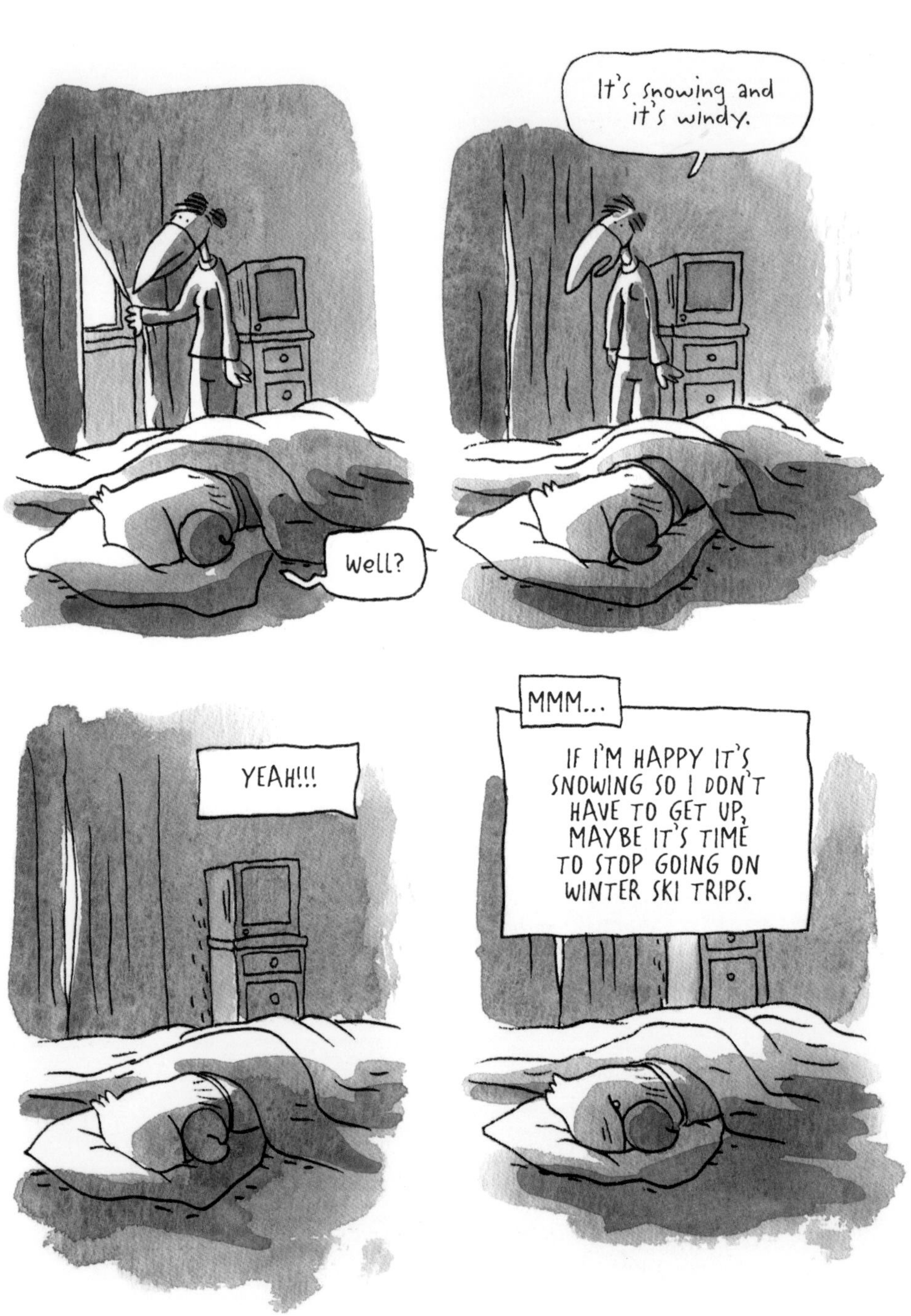
Well?
It's snowing and it's windy.
YEAH!!!
MMM...
IF I'M HAPPY IT'S SNOWING SO I DON'T HAVE TO GET UP, MAYBE IT'S TIME TO STOP GOING ON WINTER SKI TRIPS.

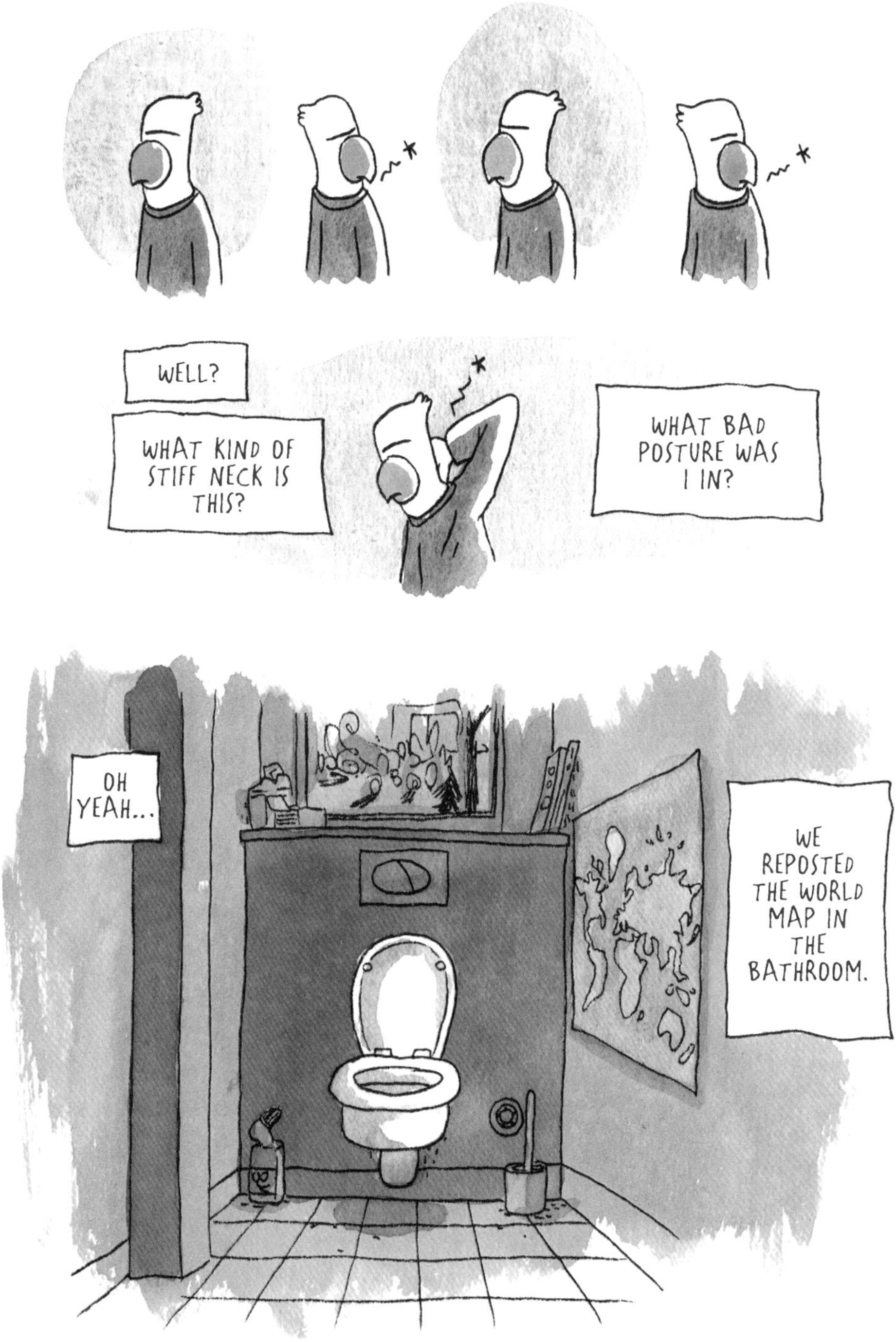
WELL?
WHAT KIND OF STIFF NECK IS THIS?
WHAT BAD POSTURE WAS I IN?
OH YEAH...
WE REPOSTED THE WORLD MAP IN THE BATHROOM.

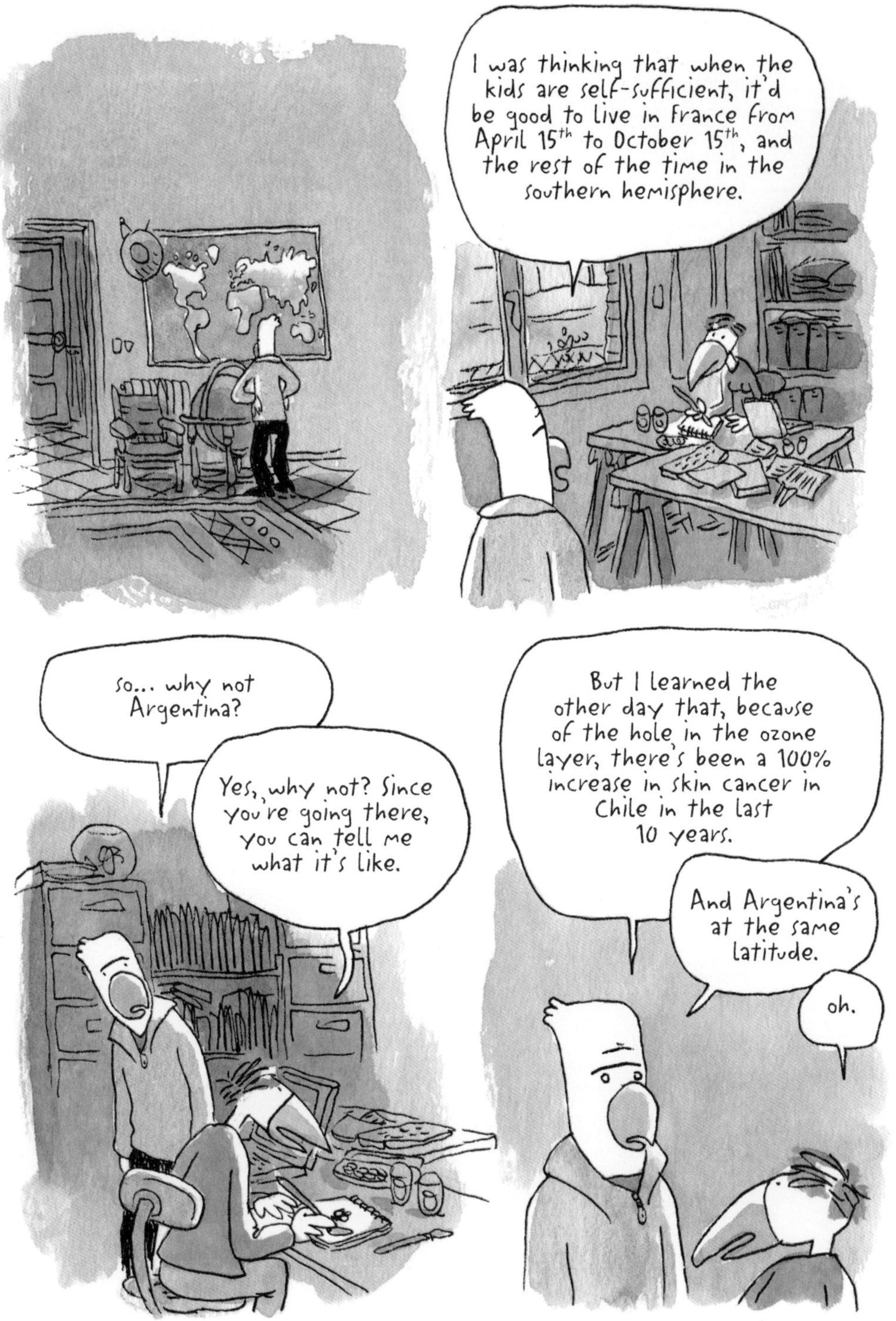
I was thinking that when the kids are self-sufficient, it'd be good to live in France from April 15th to October 15th, and the rest of the time in the southern hemisphere.
So... why not Argentina?
Yes, why not? Since you're going there, you can tell me what it's like.
But I learned the other day that, because of the hole in the ozone layer, there's been a 100% increase in skin cancer in Chile in the last 10 years.
And Argentina's at the same latitude.
oh.

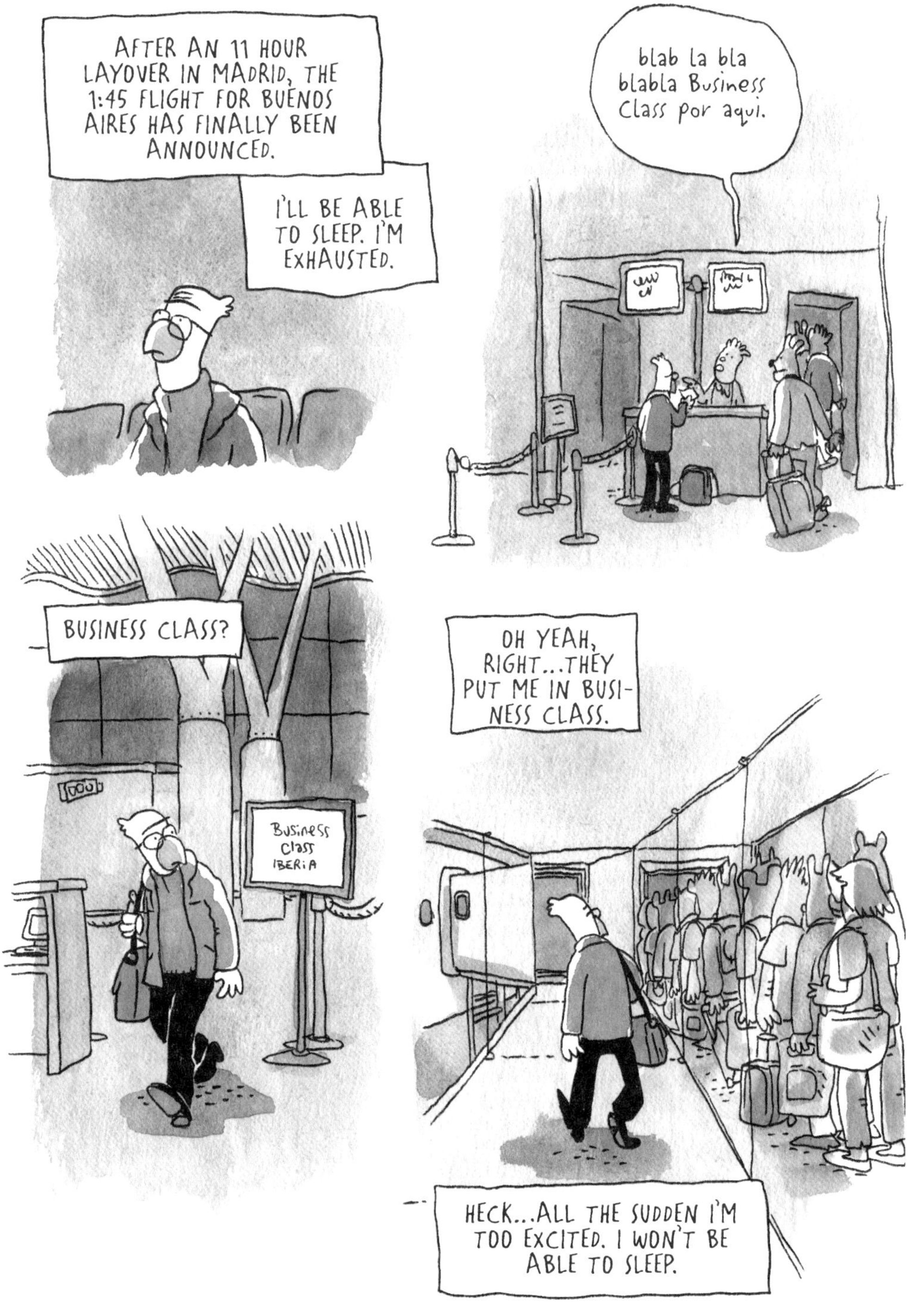
AFTER AN 11 HOUR LAYOVER IN MADRID, THE 1:45 FLIGHT FOR BUENOS AIRES HAS FINALLY BEEN ANNOUNCED.
I'LL BE ABLE TO SLEEP. I'M EXHAUSTED.
blab la bla blabla Business Class por aqui.
BUSINESS CLASS?
Business Class IBERIA
OH YEAH, RIGHT...THEY PUT ME IN BUSINESS CLASS.
HECK...ALL THE SUDDEN I'M TOO EXCITED. I WON'T BE ABLE TO SLEEP.

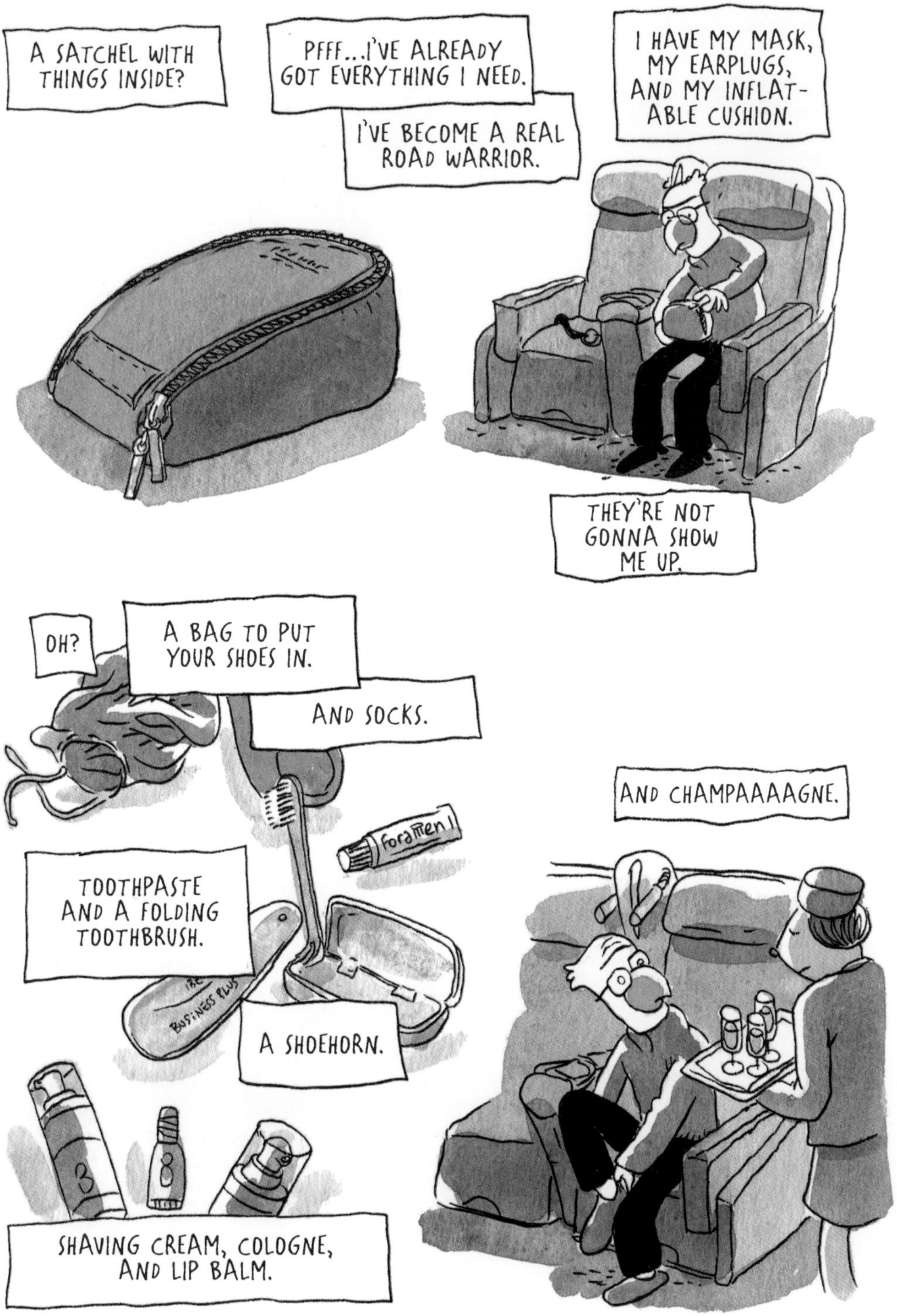
A SATCHEL WITH THINGS INSIDE?
PFFF...I'VE ALREADY GOT EVERYTHING I NEED.
I'VE BECOME A REAL ROAD WARRIOR.
I HAVE MY MASK, MY EARPLUGS, AND MY INFLAT-ABLE CUSHION.
THEY'RE NOT GONNA SHOW ME UP.
OH?
A BAG TO PUT YOUR SHOES IN.
AND SOCKS.
TOOTHPASTE AND A FOLDING TOOTHBRUSH.
A SHOEHORN.
SHAVING CREAM, COLOGNE, AND LIP BALM.
AND CHAMPAAAAGNE.

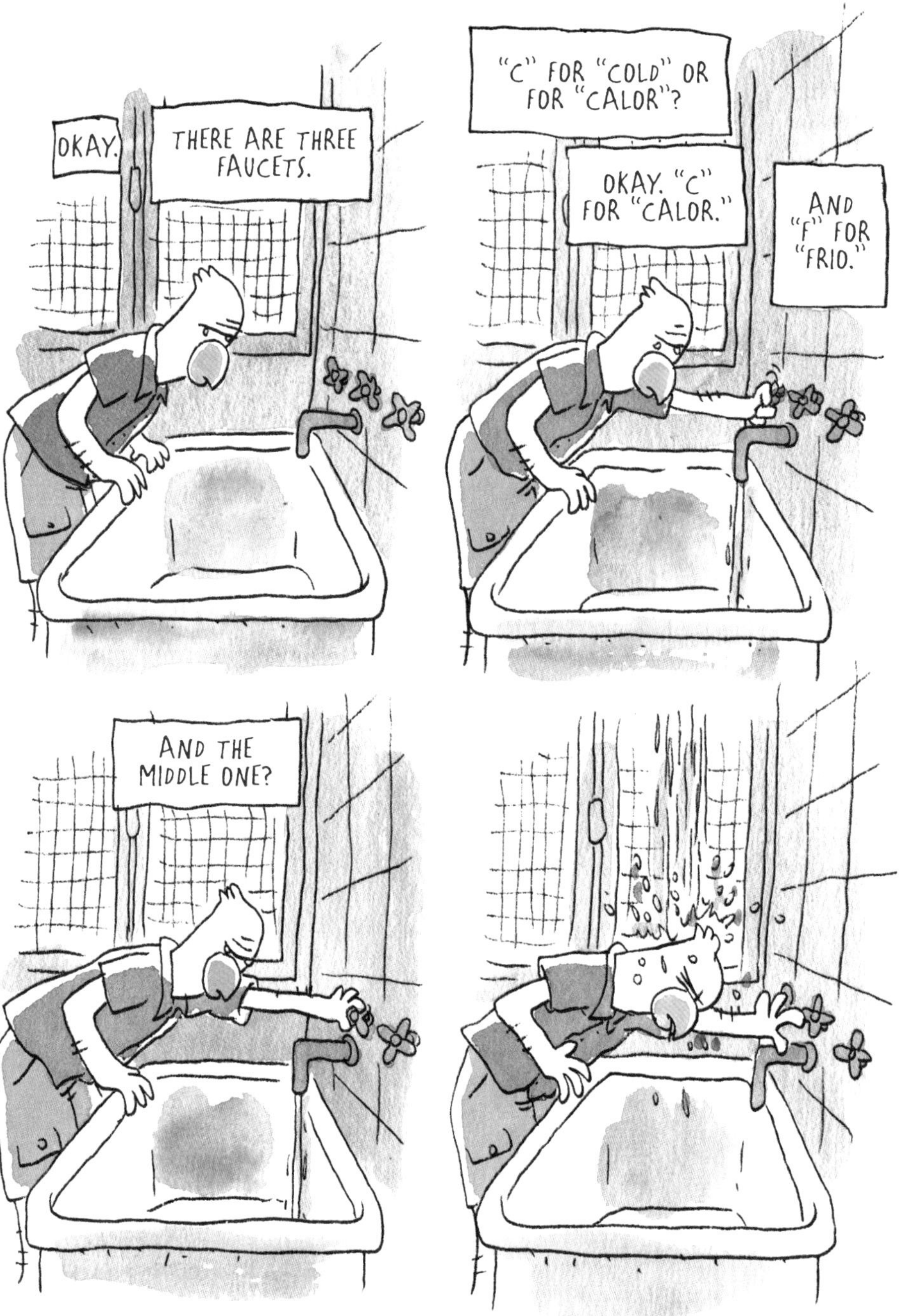
OKAY.
THERE ARE THREE FAUCETS.
"C" FOR "COLD" OR FOR "CALOR"?
OKAY. "C" FOR "CALOR."
AND "F" FOR "FRIO."
AND THE MIDDLE ONE?

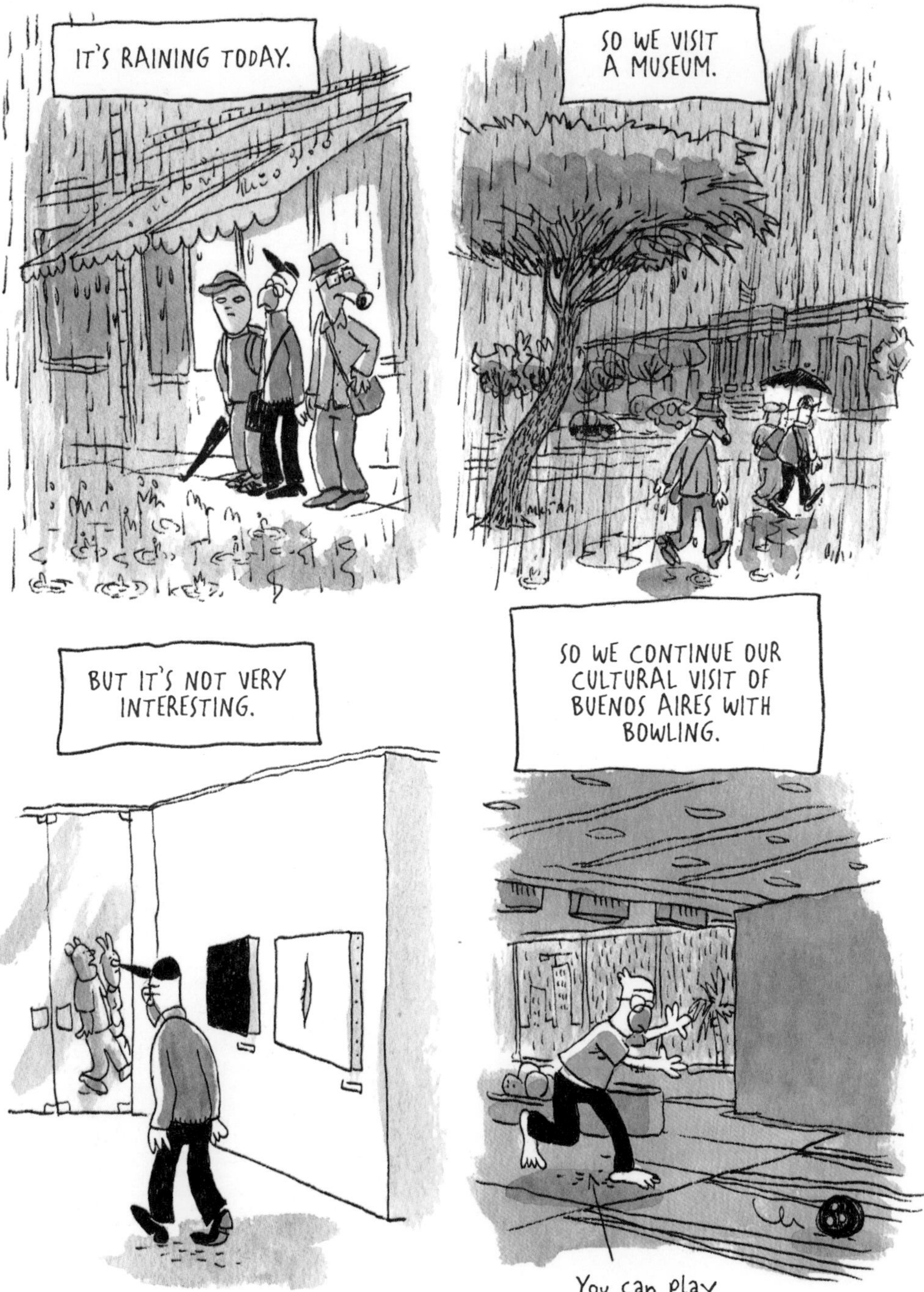
IT'S RAINING TODAY.
SO WE VISIT A MUSEUM.
BUT IT'S NOT VERY INTERESTING.
SO WE CONTINUE OUR CULTURAL VISIT OF BUENOS AIRES WITH BOWLING.
You can play barefoot!

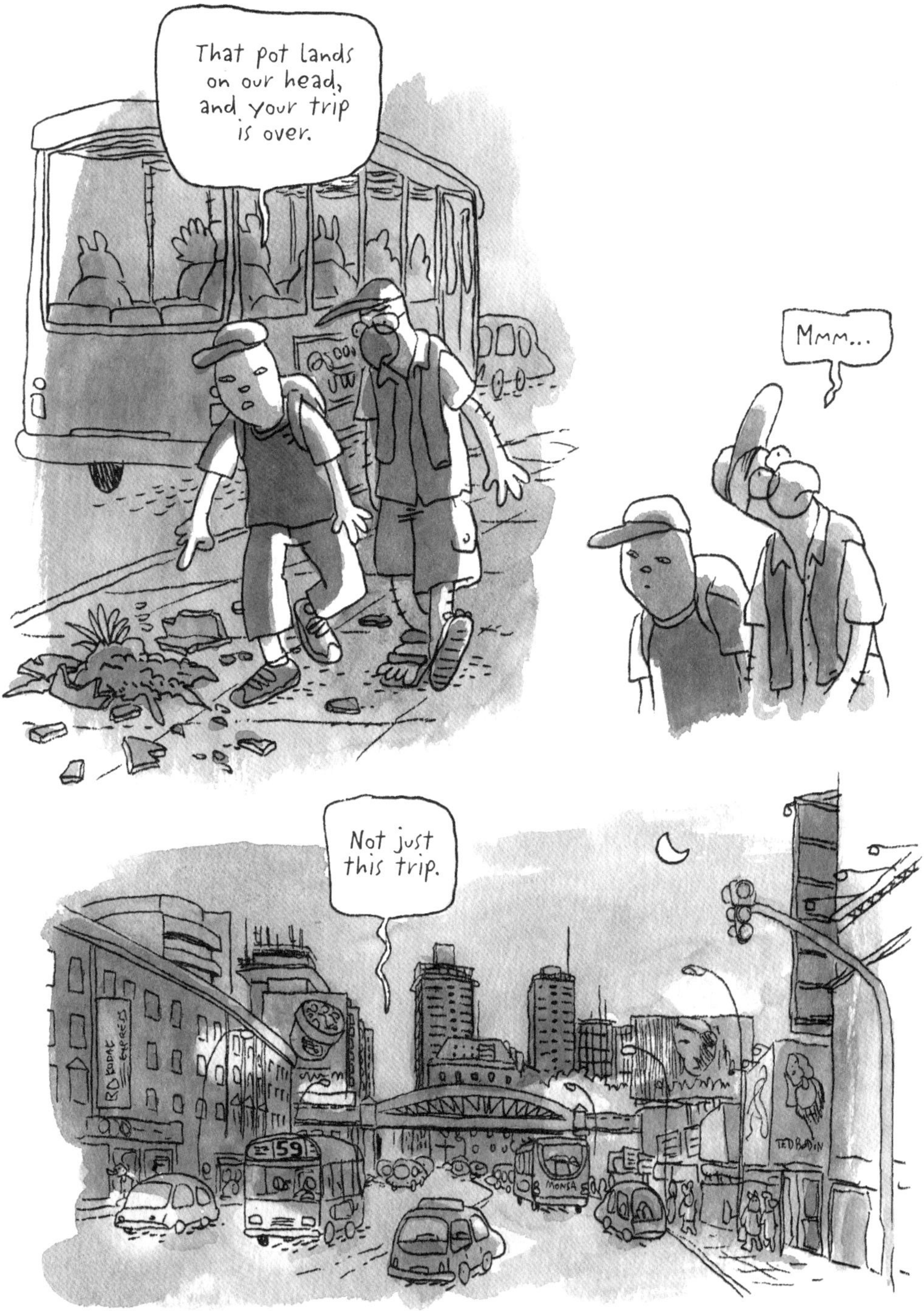
That pot lands on our head, and your trip is over.
Mmm...
Not just this trip.
59
MONSA

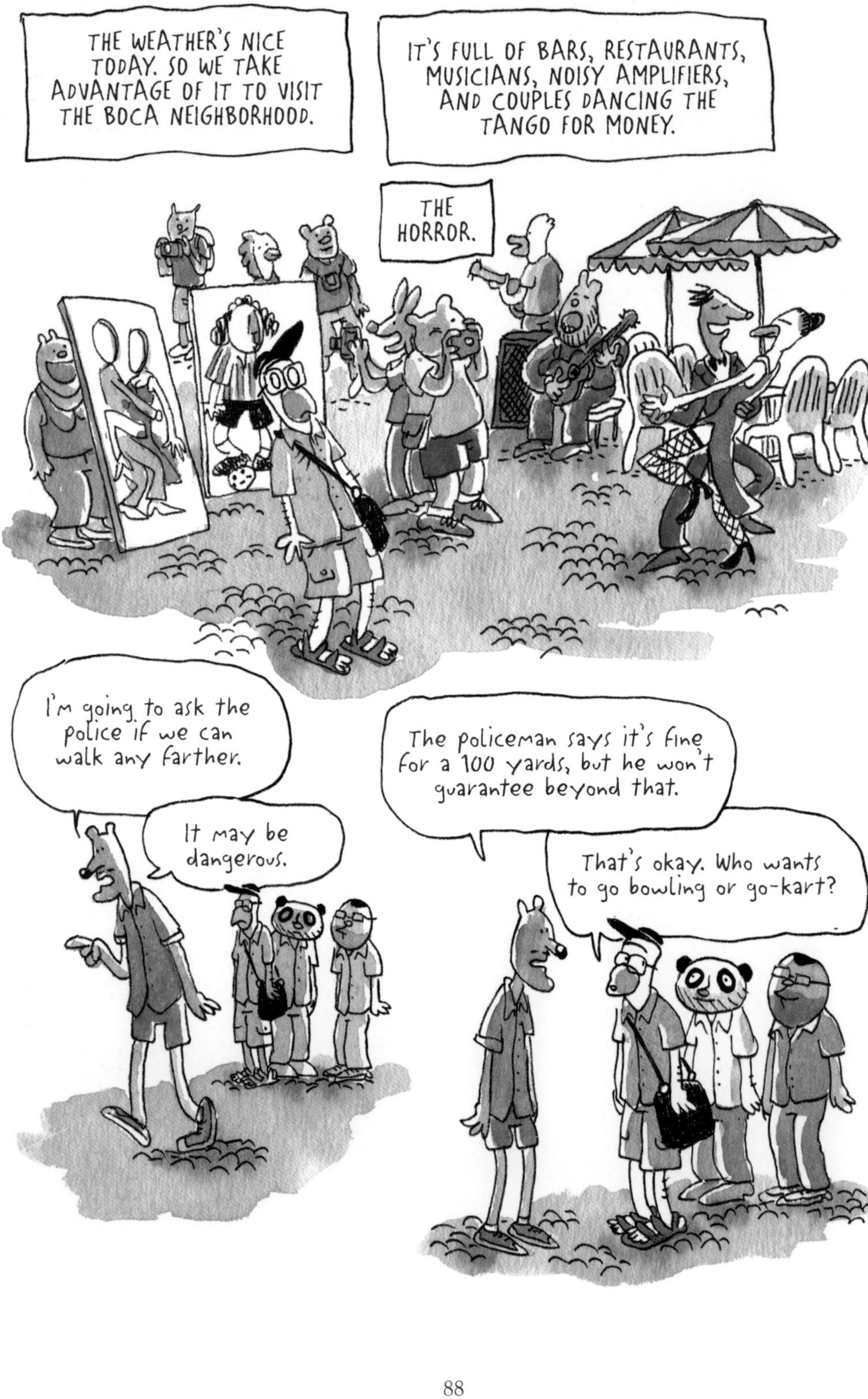
THE WEATHER'S NICE TODAY. SO WE TAKE ADVANTAGE OF IT TO VISIT THE BOCA NEIGHBORHOOD.
IT'S FULL OF BARS, RESTAURANTS, MUSICIANS, NOISY AMPLIFIERS, AND COUPLES DANCING THE TANGO FOR MONEY.
THE HORROR.
I'm going to ask the police if we can walk any farther.
It may be dangerous.
The policeman says it's fine for a 100 yards, but he won't guarantee beyond that.
That's okay. Who wants to go bowling or go-kart?

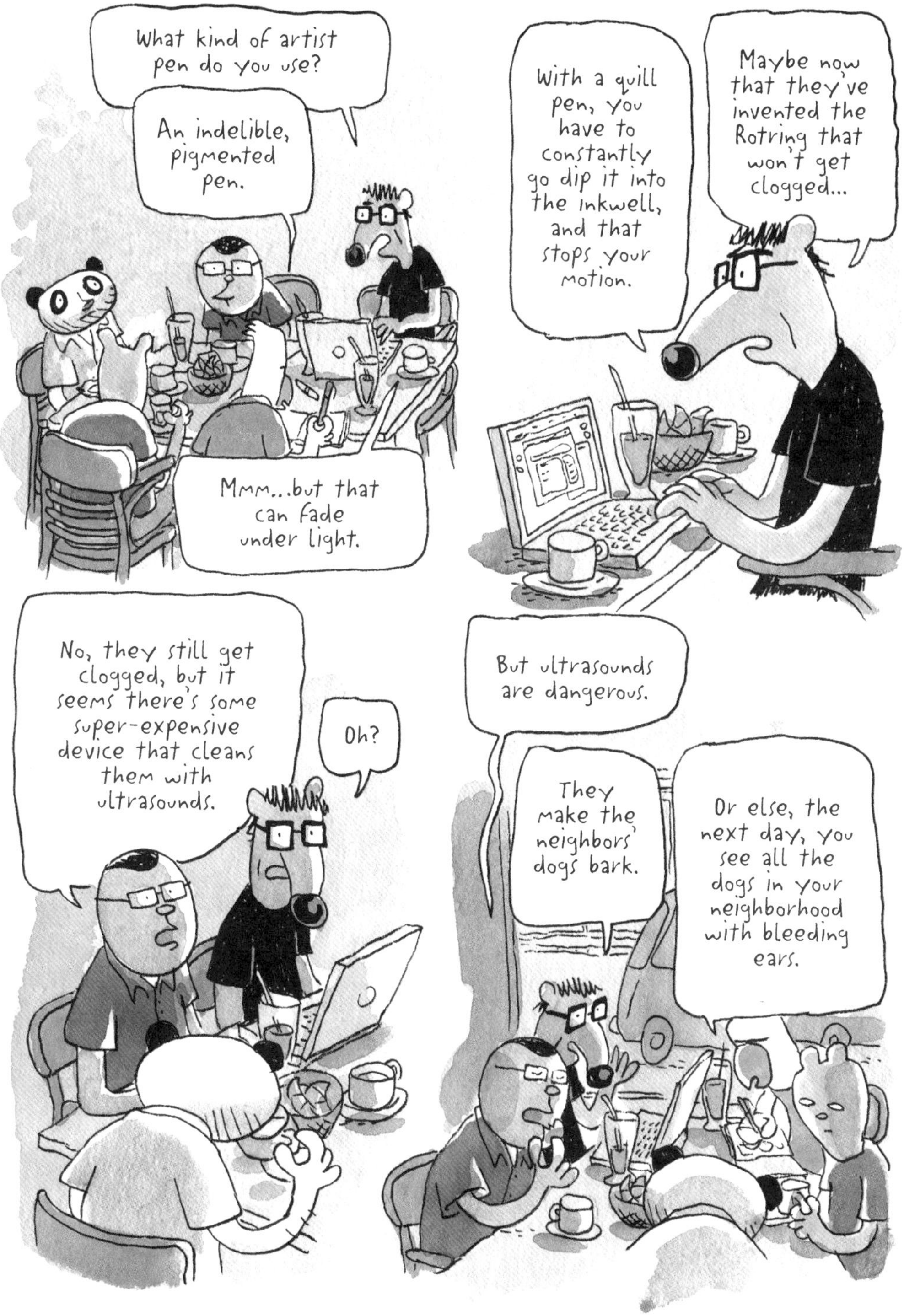
What kind of artist pen do you use?
An indelible, pigmented pen.
Mmm...but that can fade under light.
With a quill pen, you have to constantly go dip it into the inkwell, and that stops your motion.
Maybe now that they've invented the Rotring that won't get clogged...
No, they still get clogged, but it seems there's some super-expensive device that cleans them with ultrasounds.
Oh?
But ultrasounds are dangerous.
They make the neighbors' dogs bark.
Or else, the next day, you see all the dogs in your neighborhood with bleeding ears.

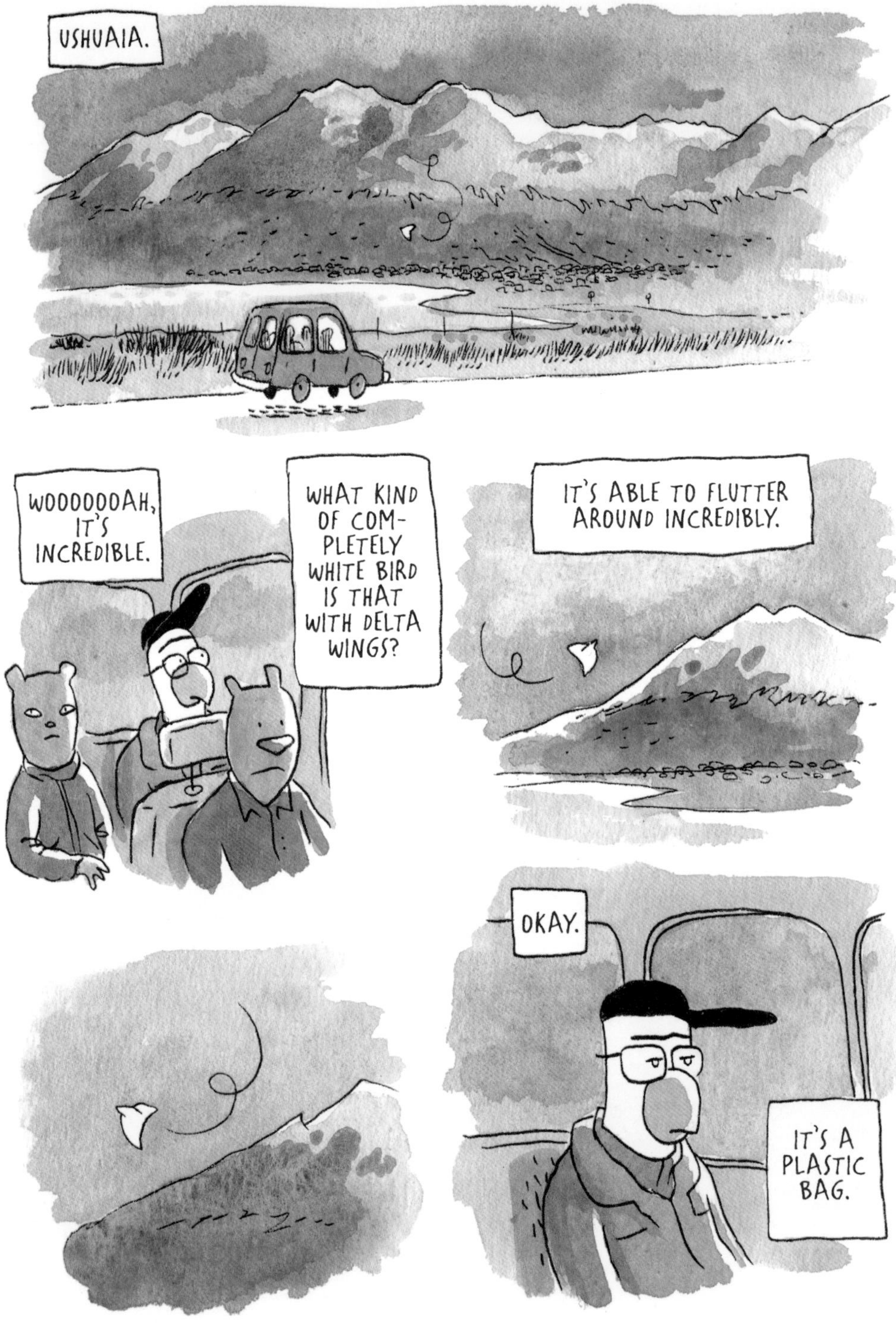
USHUAIA.
WOOOOOOAH, IT'S INCREDIBLE.
WHAT KIND OF COMPLETELY WHITE BIRD IS THAT WITH DELTA WINGS?
IT'S ABLE TO FLUTTER AROUND INCREDIBLY.
OKAY.
IT'S A PLASTIC BAG.

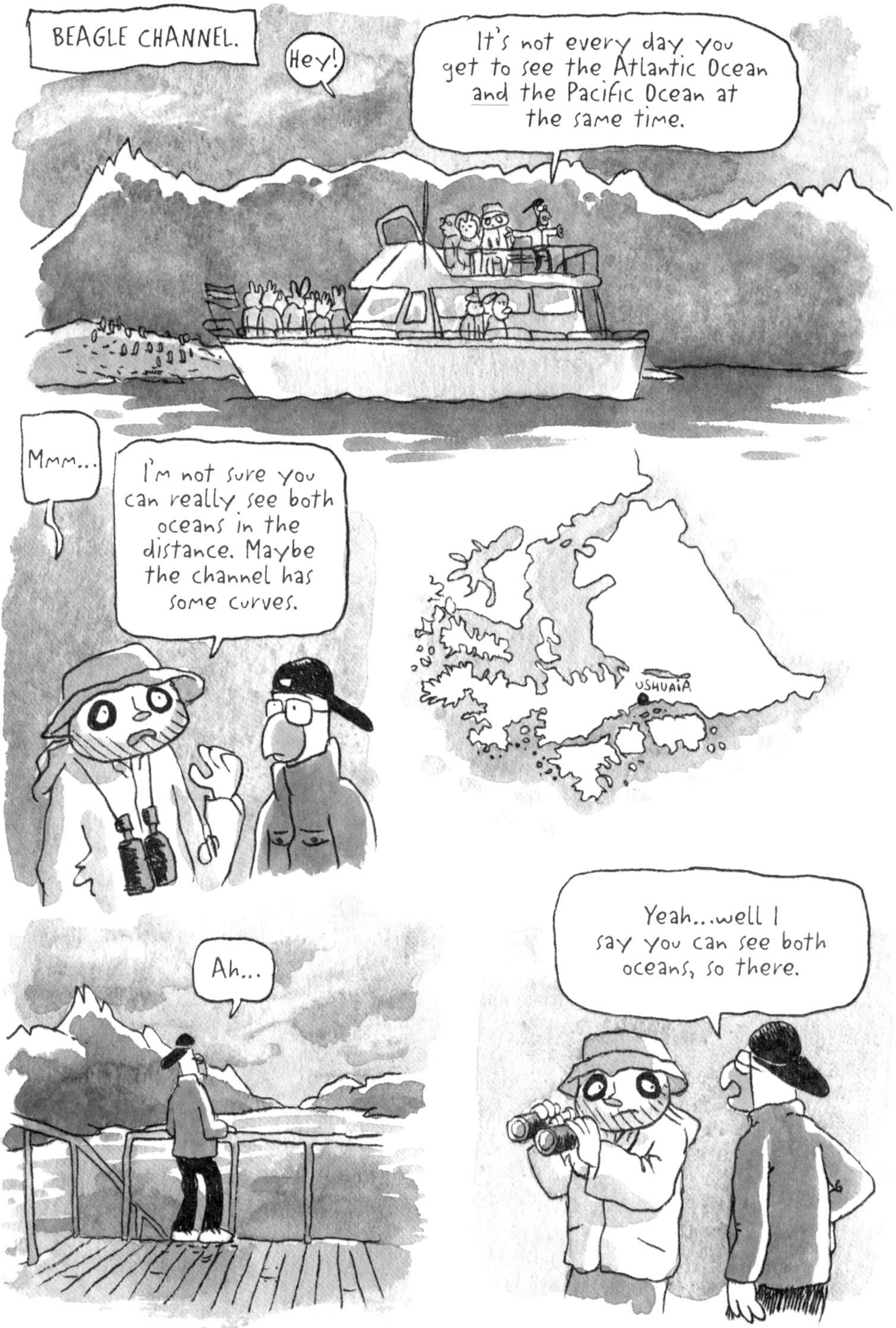
BEAGLE CHANNEL.
Hey!
It's not every day you get to see the Atlantic Ocean and the Pacific Ocean at the same time.
Mmm...
I'm not sure you can really see both oceans in the distance. Maybe the channel has some curves.
USHUAIA
Ah...
Yeah...well I say you can see both oceans, so there.

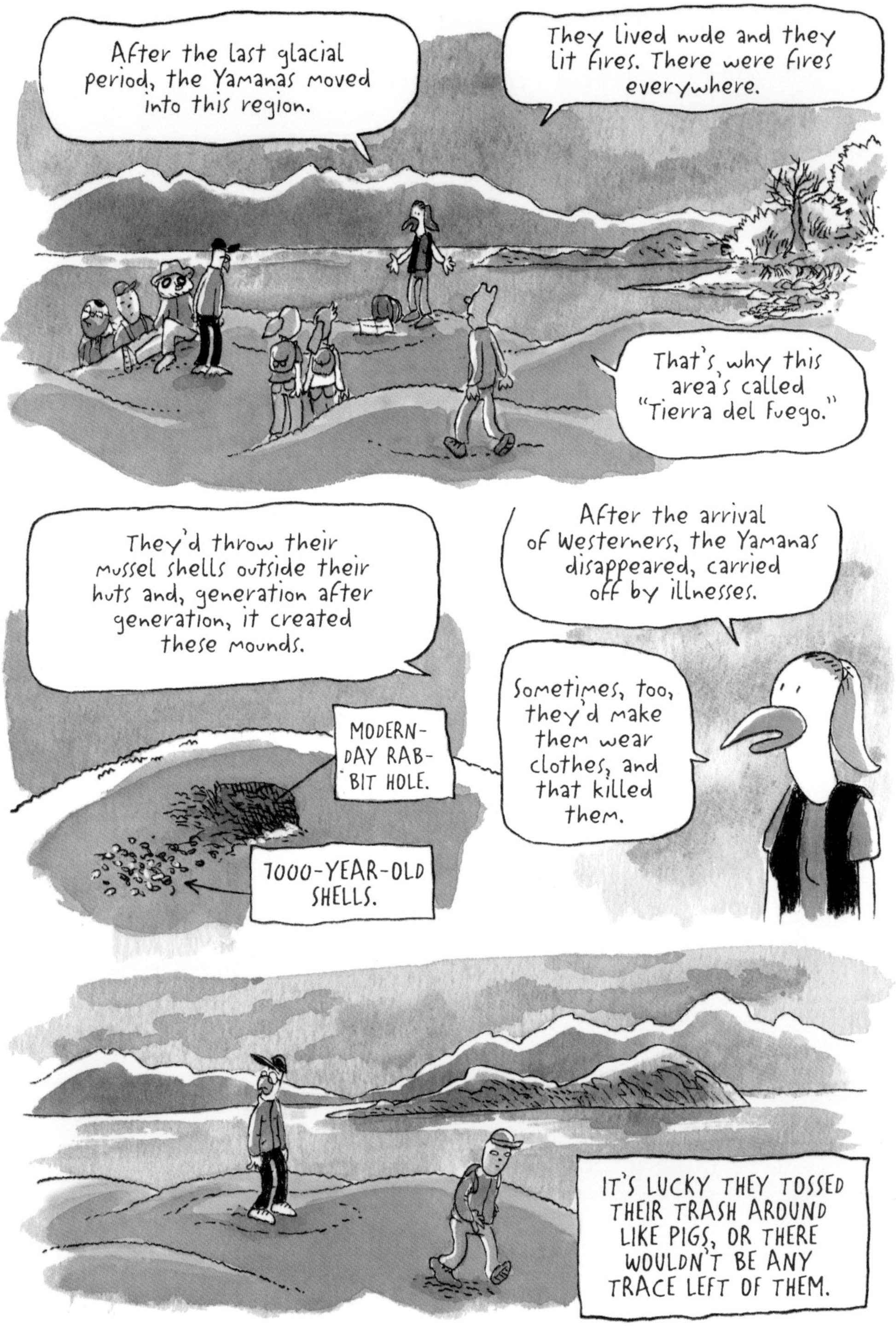
After the last glacial period, the Yamanas moved into this region.
They lived nude and they lit fires. There were fires everywhere.
That's why this area's called "Tierra del Fuego."
They'd throw their mussel shells outside their huts and, generation after generation, it created these mounds.
MODERN-DAY RAB-BIT HOLE.
7000-YEAR-OLD SHELLS.
After the arrival of Westerners, the Yamanas disappeared, carried off by illnesses.
Sometimes, too, they'd make them wear clothes, and that killed them.
IT'S LUCKY THEY TOSSED THEIR TRASH AROUND LIKE PIGS, OR THERE WOULDN'T BE ANY TRACE LEFT OF THEM.

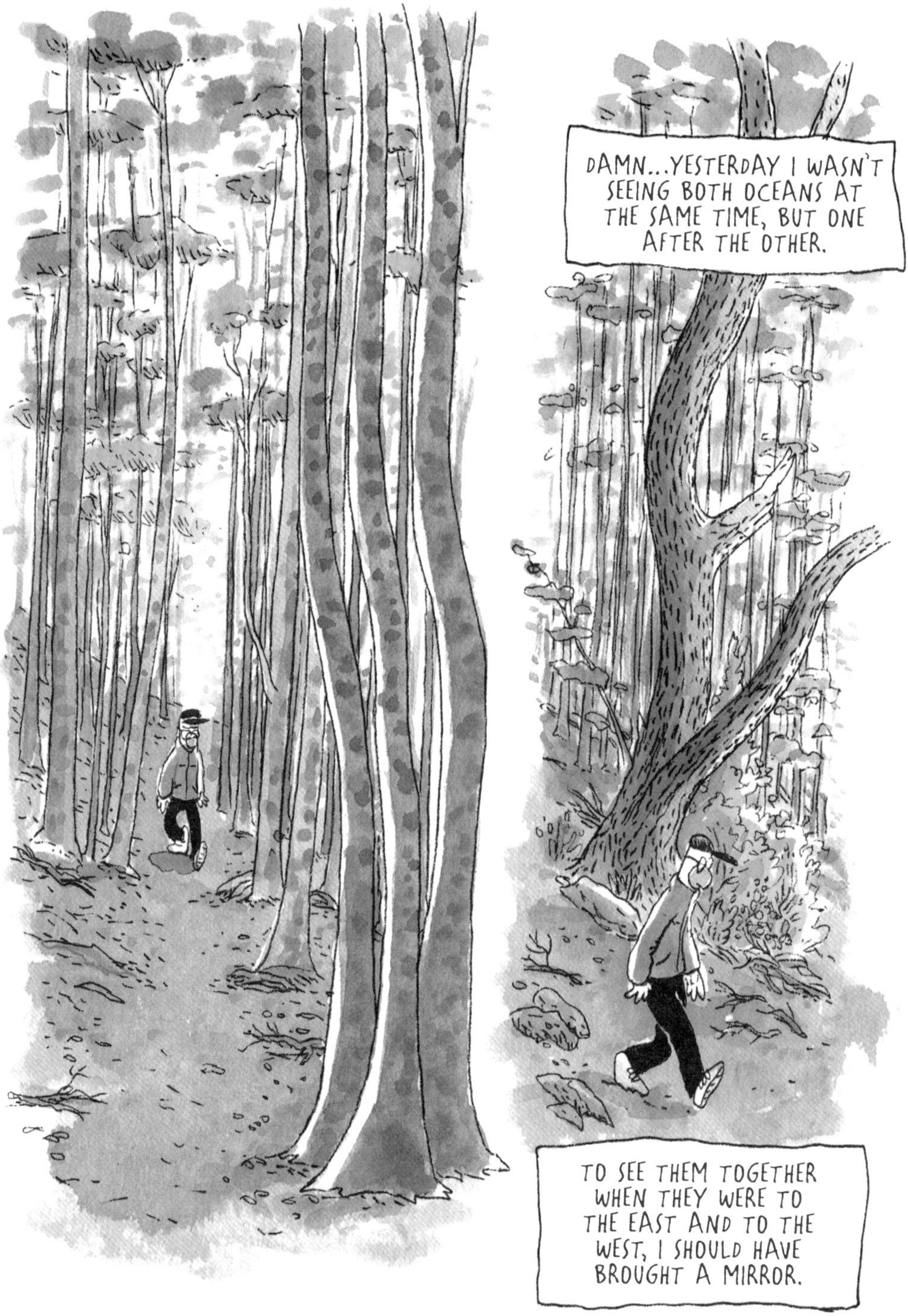
DAMN...YESTERDAY I WASN'T SEEING BOTH OCEANS AT THE SAME TIME, BUT ONE AFTER THE OTHER.
TO SEE THEM TOGETHER WHEN THEY WERE TO THE EAST AND TO THE WEST, I SHOULD HAVE BROUGHT A MIRROR.

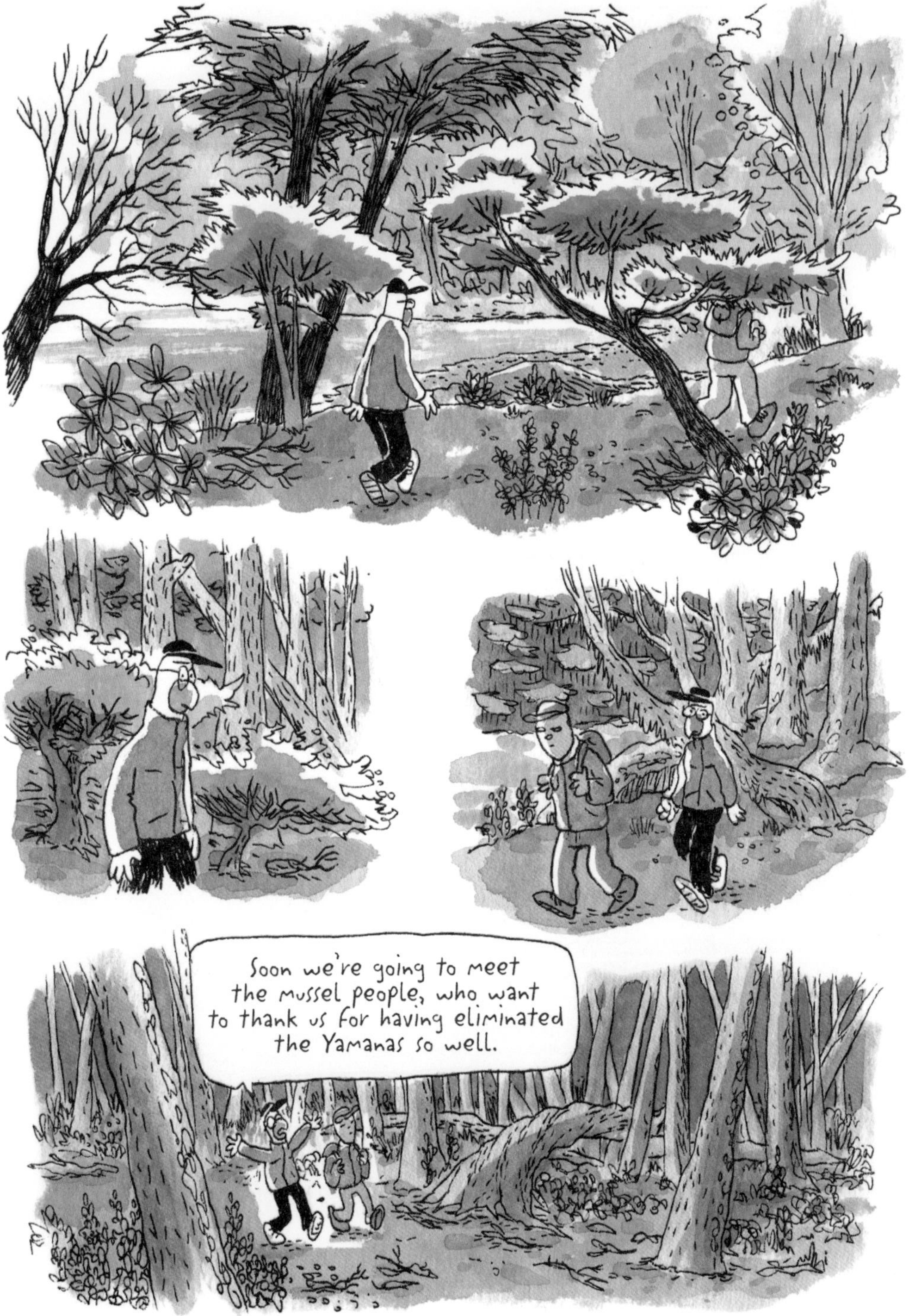
Soon we're going to meet the mussel people, who want to thank us for having eliminated the Yamanas so well.

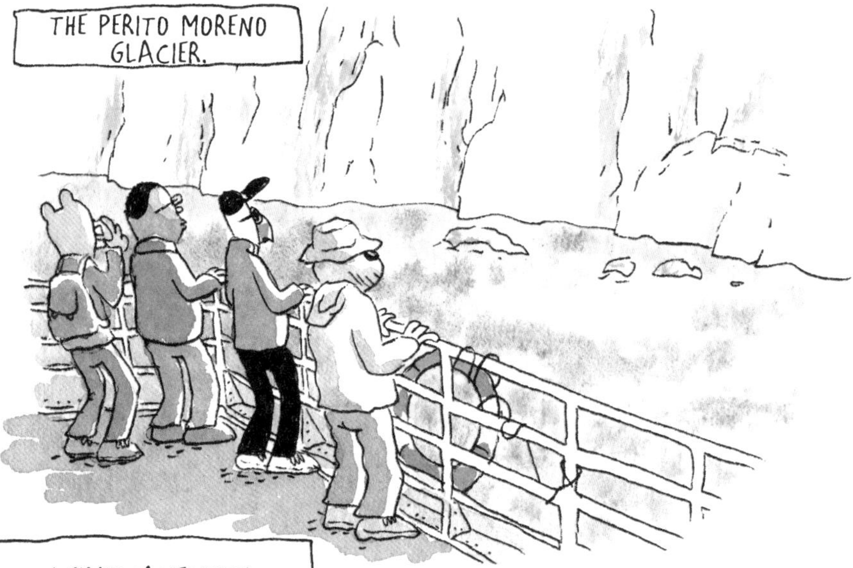
THE PERITO MORENO GLACIER.

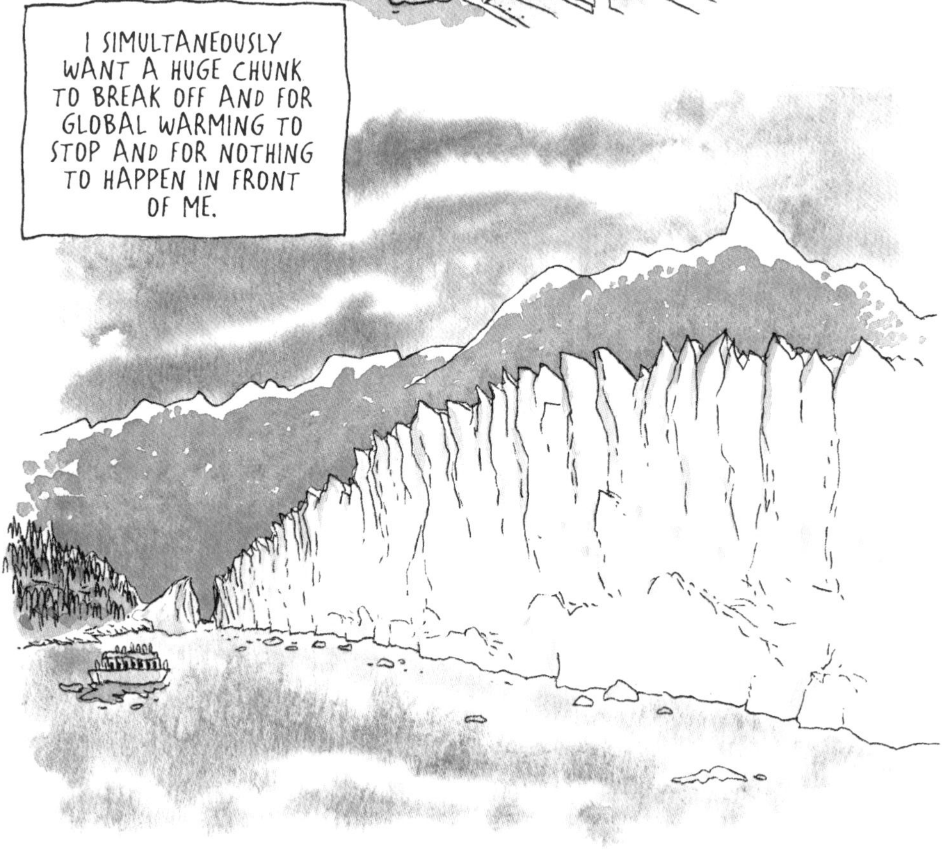
I SIMULTANEOUSLY WANT A HUGE CHUNK TO BREAK OFF AND FOR GLOBAL WARMING TO STOP AND FOR NOTHING TO HAPPEN IN FRONT OF ME.

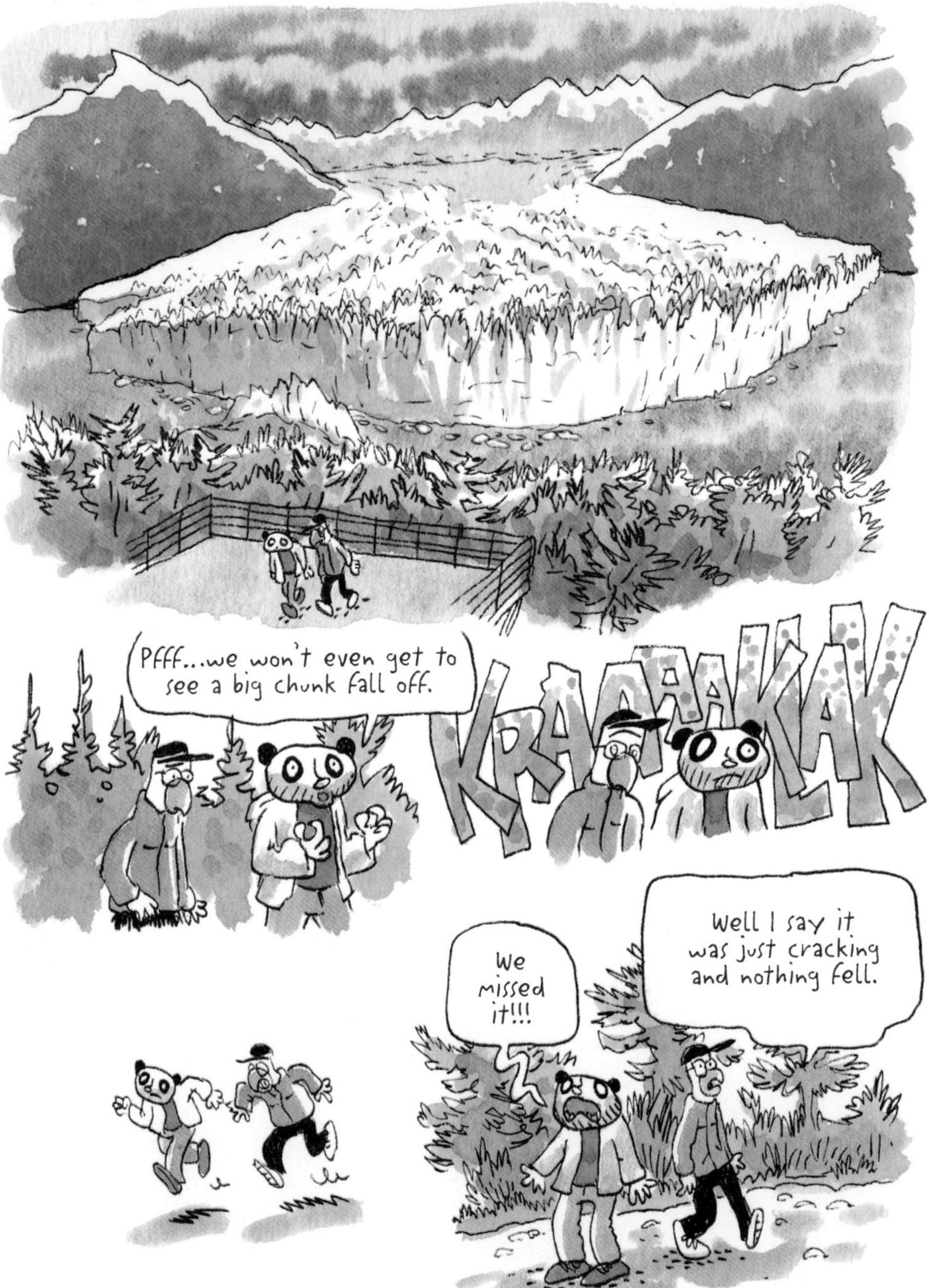
PFFF...we won't even get to see a big chunk fall off.
KRAAAAKLAK
We missed it!!!
Well I say it was just cracking and nothing fell.

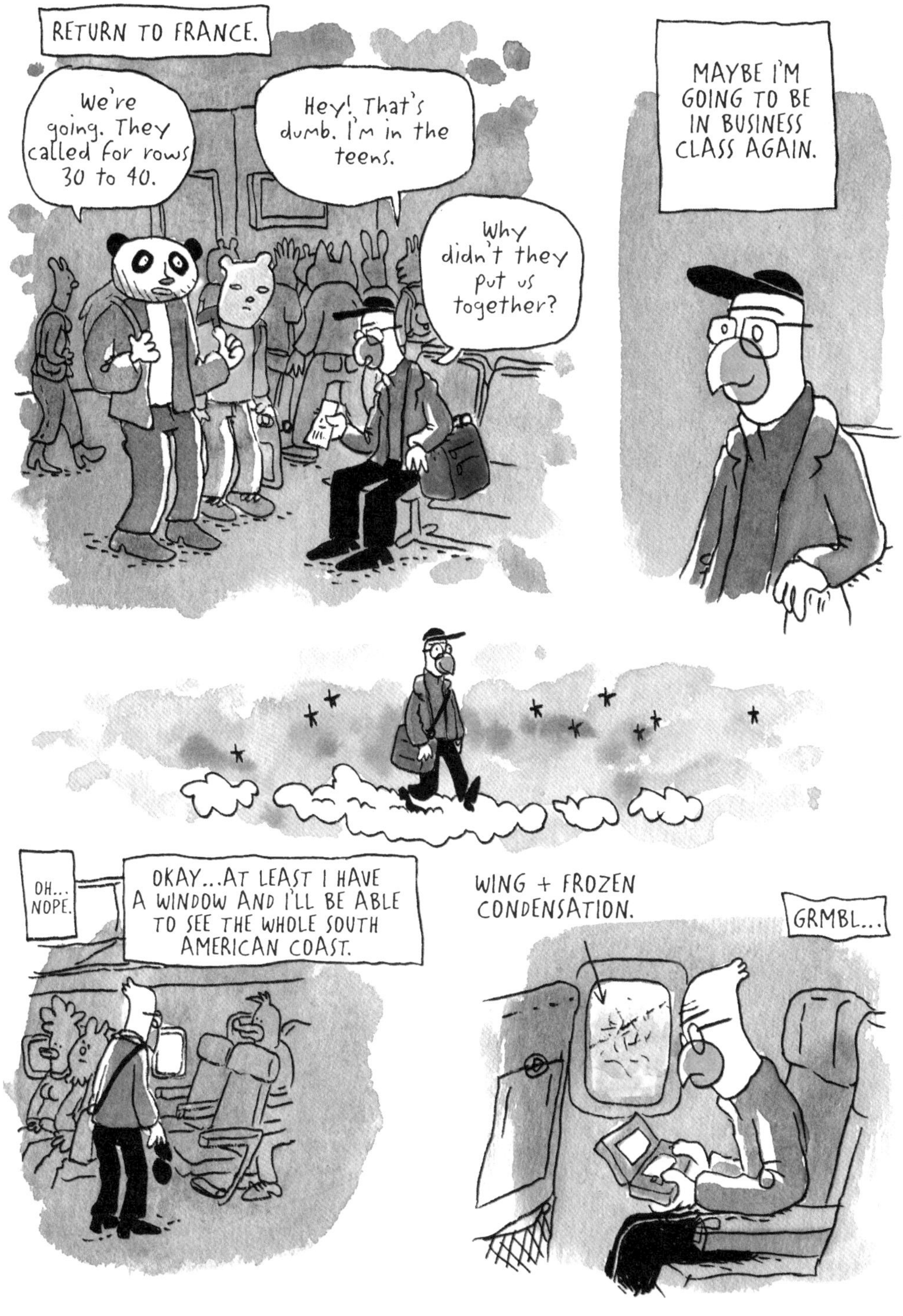

RETURN TO FRANCE.
We're going. They called for rows 30 to 40.
Hey! That's dumb. I'm in the teens.
Why didn't they put us together?
MAYBE I'M GOING TO BE IN BUSINESS CLASS AGAIN.
OKAY...AT LEAST I HAVE A WINDOW AND I'LL BE ABLE TO SEE THE WHOLE SOUTH AMERICAN COAST.
OH... NOPE.
WING + FROZEN CONDENSATION.
GRMBL...

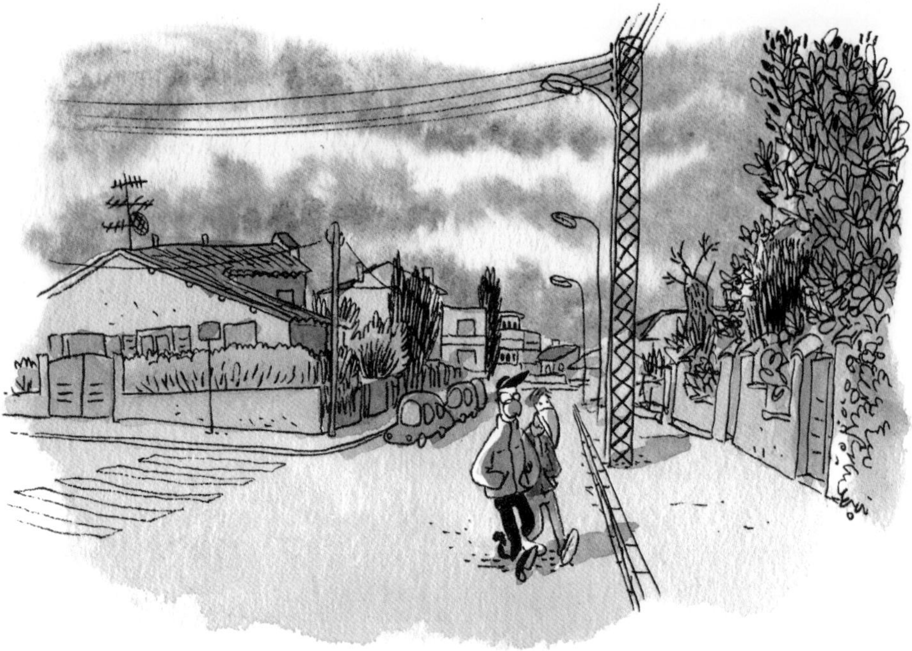

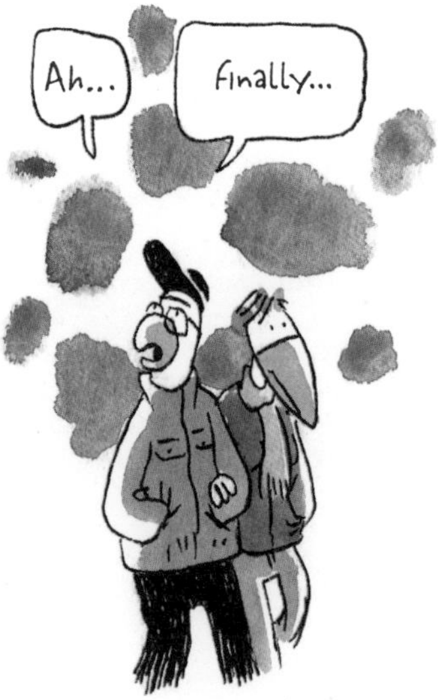
Ah...
finally...

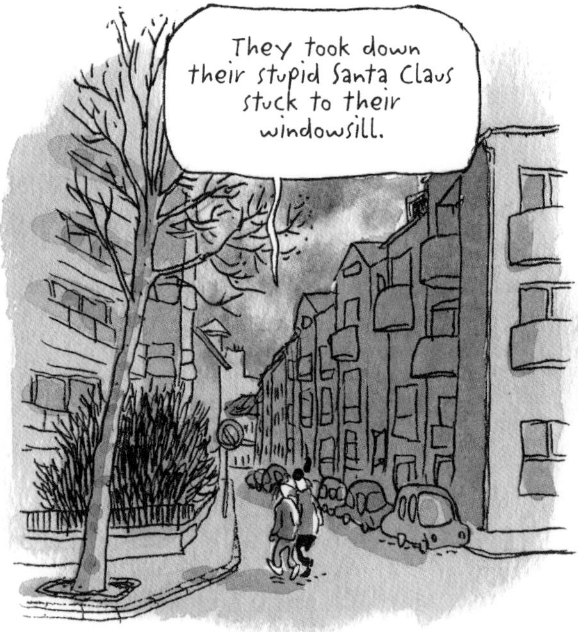
They took down their stupid Santa Claus stuck to their windowsill.

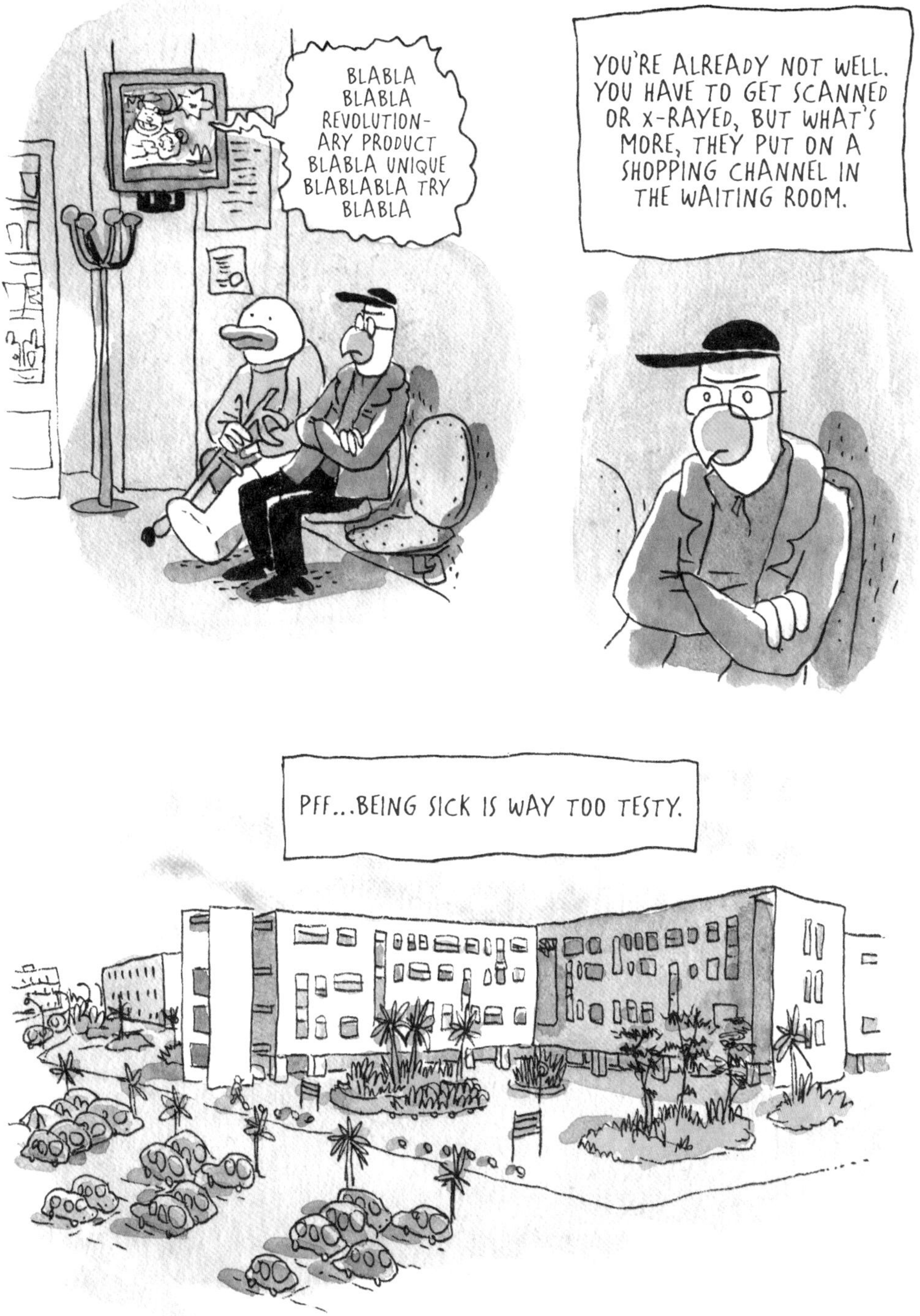
BLABLA BLABLA REVOLUTIONARY PRODUCT BLABLA UNIQUE BLABLABLA TRY BLABLA
YOU'RE ALREADY NOT WELL. YOU HAVE TO GET SCANNED OR X-RAYED, BUT WHAT'S MORE, THEY PUT ON A SHOPPING CHANNEL IN THE WAITING ROOM.
PFF...BEING SICK IS WAY TOO TESTY.

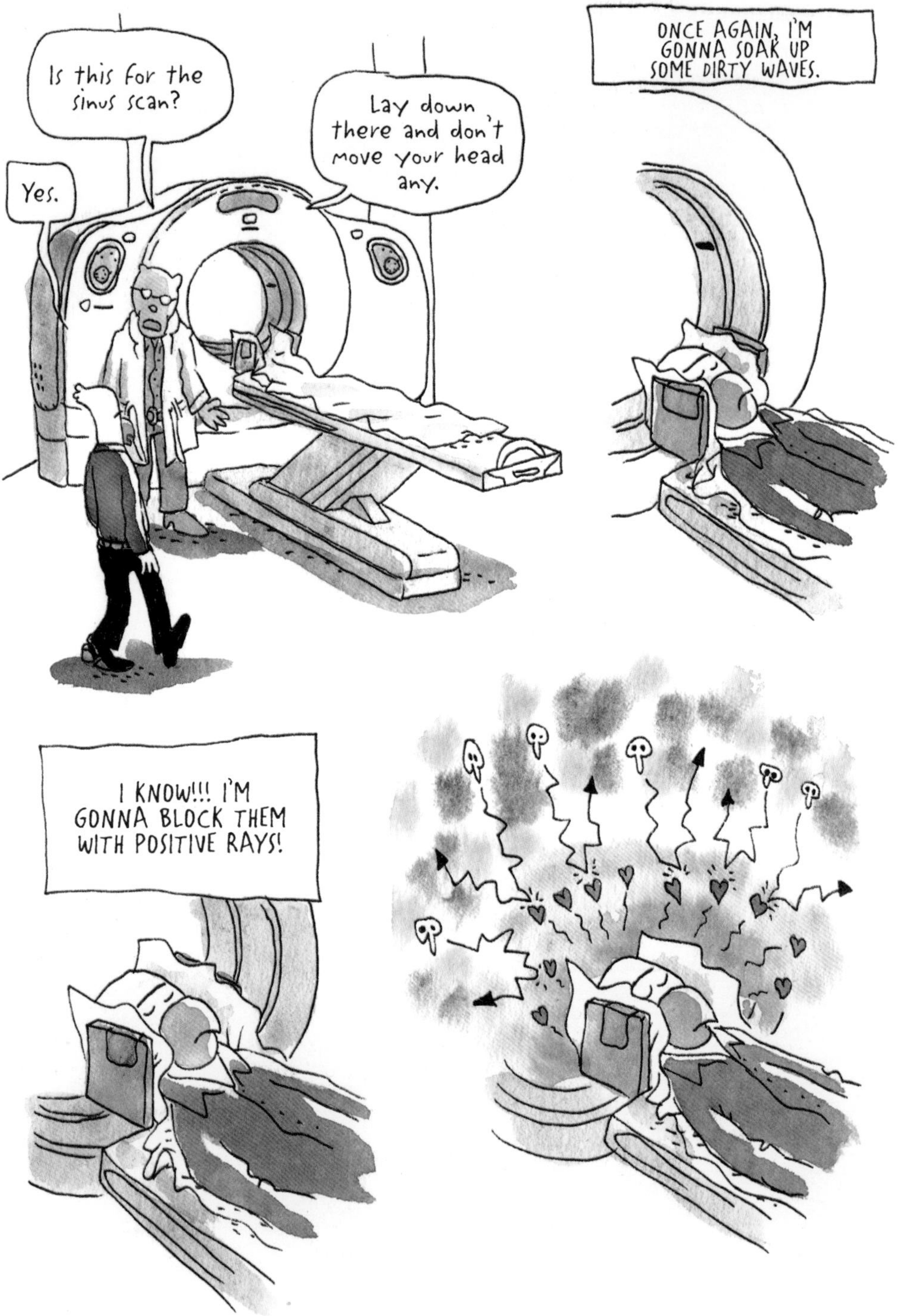
Is this for the sinus scan?
Yes.
Lay down there and don't move your head any.
ONCE AGAIN, I'M GONNA SOAK UP SOME DIRTY WAVES.
I KNOW!!! I'M GONNA BLOCK THEM WITH POSITIVE RAYS!

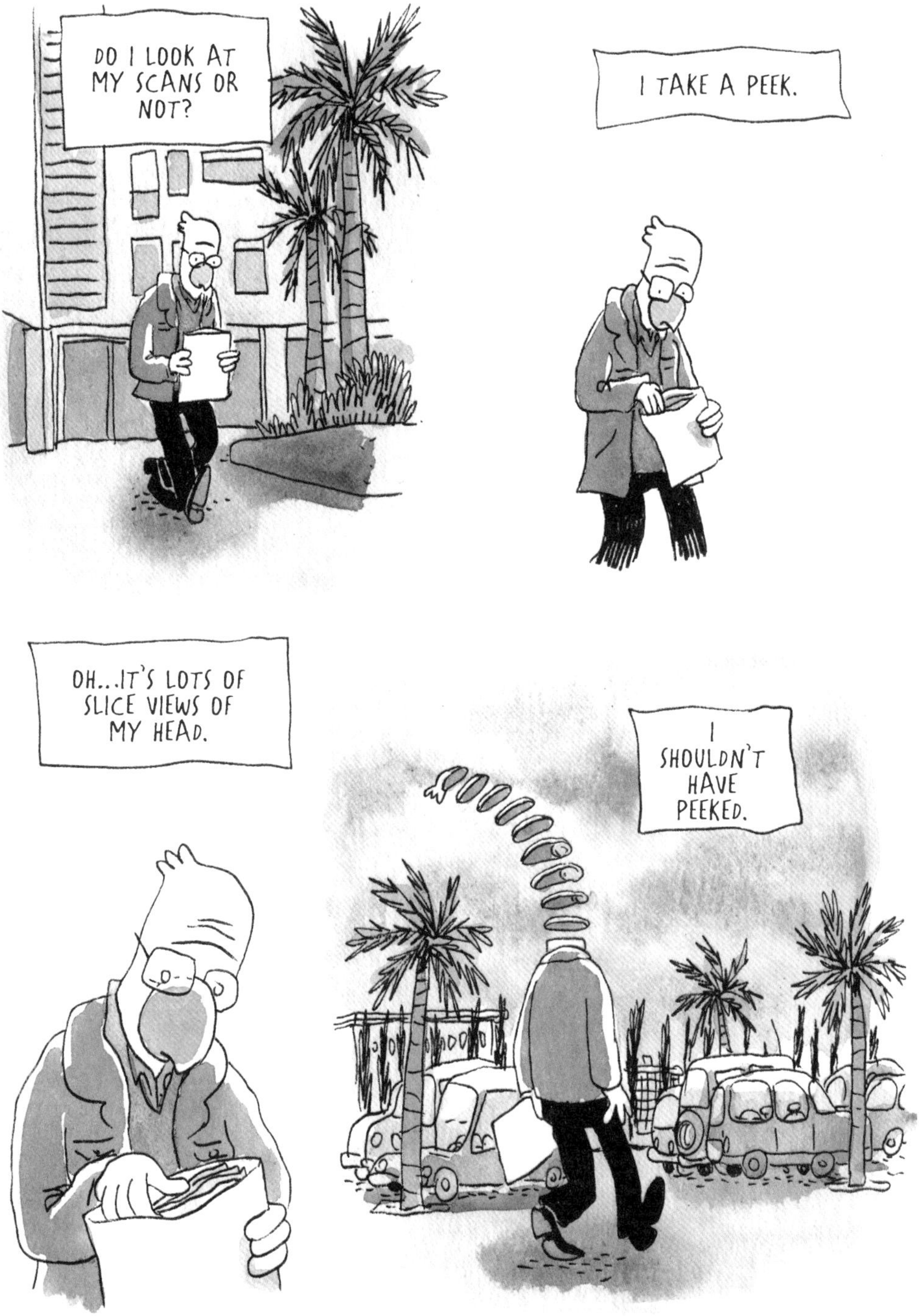
DO I LOOK AT MY SCANS OR NOT?
I TAKE A PEEK.
OH...IT'S LOTS OF SLICE VIEWS OF MY HEAD.
I SHOULDN'T HAVE PEEKED.

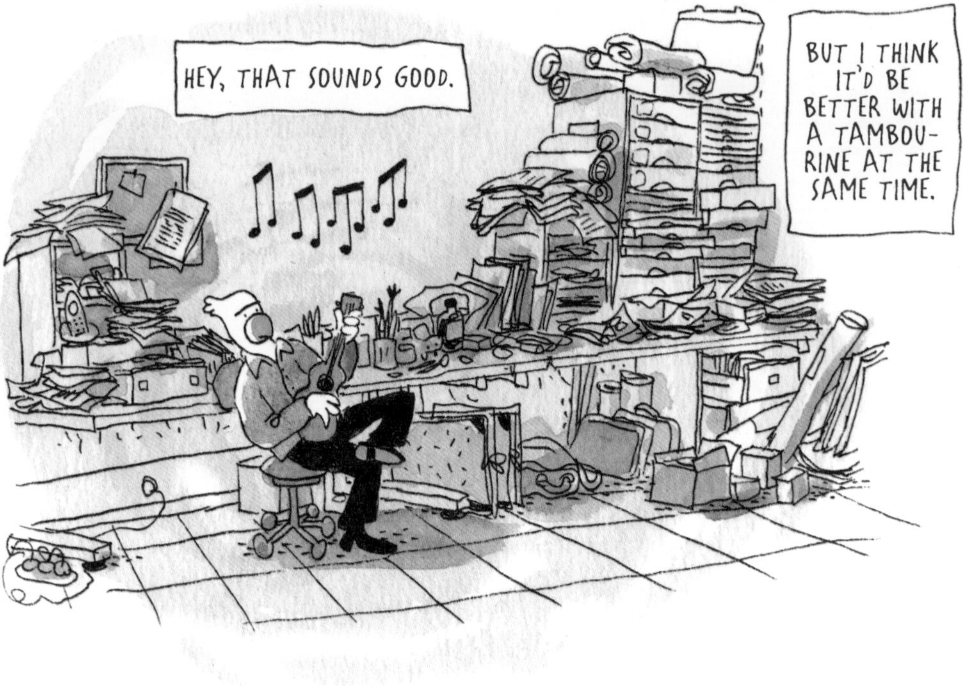
HEY, THAT SOUNDS GOOD.
BUT I THINK IT'D BE BETTER WITH A TAMBOURINE AT THE SAME TIME.

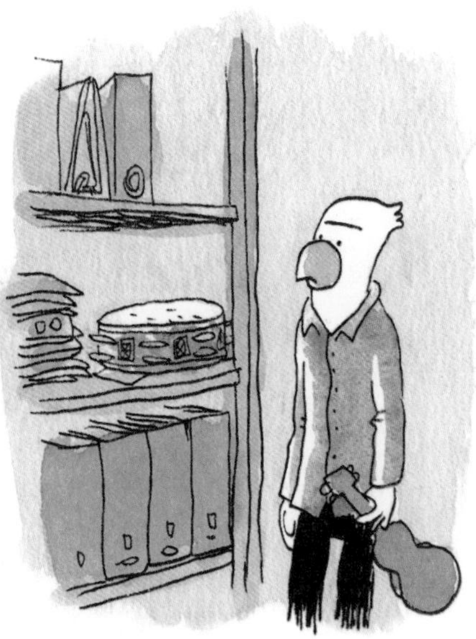

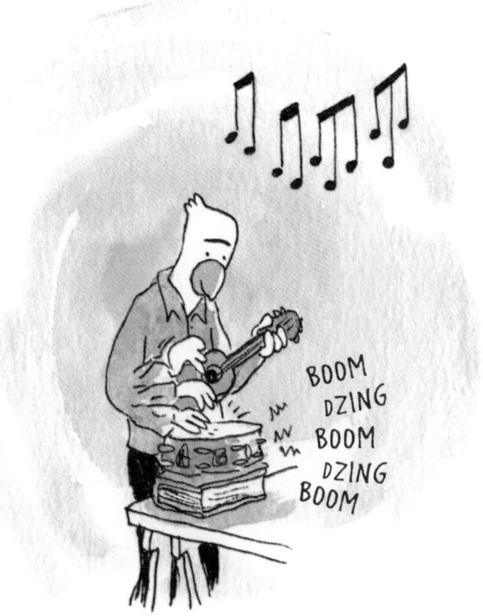
BOOM
DZING
BOOM
DZING
BOOM

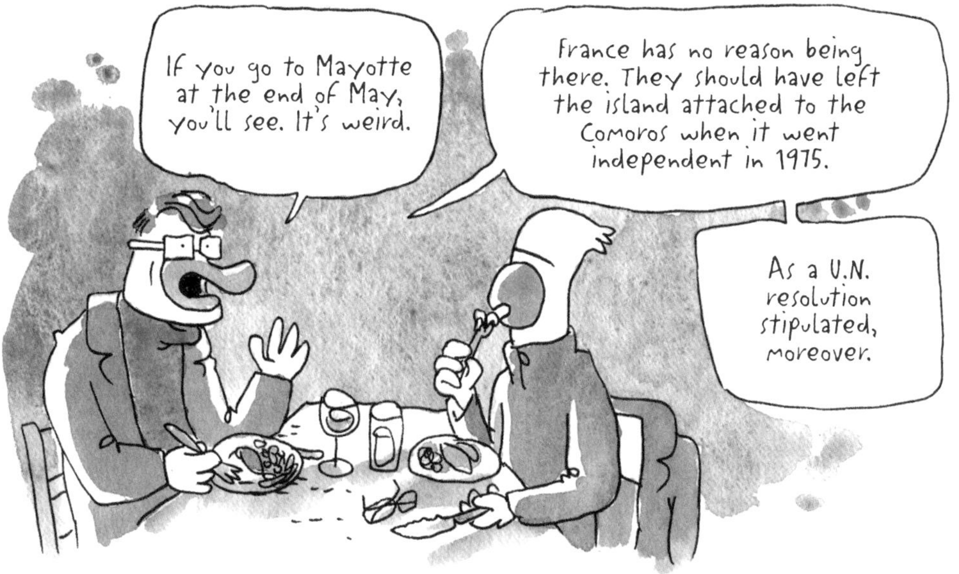
If you go to Mayotte at the end of May, you'll see. It's weird.
France has no reason being there. They should have left the island attached to the Comoros when it went independent in 1975.
As a U.N. resolution stipulated, moreover.

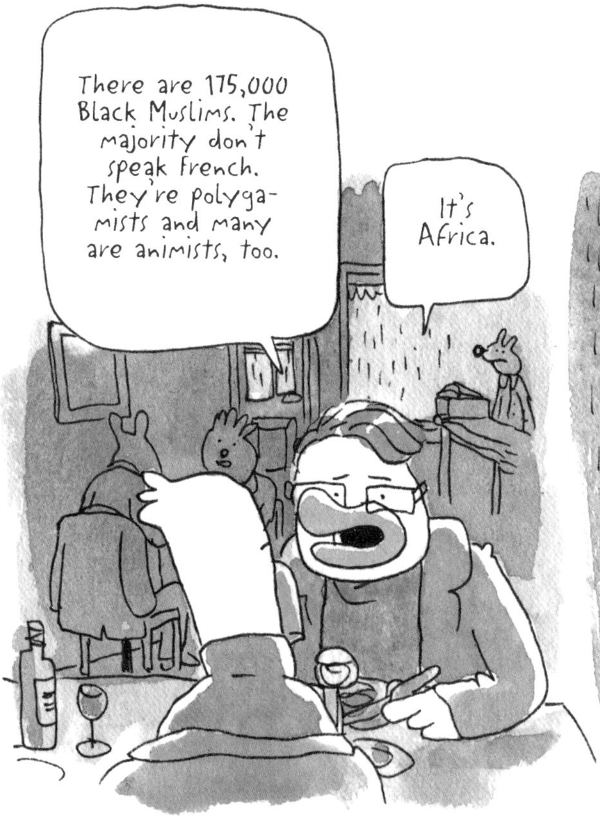
There are 175,000 Black Muslims. The majority don't speak French. They're polygamists and many are animists, too.
It's Africa.

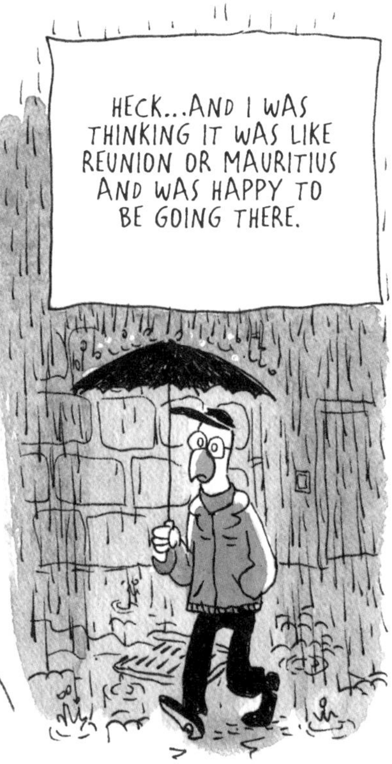
HECK...AND I WAS THINKING IT WAS LIKE REUNION OR MAURITIUS AND WAS HAPPY TO BE GOING THERE.

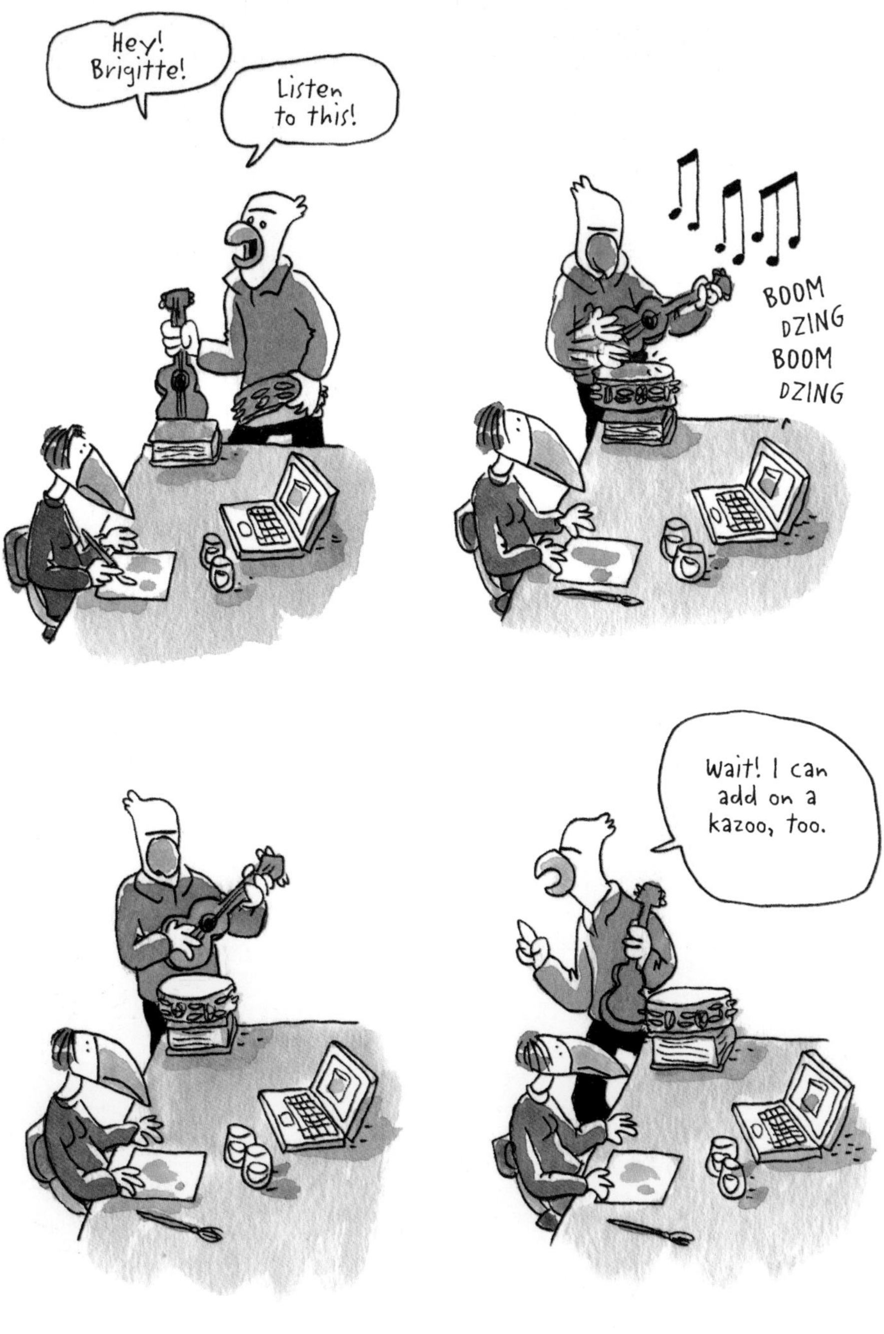
Hey! Brigitte!
Listen to this!
BOOM DZING BOOM DZING
Wait! I can add on a kazoo, too.

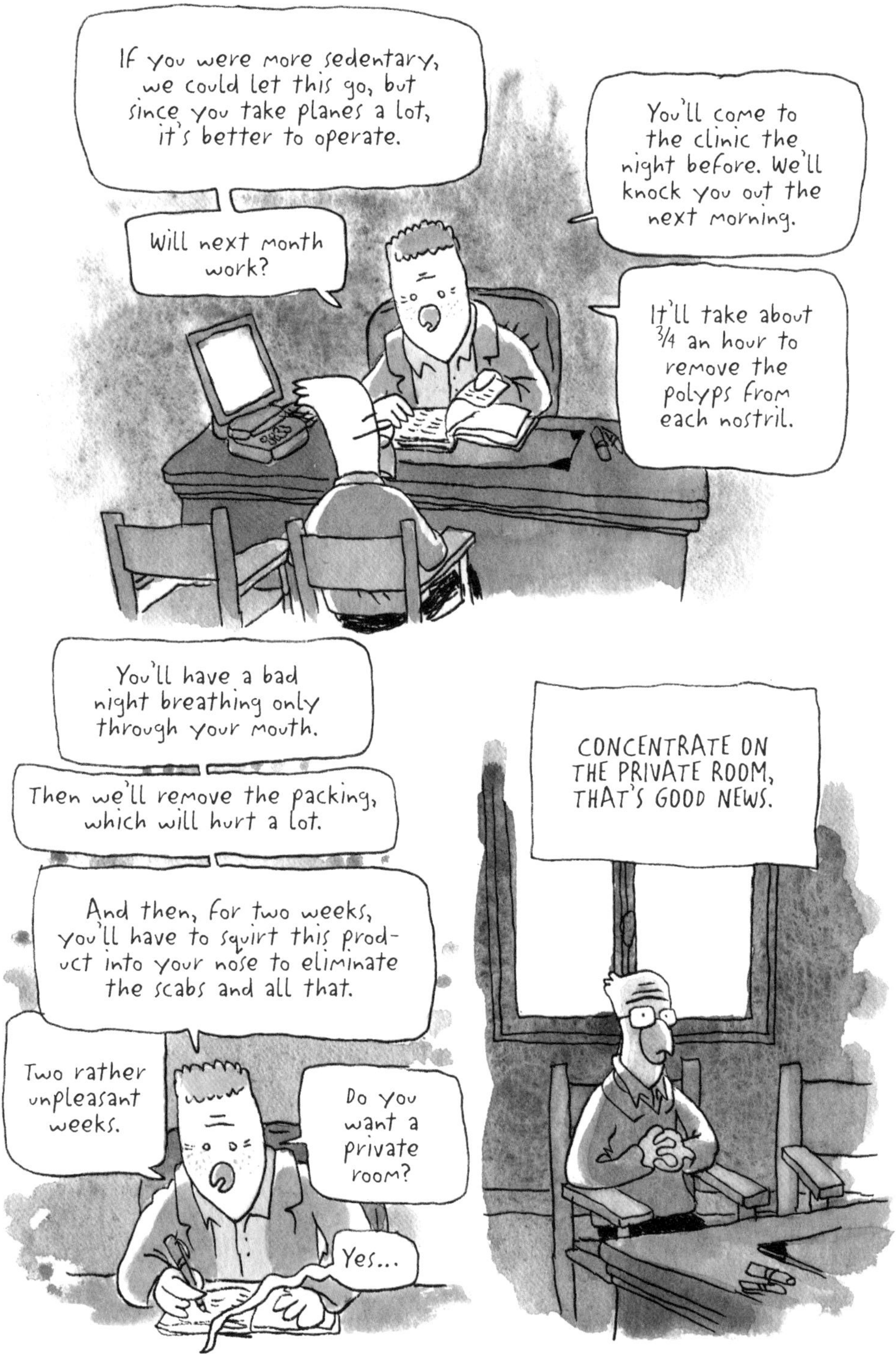
If you were more sedentary, we could let this go, but since you take planes a lot, it's better to operate.
Will next month work?
You'll come to the clinic the night before. We'll knock you out the next morning.
It'll take about 3/4 an hour to remove the polyps from each nostril.
You'll have a bad night breathing only through your mouth.
Then we'll remove the packing, which will hurt a lot.
And then, for two weeks, you'll have to squirt this product into your nose to eliminate the scabs and all that.
Two rather unpleasant weeks.
Do you want a private room?
Yes...
CONCENTRATE ON THE PRIVATE ROOM, THAT'S GOOD NEWS.

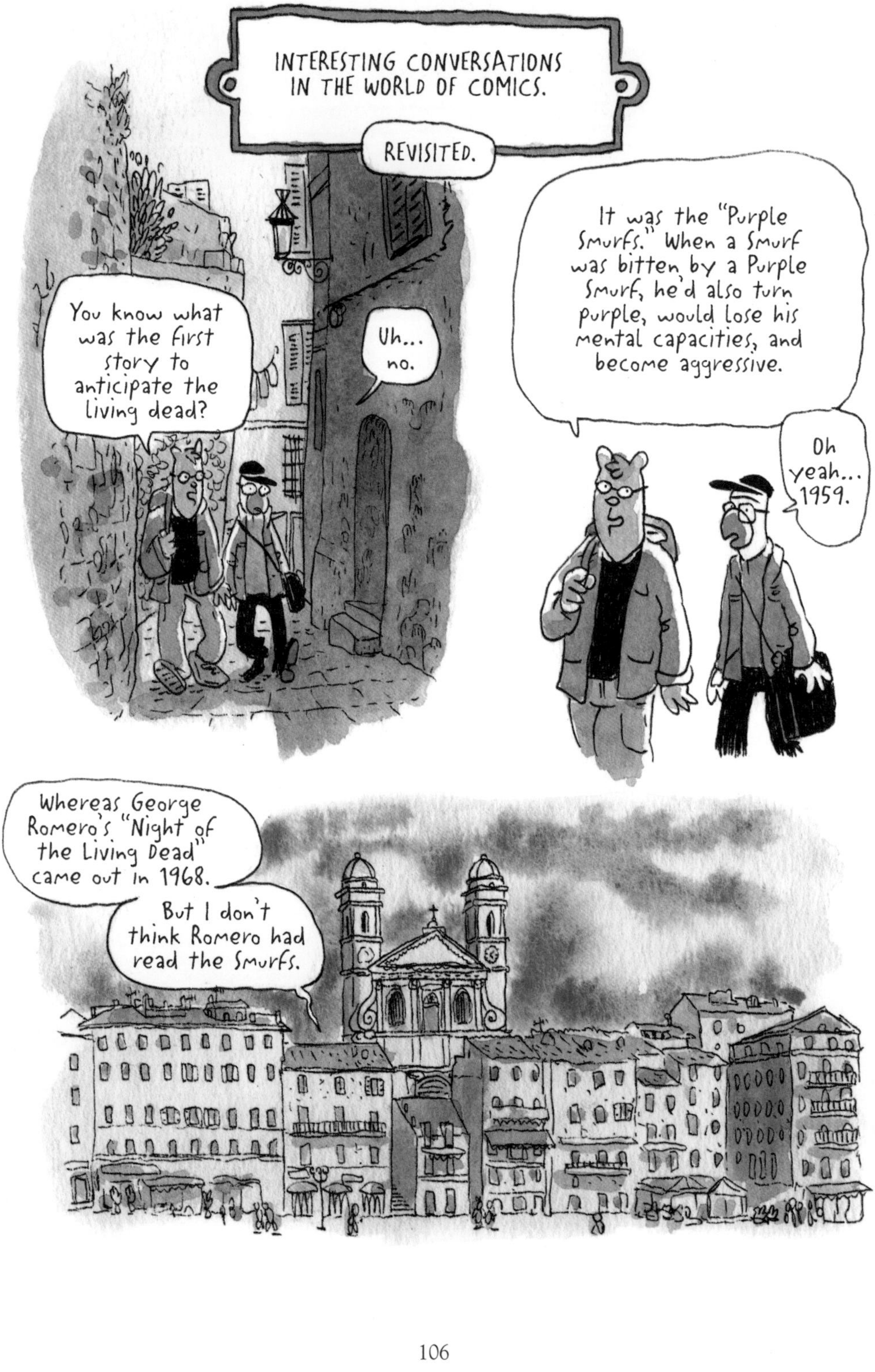

INTERESTING CONVERSATIONS IN THE WORLD OF COMICS.
REVISITED.
You know what was the first story to anticipate the living dead?
Uh... no.
It was the "Purple Smurfs." When a Smurf was bitten by a Purple Smurf, he'd also turn purple, would lose his mental capacities, and become aggressive.
Oh yeah... 1959.
Whereas George Romero's "Night of the Living Dead" came out in 1968.
But I don't think Romero had read the Smurfs.

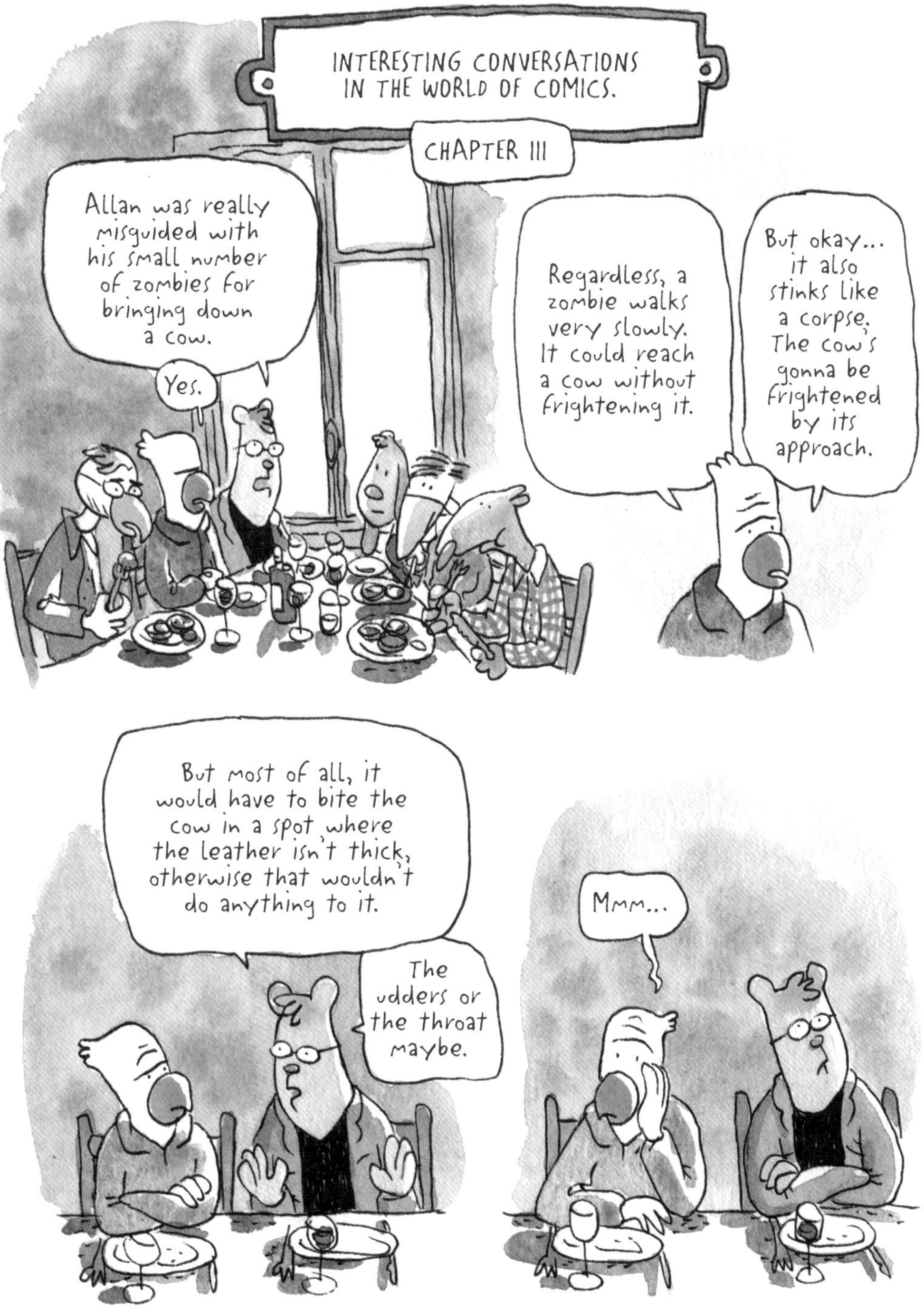
INTERESTING CONVERSATIONS IN THE WORLD OF COMICS.
CHAPTER III
Allan was really misguided with his small number of zombies for bringing down a cow.
Yes.
Regardless, a zombie walks very slowly. It could reach a cow without frightening it.
But okay... it also stinks like a corpse. The cow's gonna be frightened by its approach.
But most of all, it would have to bite the cow in a spot where the leather isn't thick, otherwise that wouldn't do anything to it.
The udders or the throat maybe.
Mmm...

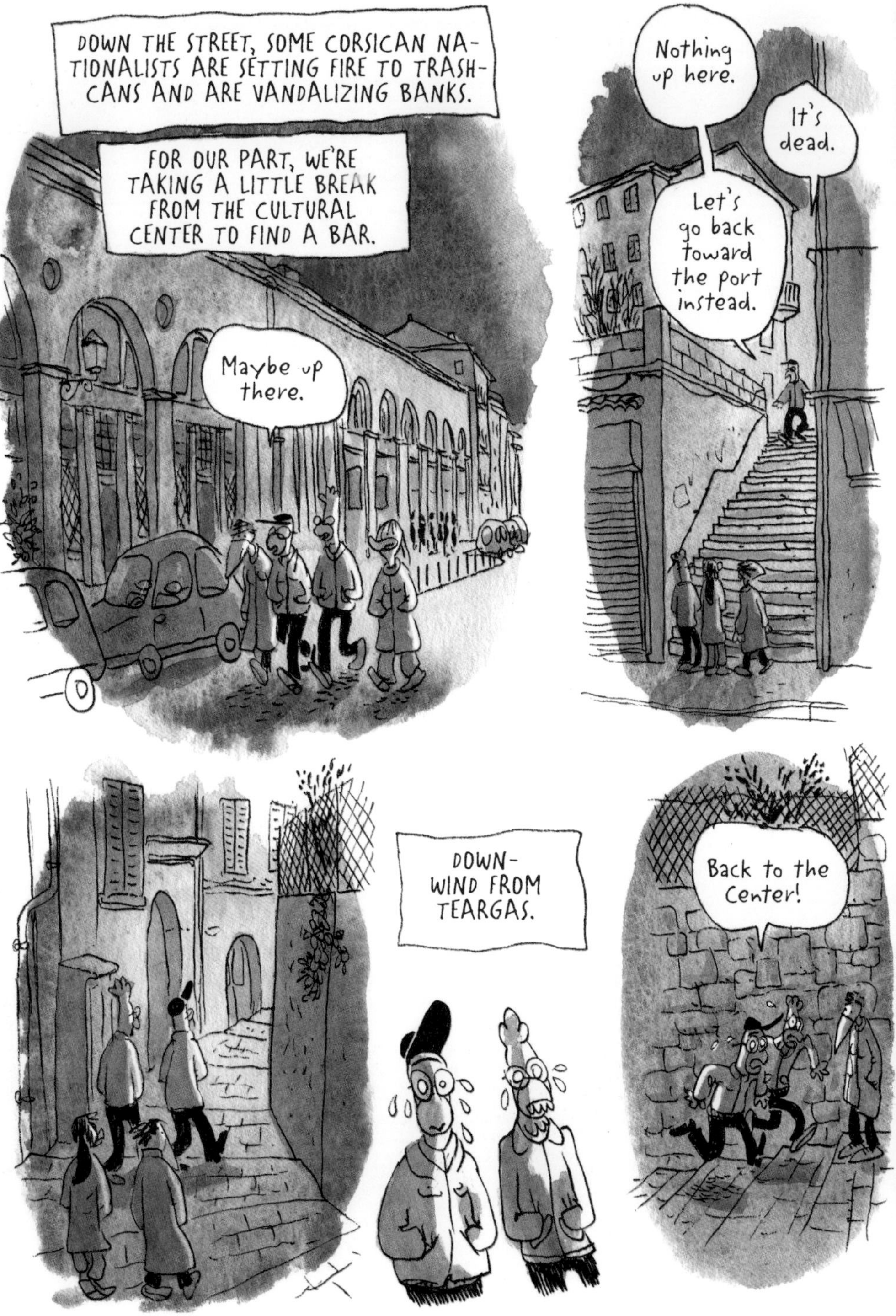
DOWN THE STREET, SOME CORSICAN NATIONALISTS ARE SETTING FIRE TO TRASHCANS AND ARE VANDALIZING BANKS.
FOR OUR PART, WE'RE TAKING A LITTLE BREAK FROM THE CULTURAL CENTER TO FIND A BAR.
Maybe up there.
Nothing up here.
It's dead.
Let's go back toward the port instead.
DOWN-WIND FROM TEARGAS.
Back to the Center!

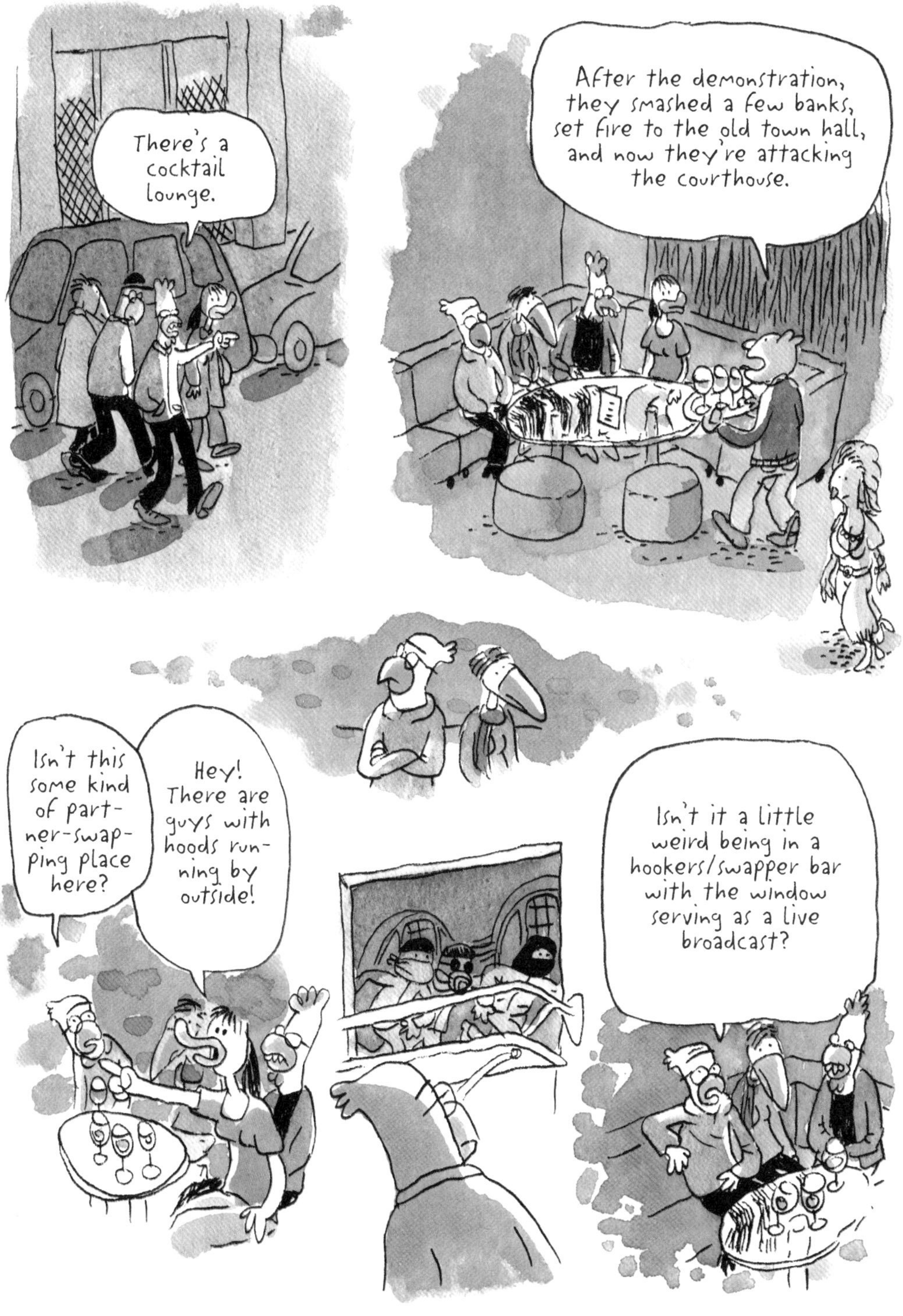
There's a cocktail lounge.
After the demonstration, they smashed a few banks, set fire to the old town hall, and now they're attacking the courthouse.
Isn't this some kind of part-ner-swap-ping place here?
Hey! There are guys with hoods run-ning by outside!
Isn't it a little weird being in a hookers/swapper bar with the window serving as a live broadcast?

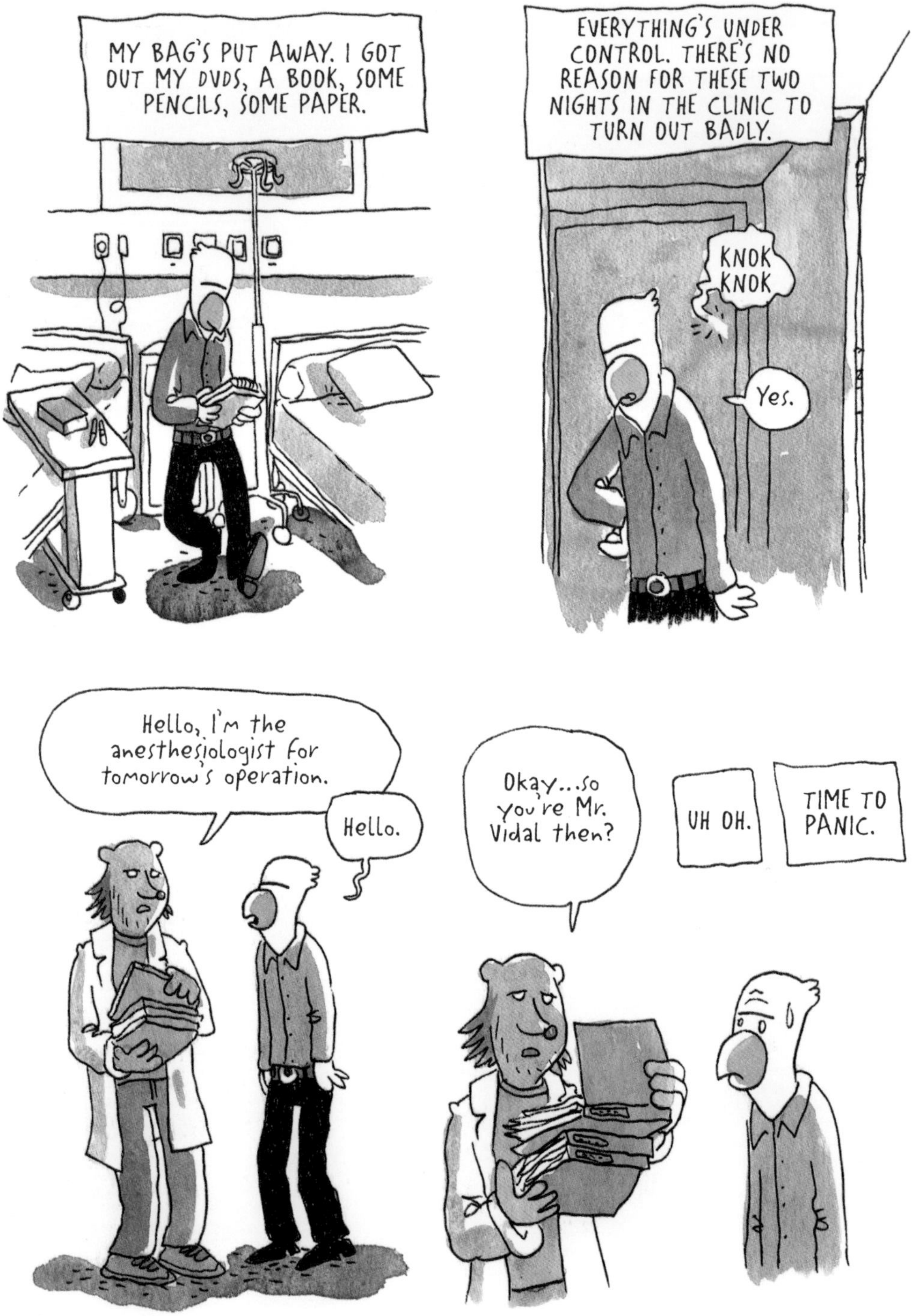
MY BAG'S PUT AWAY. I GOT OUT MY DVDS, A BOOK, SOME PENCILS, SOME PAPER.
EVERYTHING'S UNDER CONTROL. THERE'S NO REASON FOR THESE TWO NIGHTS IN THE CLINIC TO TURN OUT BADLY.
KNOK KNOK
Yes.
Hello, I'm the anesthesiologist for tomorrow's operation.
Hello.
Okay...so you're Mr. Vidal then?
UH OH.
TIME TO PANIC.

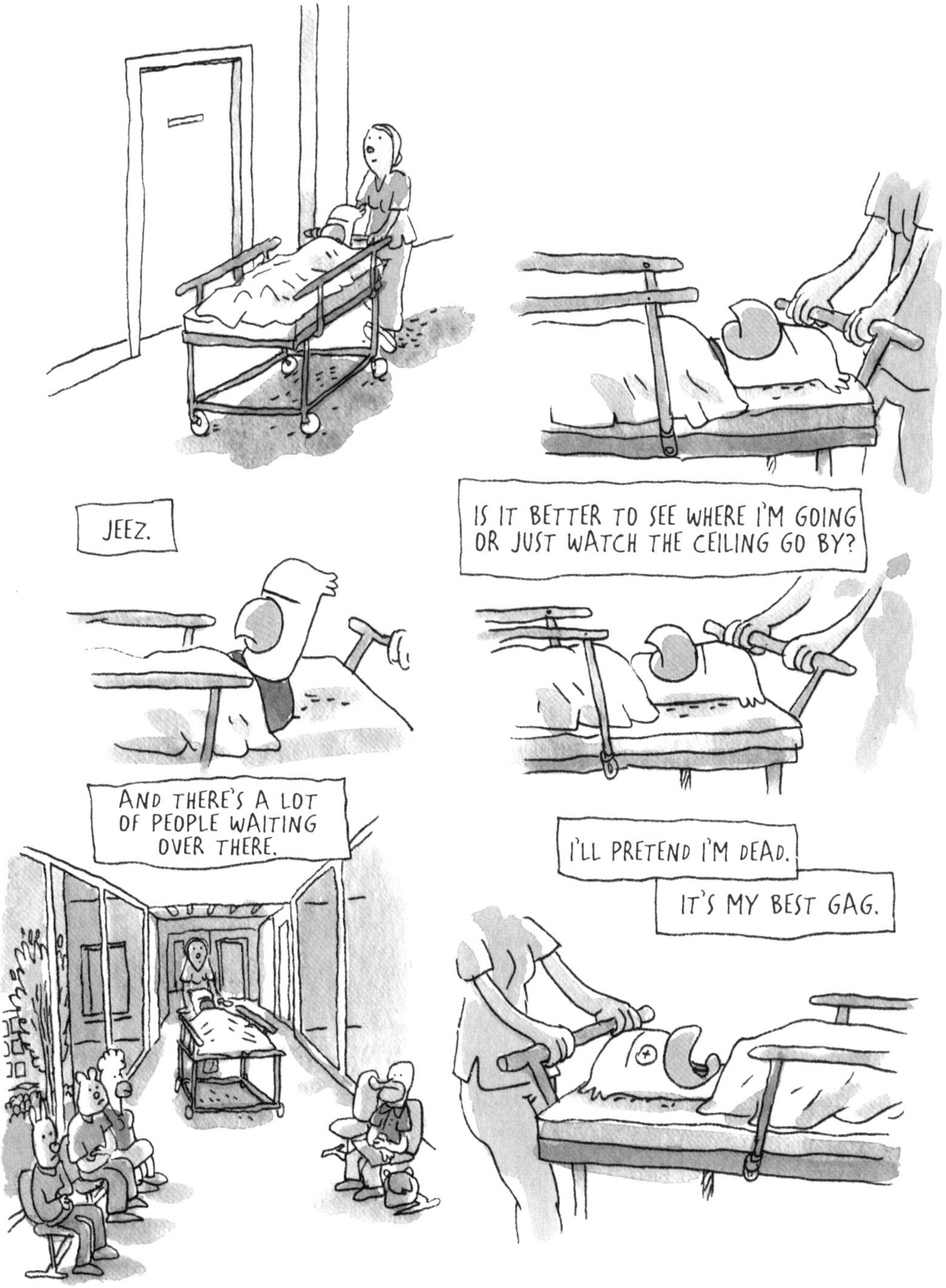
JEEZ.
IS IT BETTER TO SEE WHERE I'M GOING OR JUST WATCH THE CEILING GO BY?
AND THERE'S A LOT OF PEOPLE WAITING OVER THERE.
I'LL PRETEND I'M DEAD.
IT'S MY BEST GAG.

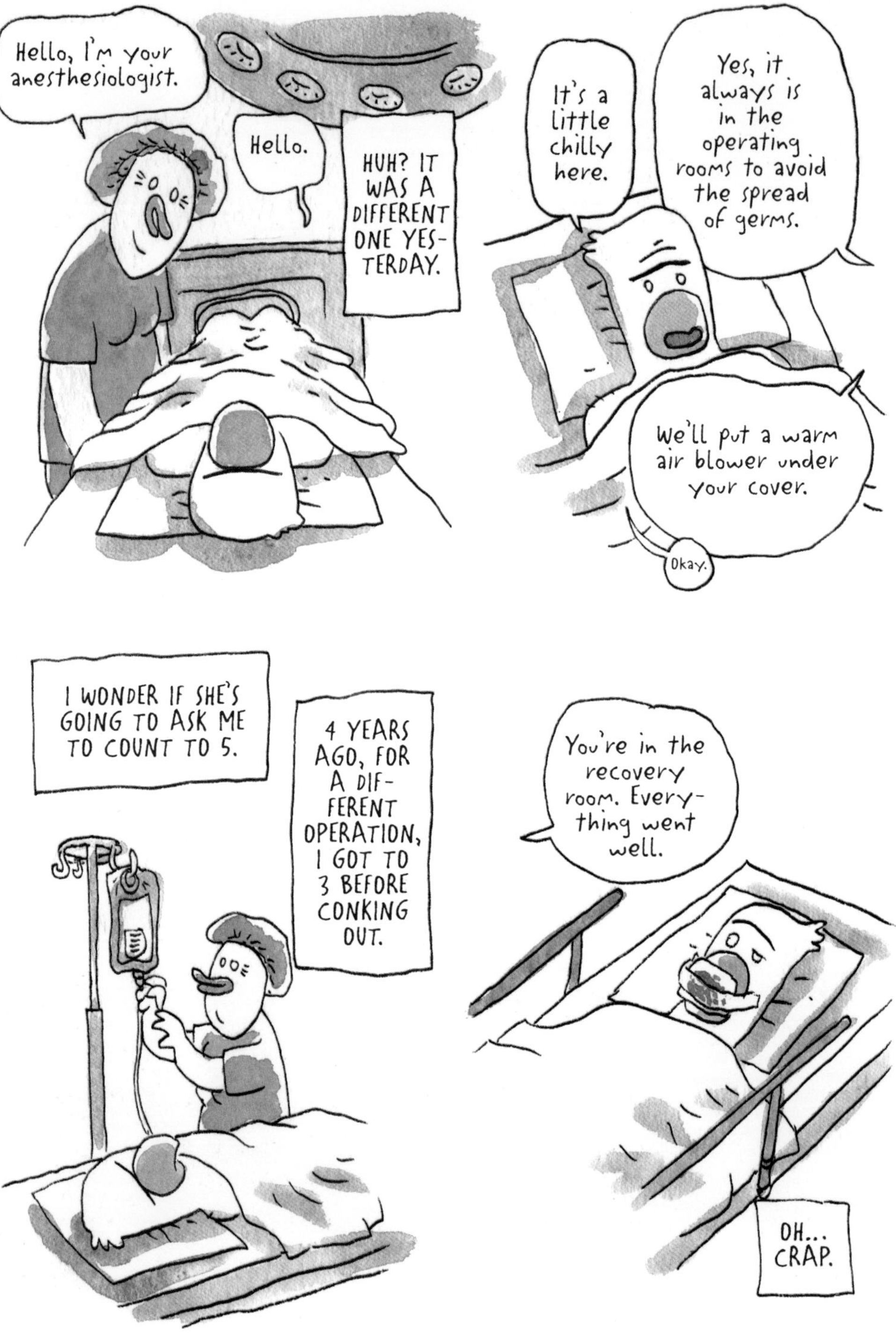
Hello, I'm your anesthesiologist.
Hello.
HUH? IT WAS A DIFFERENT ONE YESTERDAY.
It's a little chilly here.
Yes, it always is in the operating rooms to avoid the spread of germs.
We'll put a warm air blower under your cover.
Okay.
I WONDER IF SHE'S GOING TO ASK ME TO COUNT TO 5.
4 YEARS AGO, FOR A DIFFERENT OPERATION, I GOT TO 3 BEFORE CONKING OUT.
You're in the recovery room. Everything went well.
OH... CRAP.

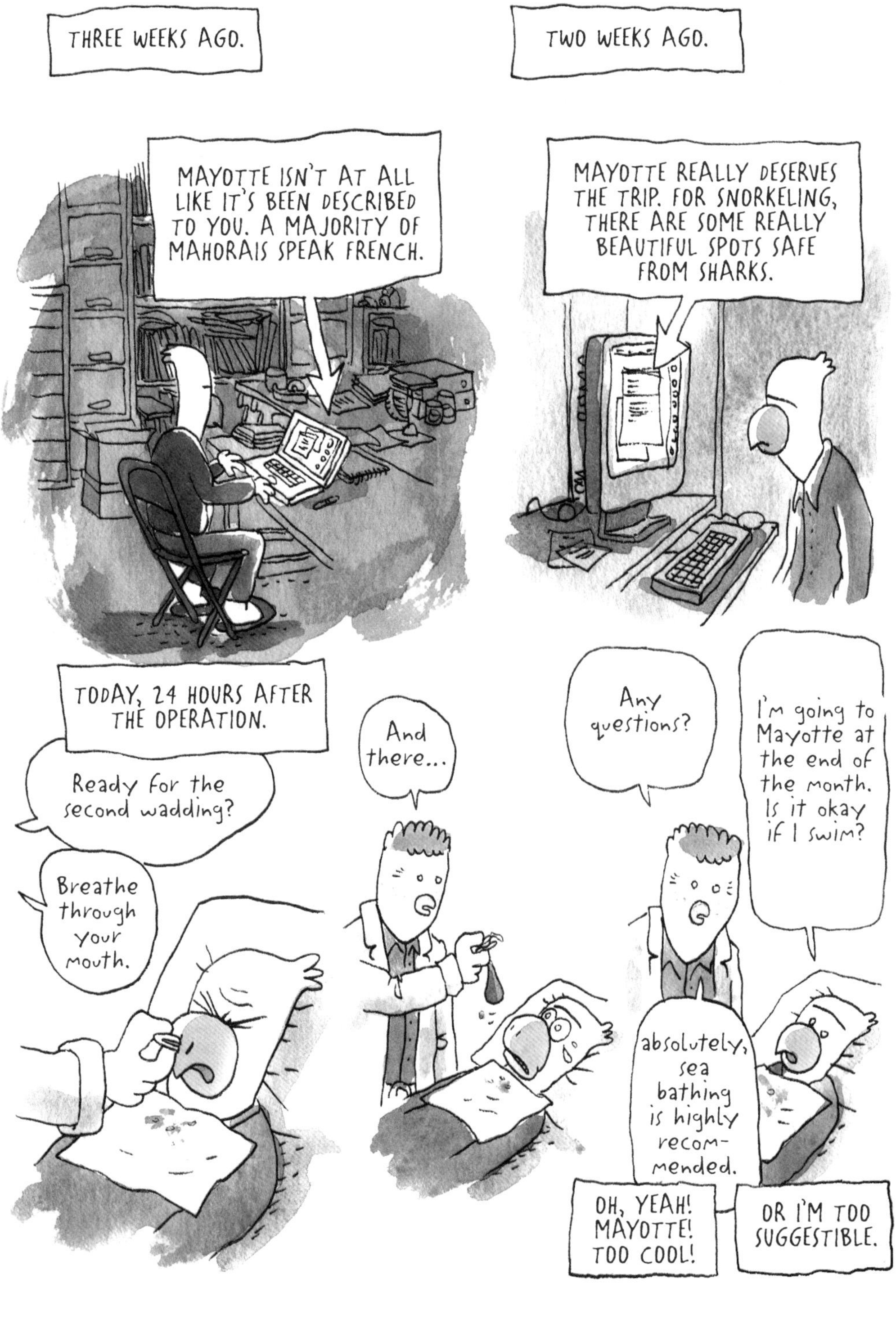
THREE WEEKS AGO.
MAYOTTE ISN'T AT ALL LIKE IT'S BEEN DESCRIBED TO YOU. A MAJORITY OF MAHORAIS SPEAK FRENCH.
TWO WEEKS AGO.
MAYOTTE REALLY DESERVES THE TRIP. FOR SNORKELING, THERE ARE SOME REALLY BEAUTIFUL SPOTS SAFE FROM SHARKS.
TODAY, 24 HOURS AFTER THE OPERATION.
Ready for the second wadding?
Breathe through your mouth.
And there...
Any questions?
I'm going to Mayotte at the end of the month. Is it okay if I swim?
absolutely, sea bathing is highly recom-mended.
OH, YEAH! MAYOTTE! TOO COOL!
OR I'M TOO SUGGESTIBLE.

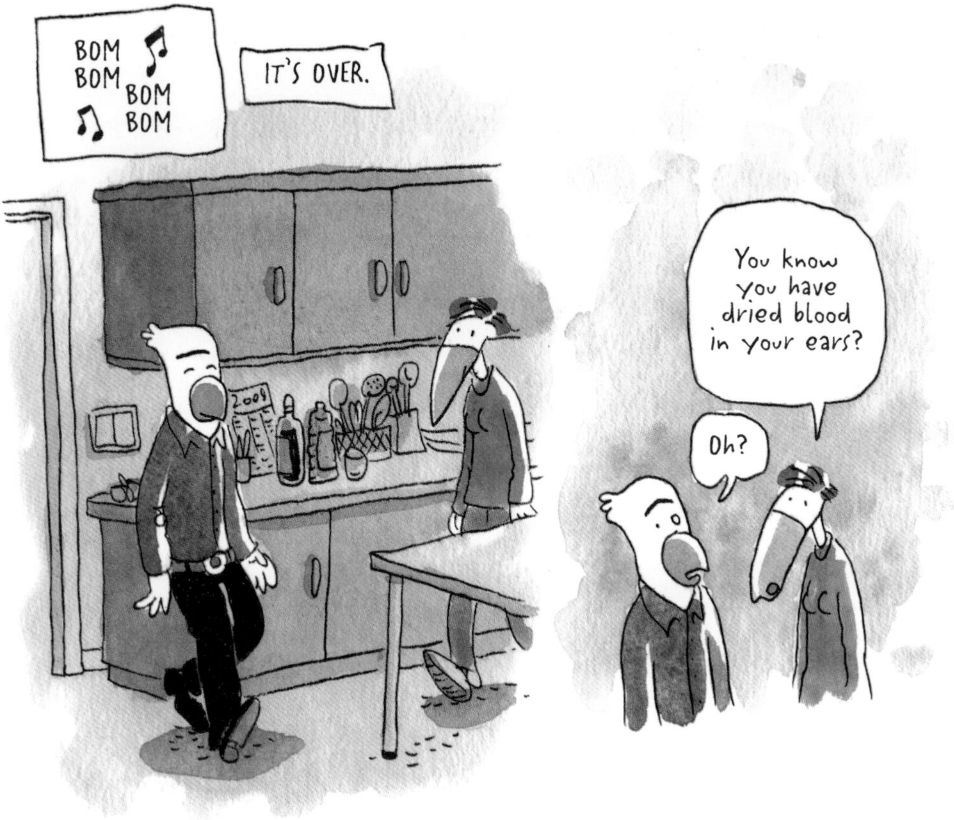
BOM BOM BOM BOM
IT'S OVER.
You know you have dried blood in your ears?
Oh?

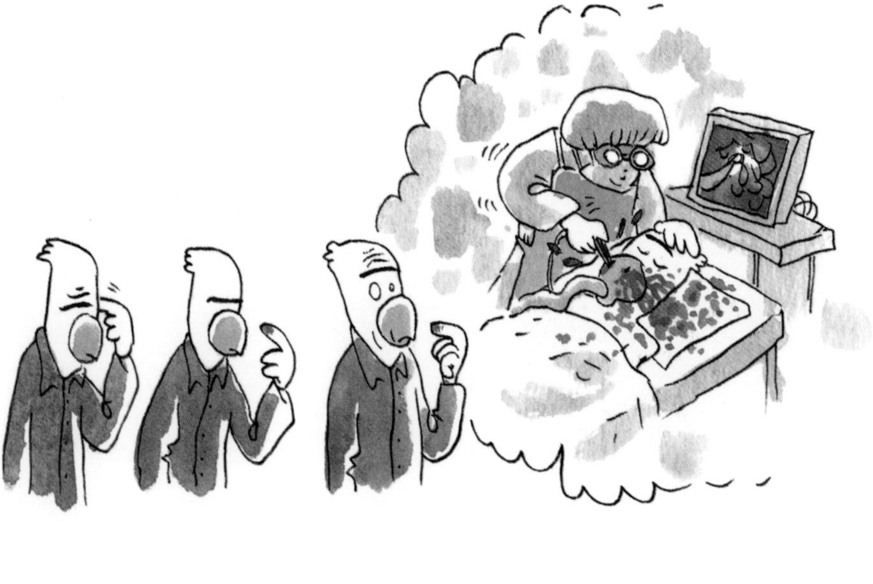

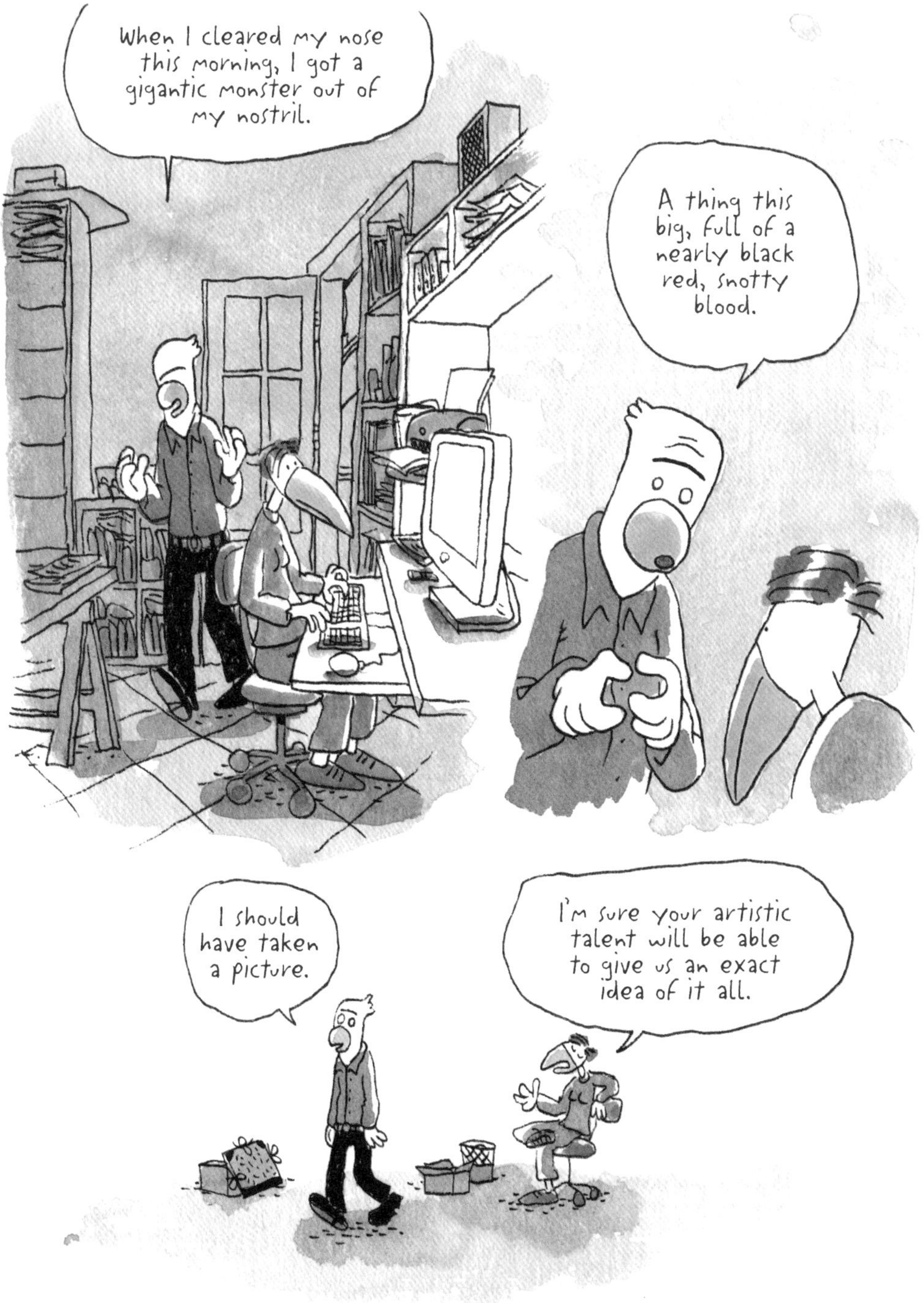
When I cleared my nose this morning, I got a gigantic monster out of my nostril.
A thing this big, full of a nearly black red, snotty blood.
I should have taken a picture.
I'm sure your artistic talent will be able to give us an exact idea of it all.

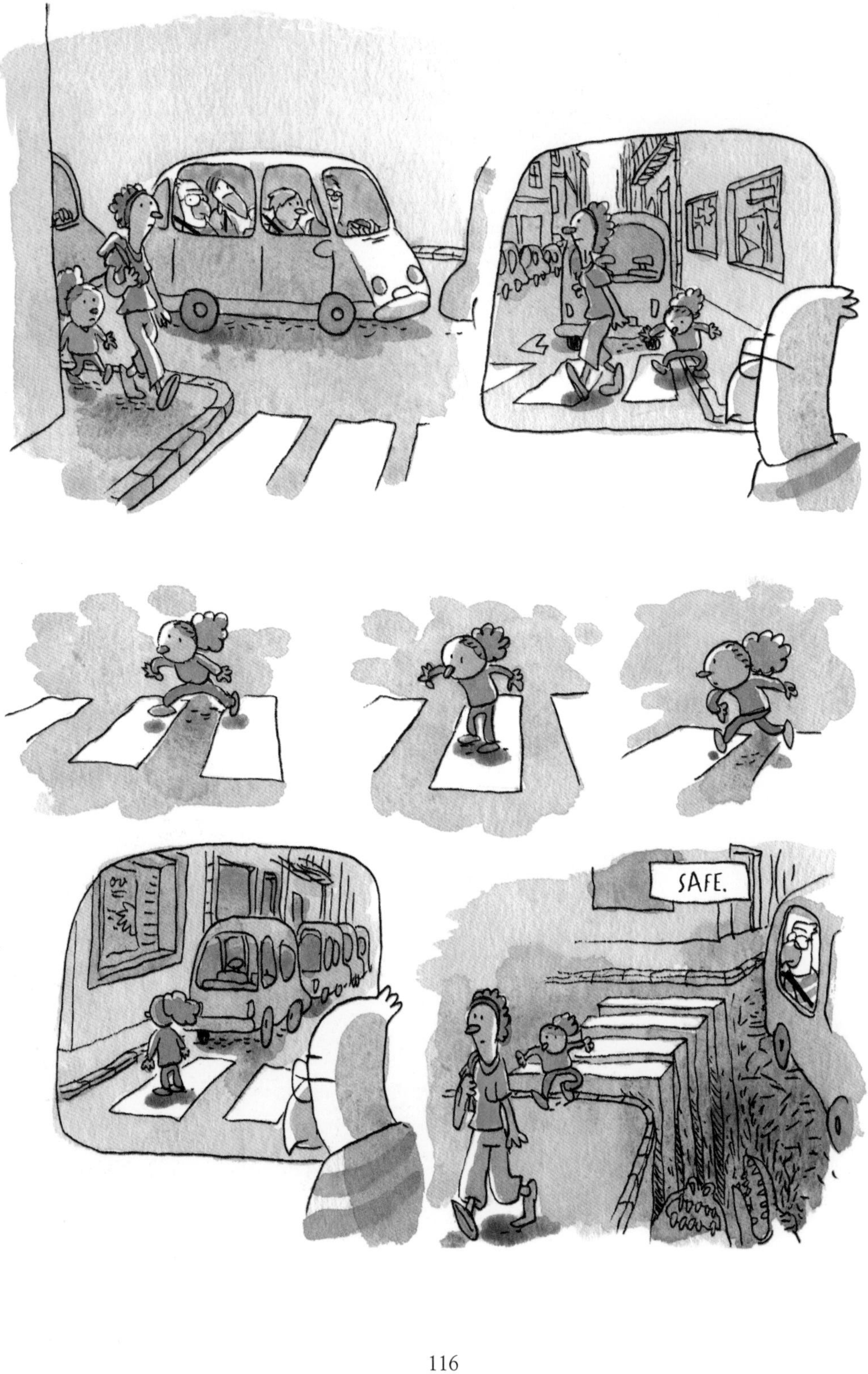
SAFE.

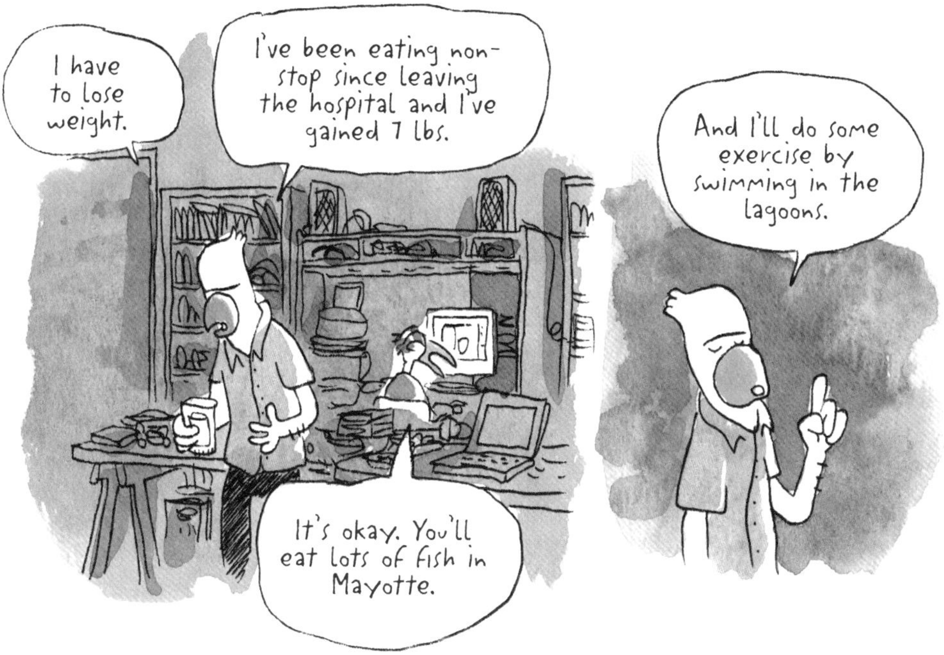
I have to lose weight.
I've been eating non-stop since leaving the hospital and I've gained 7 lbs.
It's okay. You'll eat lots of fish in Mayotte.
And I'll do some exercise by swimming in the lagoons.

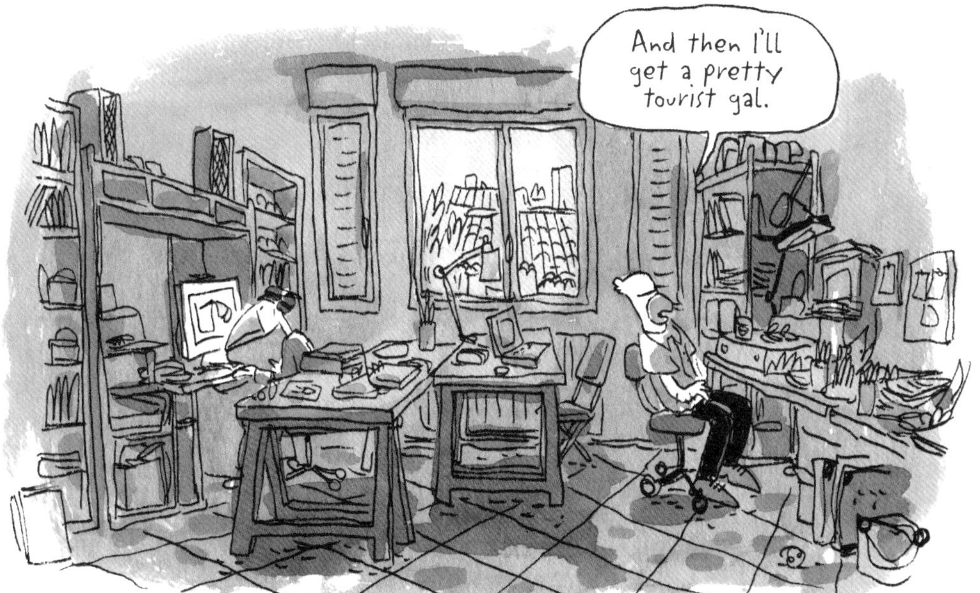
And then I'll get a pretty tourist gal.

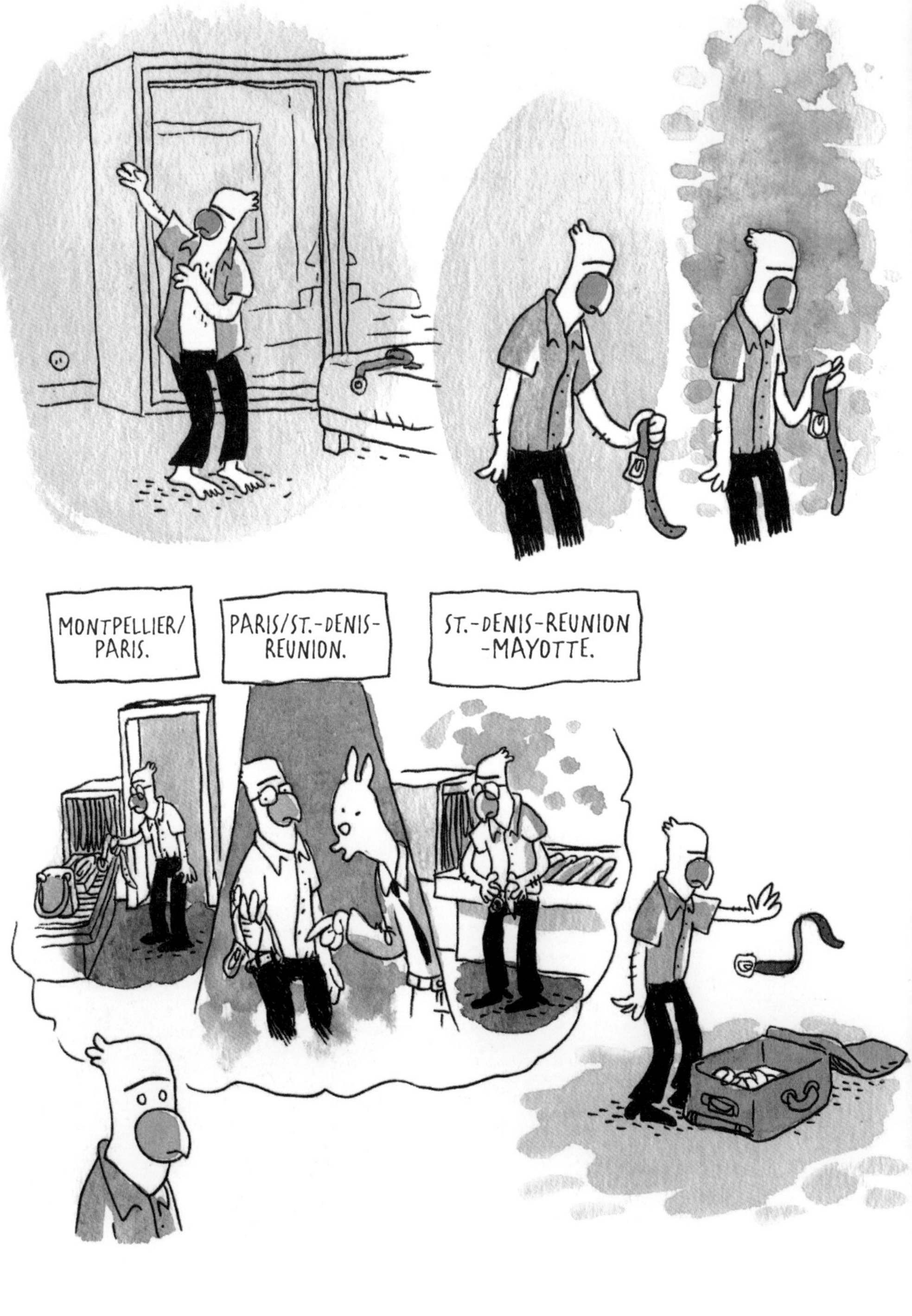
MONTPELLIER/ PARIS.
PARIS/ST.-DENIS-REUNION.
ST.-DENIS-REUNION -MAYOTTE.

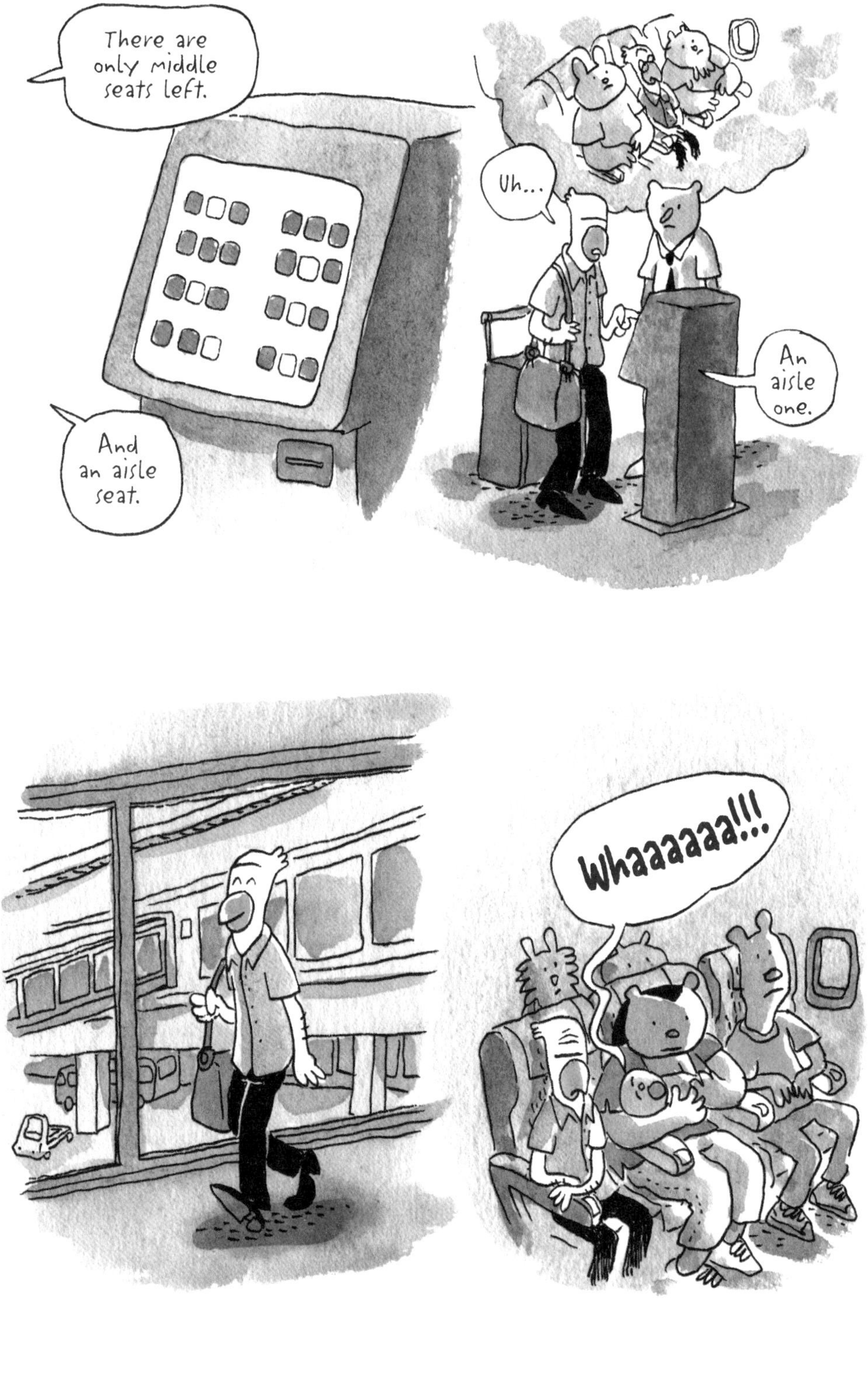
There are only middle seats left.
And an aisle seat.
Uh...
An aisle one.
Whaaaaaa!!!

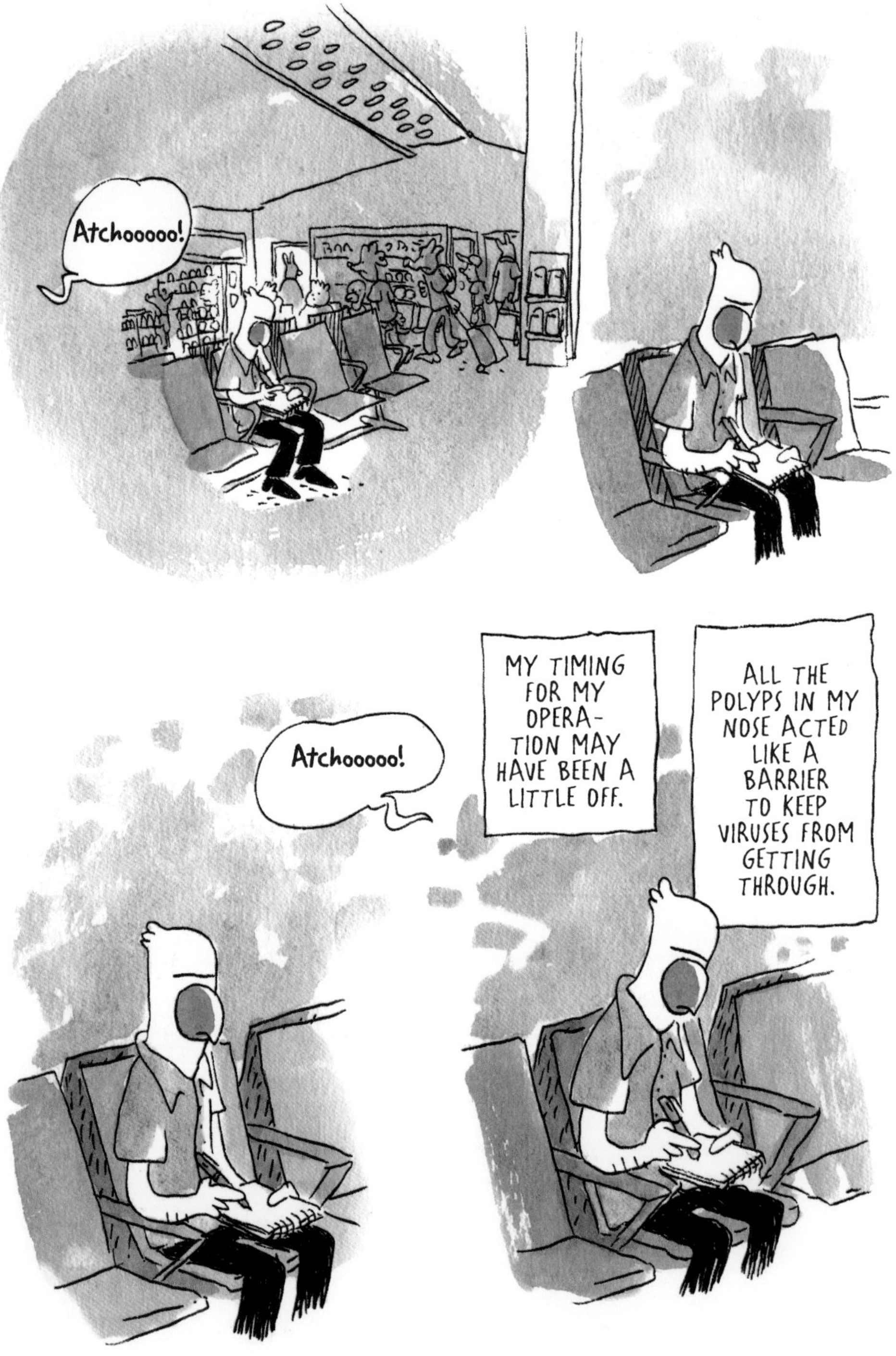
Atchooooo!
Atchooooo!
MY TIMING FOR MY OPERATION MAY HAVE BEEN A LITTLE OFF.
ALL THE POLYPS IN MY NOSE ACTED LIKE A BARRIER TO KEEP VIRUSES FROM GETTING THROUGH.

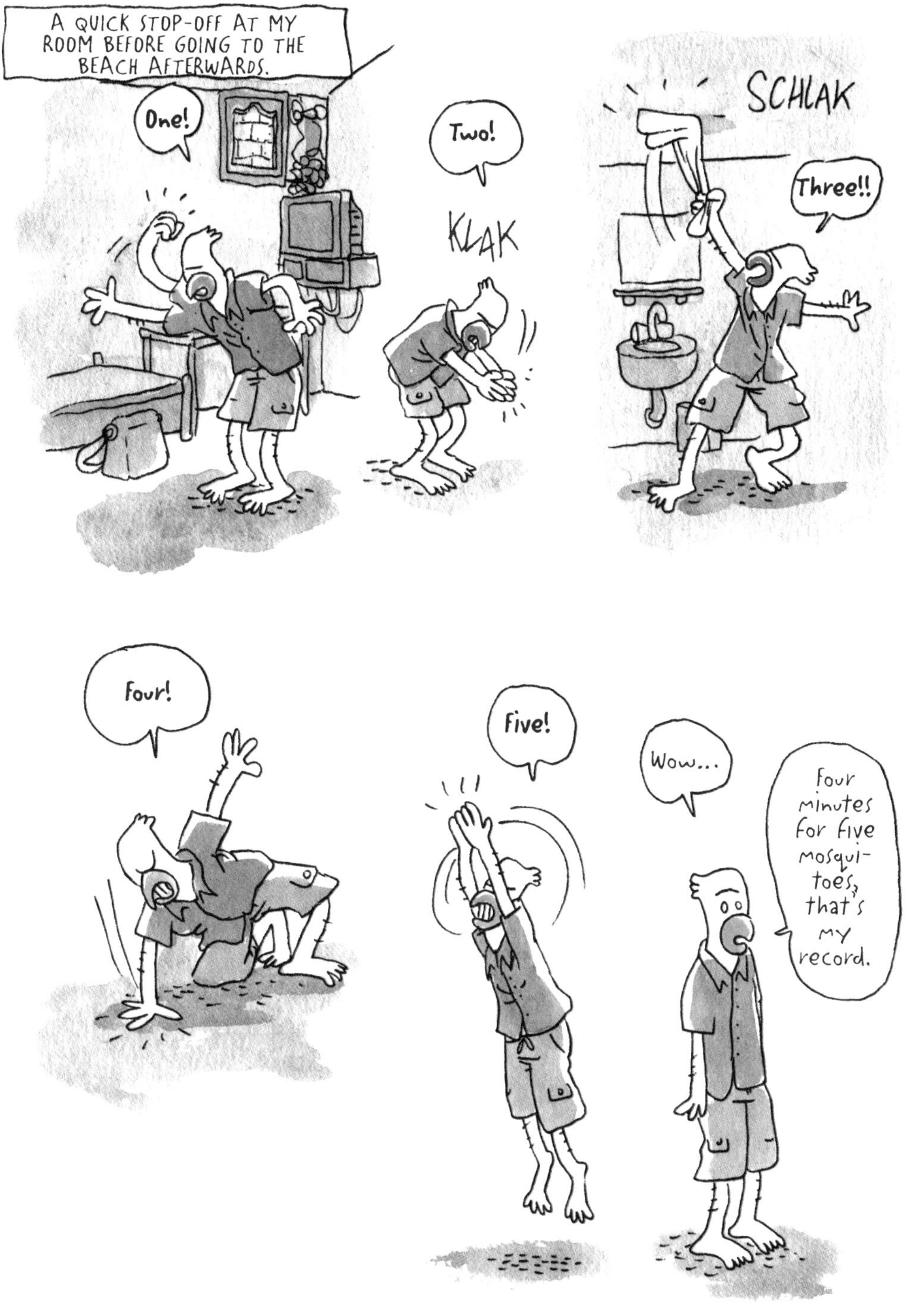
A QUICK STOP-OFF AT MY ROOM BEFORE GOING TO THE BEACH AFTERWARDS.
One!
Two!
KLAK
SCHLAK
Three!!
Four!
Five!
Wow...
Four minutes for five mosquitoes, that's my record.

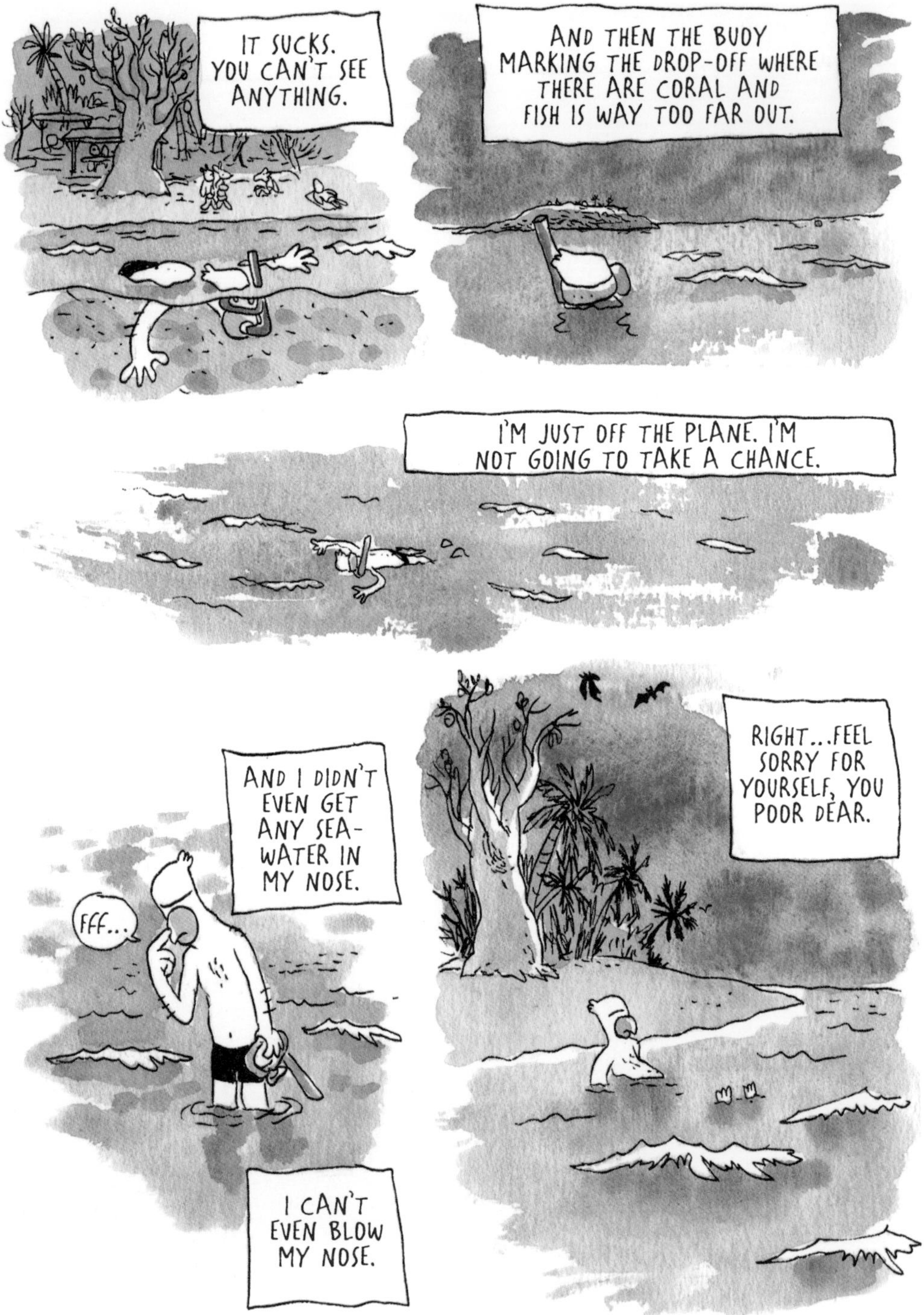
IT SUCKS. YOU CAN'T SEE ANYTHING.
AND THEN THE BUOY MARKING THE DROP-OFF WHERE THERE ARE CORAL AND FISH IS WAY TOO FAR OUT.
I'M JUST OFF THE PLANE. I'M NOT GOING TO TAKE A CHANCE.
AND I DIDN'T EVEN GET ANY SEA-WATER IN MY NOSE.
FFF...
I CAN'T EVEN BLOW MY NOSE.
RIGHT...FEEL SORRY FOR YOURSELF, YOU POOR DEAR.

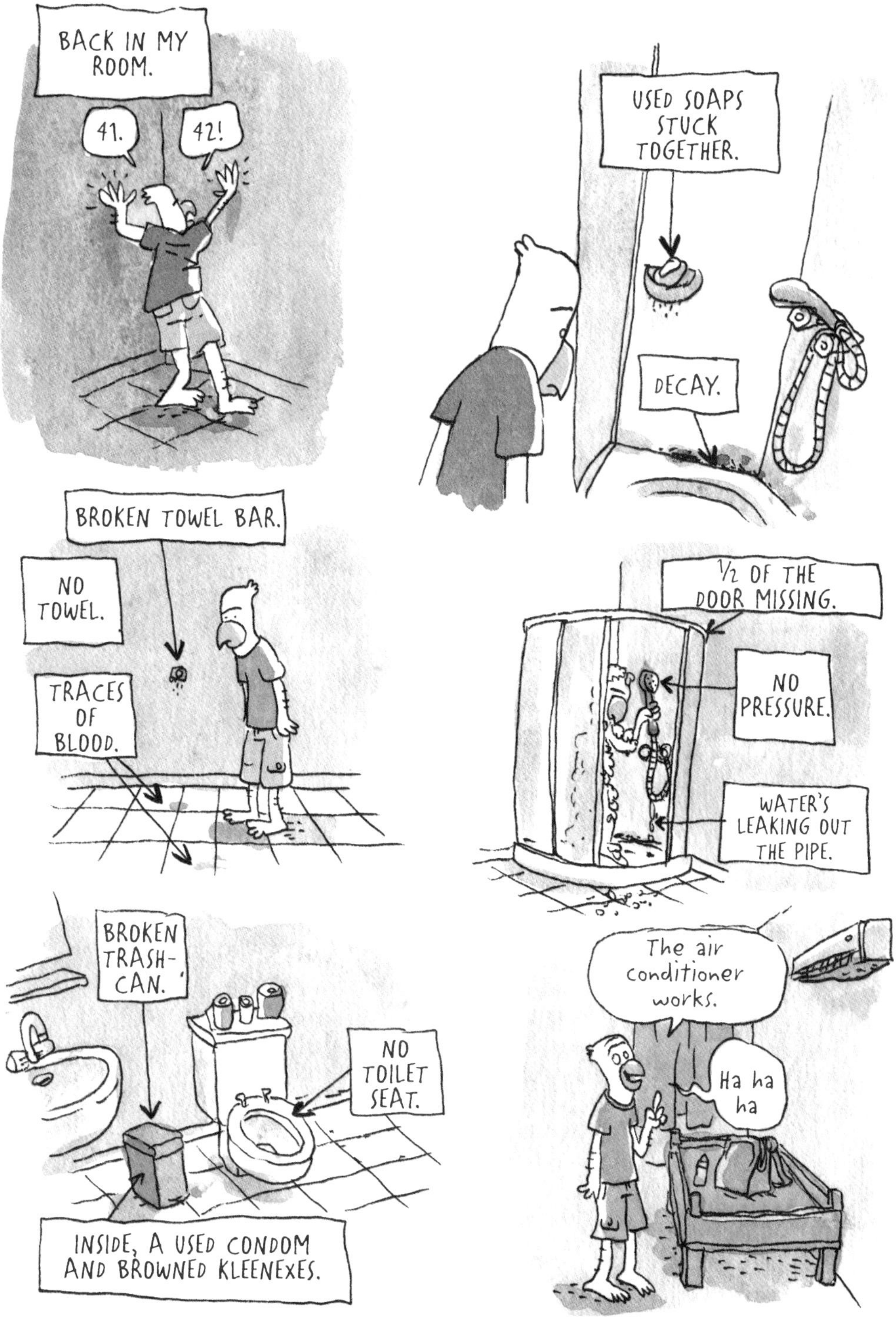
BACK IN MY ROOM.
41.
42!
USED SOAPS STUCK TOGETHER.
DECAY.
BROKEN TOWEL BAR.
NO TOWEL.
TRACES OF BLOOD.
½ OF THE DOOR MISSING.
NO PRESSURE.
WATER'S LEAKING OUT THE PIPE.
BROKEN TRASH-CAN.
NO TOILET SEAT.
INSIDE, A USED CONDOM AND BROWNED KLEENEXES.
The air conditioner works.
Ha ha ha

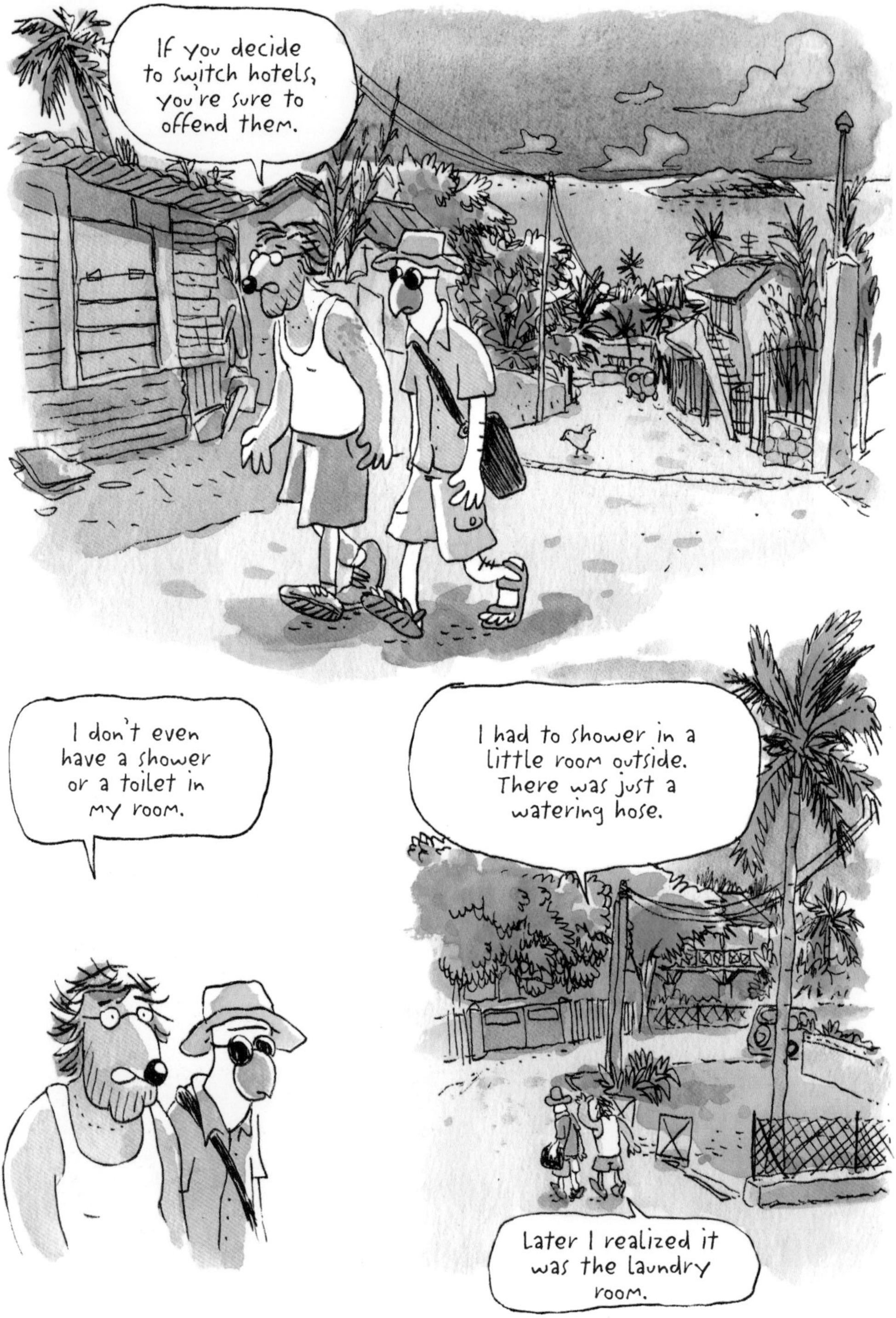
If you decide to switch hotels, you're sure to offend them.
I don't even have a shower or a toilet in my room.
I had to shower in a little room outside. There was just a watering hose.
Later I realized it was the laundry room.

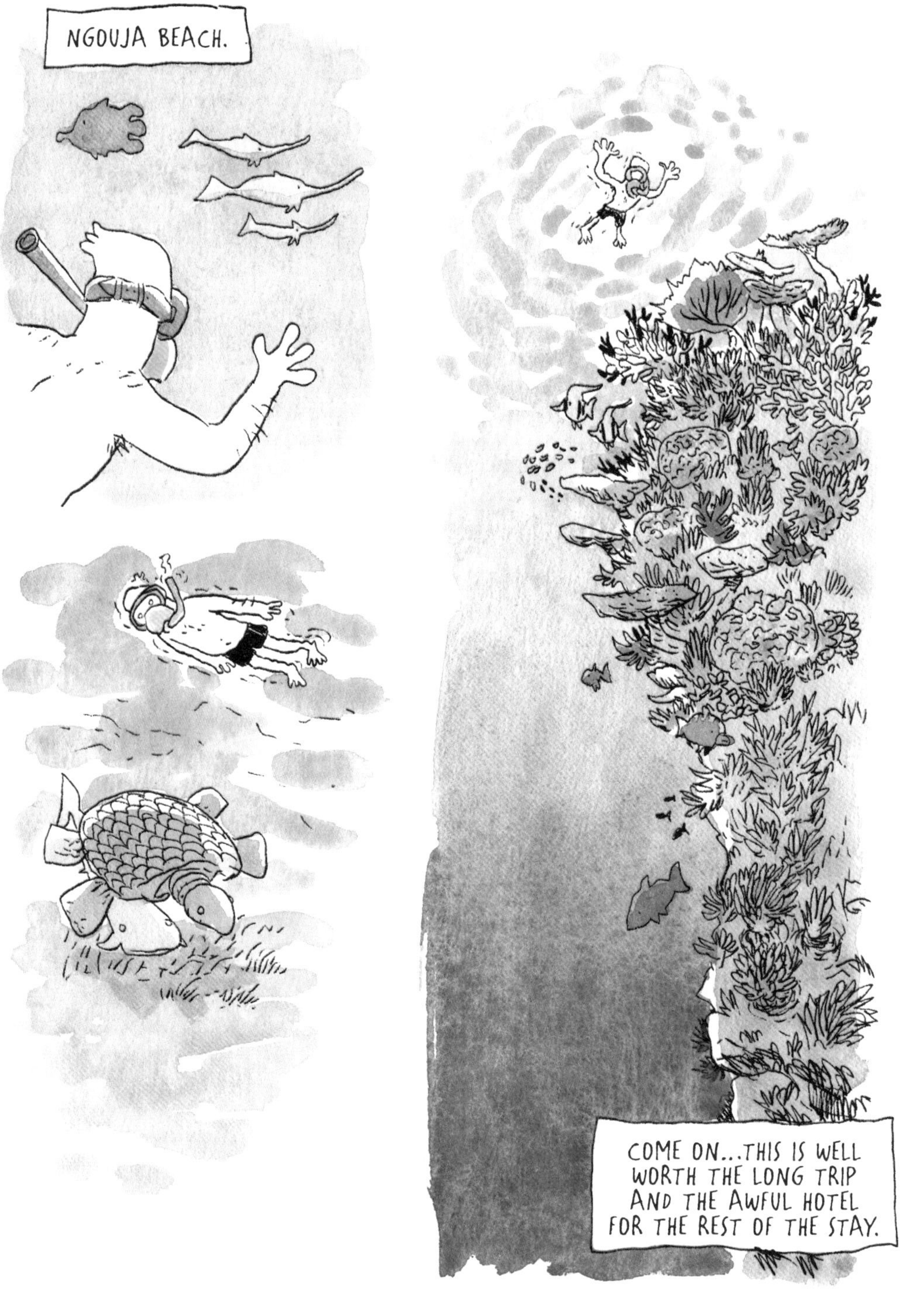
NGOUJA BEACH.
COME ON...THIS IS WELL WORTH THE LONG TRIP AND THE AWFUL HOTEL FOR THE REST OF THE STAY.

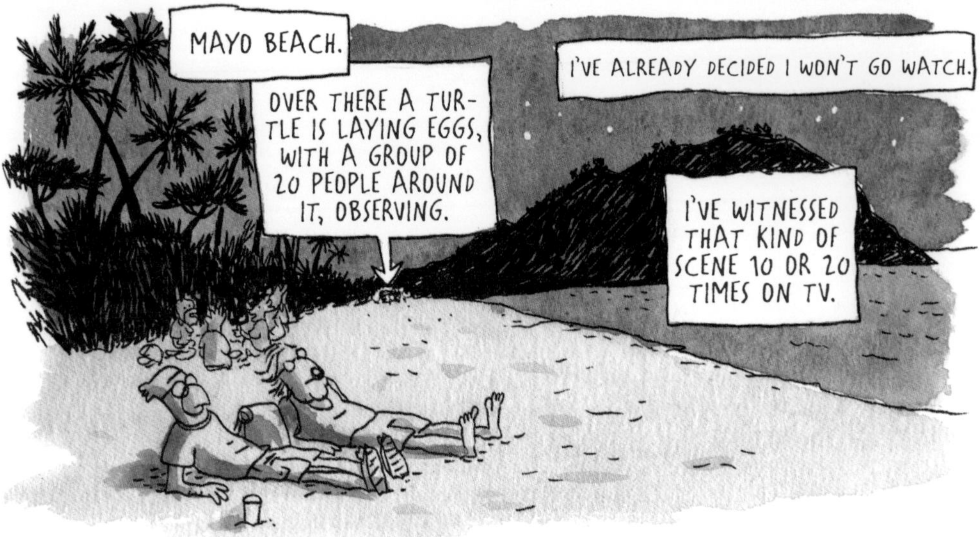
MAYO BEACH.
OVER THERE A TURTLE IS LAYING EGGS, WITH A GROUP OF 20 PEOPLE AROUND IT, OBSERVING.
I'VE ALREADY DECIDED I WON'T GO WATCH.
I'VE WITNESSED THAT KIND OF SCENE 10 OR 20 TIMES ON TV.

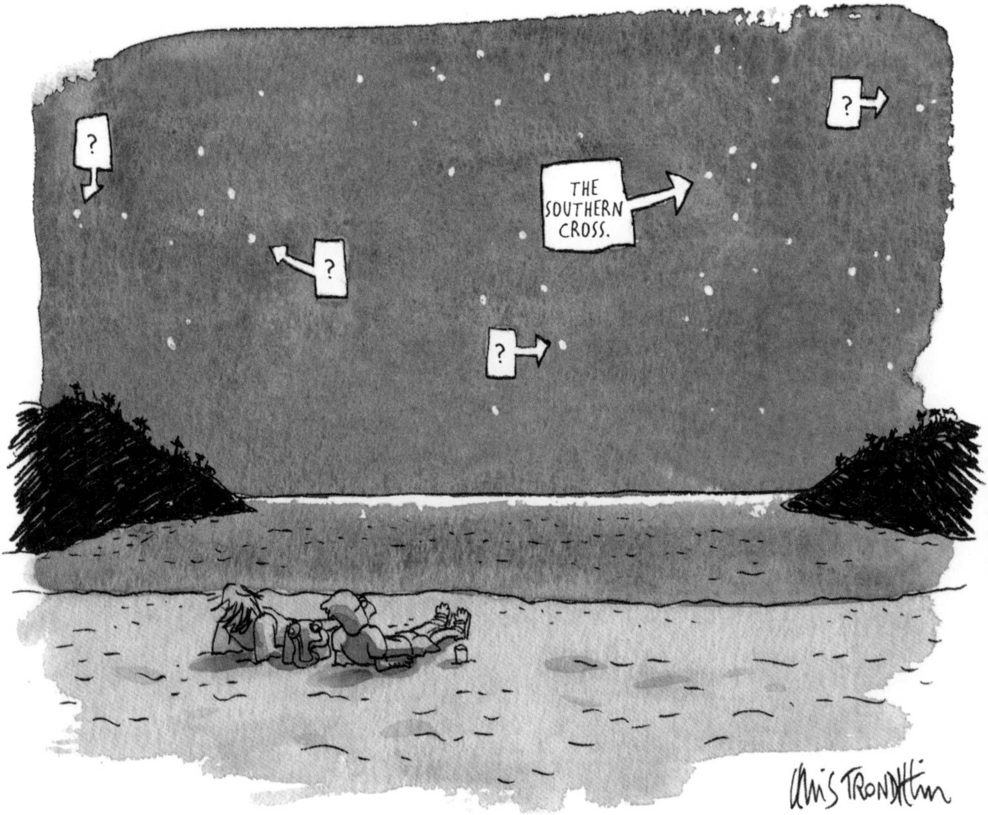
?
?
THE SOUTHERN CROSS.
?
?
Lewis Trondheim

Other books by Trondheim from NBM:
Little Nothings:
Vol. 1: The Curse of the Umbrella, $14.95
Vol. 2: The Prisoner Syndrome, $14.95
Vol. 3: Uneasy Happiness, $14.95

Mr. I, $13.95
with Joann Sfar:
Dungeon, Zenith, vols. 1, 2, $14.95 each, 3, $12.95
Dungeon Early Years, vols. 1, 2 $12.95 each
Dungeon, Twilight, vols. 1, $12.95, 2, $14.95, 3, $12.99
Dungeon, Parade, vols. 1, 2, $9.95 each
Dungeon, Monstres, vols. 1, 2, $12.95 each,
3, $12.99, 4, $14.99
with Thierry Robin:
Li'l Santa, $14.95
Happy Halloween, Li'l Santa, $14.95

From Papercutz:
Monster Christmas, $9.99

Add $4 P&H first item $1 each additional.

Write for our complete catalog
of over 200 graphic novels:
NBM
40 Exchange Pl., Suite 1308
New York, NY 10005
www.nbmpublishing.com

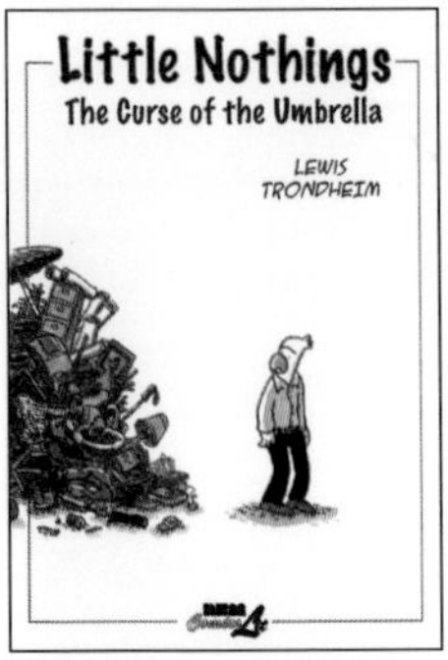
Little Nothings
The Curse of the Umbrella
LEWIS TRONDHEIM

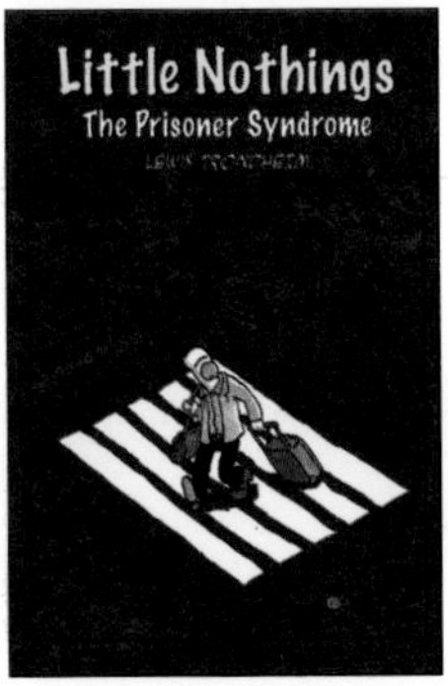
Little Nothings
The Prisoner Syndrome

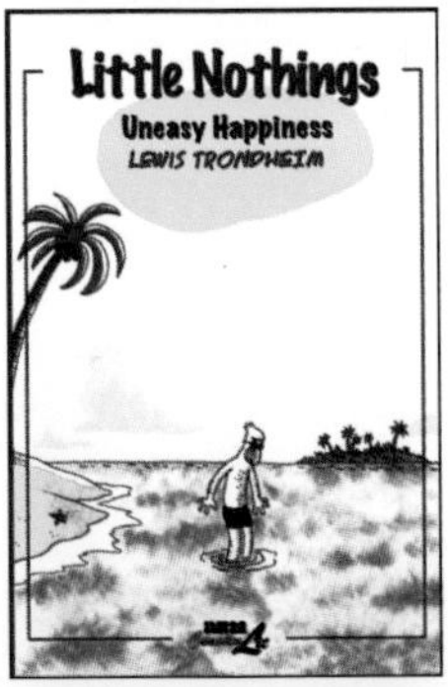
Little Nothings
Uneasy Happiness
LEWIS TRONDHEIM

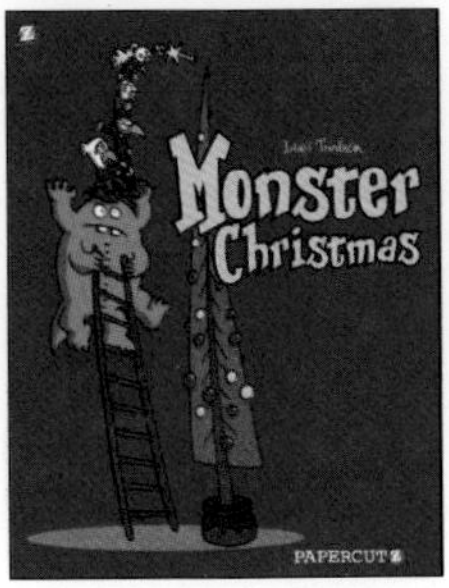
Monster Christmas
PAPERCUTZ